Pokhran and Beyond

POKHRAN AND BEYOND
India's Nuclear Behaviour

Ashok Kapur

OXFORD
UNIVERSITY PRESS

OXFORD

UNIVERSITY PRESS

YMCA Library Building, Jai Singh Road, New Delhi 110 001

Oxford University Press is a department of the University of Oxford. It furthers the
University's objective of excellence in research, scholarship, and education
by publishing worldwide in

Oxford   New York

Athens   Auckland   Bangkok   Bogota   Buenos Aires   Cape Town
Chennai   Dar es Salaam   Delhi   Florence   Hong Kong   Istanbul   Karachi
Kolkata   Kuala Lumpur   Madrid   Melbourne   Mexico City   Mumbai
Nairobi   Paris   São Paolo   Shanghai   Singapore   Taipei   Tokyo   Toronto   Warsaw

with associated companies in   Berlin   Ibadan

Oxford is a registered trade mark of Oxford University Press
in the UK and in certain other countries

Published in India
By Oxford University Press, New Delhi

ISBN 019 564 9435

Typeset by Urvashi Press, Vaidwara, Meerut
Printed in India by Rashtriya Printers
Published by Manzar Khan, Oxford University Press
YMCA Library Building; Jai Singh Road, New Delhi 110 001

Preface

India's nuclear tests in May 1998 initially evoked strong negative international reactions. Several Western commentators felt that the decision to test reflected compulsions of Indian domestic politics rather than external security considerations. American and European commentators generally ignored the China factor, the role of Chinese nuclear and missile supplies to Pakistan and White House's unwillingness to confront China on this issue despite US intelligence reports. The US State Department's approach to India in recent years has been dominated by the 'Pickering doctrine' (i.e. India must cap, then reduce and finally eliminate nuclear weapons), but it acknowledged that China was a security issue in India's strategic thinking. Washington accepted the importance of harmonizing American non-proliferation norms with Indian security concerns. The Indo-American strategic dialogue conducted by Strobe Talbott and Jaswant Singh was based on this approach. Despite initial opposition to Indian tests which led to economic and technological sanctions, Australia and Japan have now renewed ties with India.

The international reactions and debates generated in the aftermath of Pokhran II have received scholarly attention. Two studies stand out. George Perkovich's *India's Nuclear Bomb* was completed in late 1998 before international opinion about the Indian tests had calmed down. This is a timely, well-written history of Indian nuclear debates and decision-making processes. It makes good use of declassified US government materials and interviews with contemporary Indian and American experts, apart from published works. Perkovich holds that domestic not external considerations were crucial in arriving at the decision to test although an 'economy-first' position is in his opinion, the rational choice in dealing with Indian security. He says that the international community believes that India has gained nothing from its 1998 tests and the missile programme. In Perkovich's view the Indian policy process is *ad hoc* and uncoordinated.

Except for the last point, Perkovich's conclusions can be contested. Publications in the fifties emanating from the Indian atomic energy establishment on the radiation effects of atomic tests clearly demonstrated to Western scientific audiences that Bhabha and his colleagues had the know-how to make an atomic bomb. Declassified Canadian files show that Canadian scientists were aware of this and for this reason believed that it was essential to have stronger international safeguards and legal restraints against diversion of Canadian materials into bomb use.

There is room for honest disagreement as to the components of 'security'. What is the mix of economic and military strength, and political will, organization and strategy that are conducive to national security in a country given its internal and external circumstances? In India, during the 1940s–50s, 'security' referred to the danger of losing Indian control over Indian missile materials like thorium which were earmarked for future use; hence the opposition to international controls by the USA or by the IAEA. The political, legal and diplomatic fights on this issue were conducted by the Ministry of External Affairs in international conferences. These fights reflected tangible Indian national security interests rather than ideological preferences of leaders or the narrow interests of institutions or individuals. The larger context of the emerging international order rather than security problems relating to Pakistan and China was dominant. This policy frame was evolved by a coalition (the Indian 'strategic enclave') consisting of the Prime Minister's Office, the Ministry of External Affairs and the atomic energy establishment. In subsequent years, the parameters of Indian security became broader and deeper in the context of changes in India's external environment at the global and regional levels. Perkovich ignores the effect of a fluid strategic environment on Indian decision-making.

In emphasizing the role of Indian weaponeers in shaping the political decision process, Perkovich also ignores the role of another 'strategic enclave' which centred around American and British efforts in organizing a coalition of anti-bomb, pro-NPT and pro-CTBT coalition during the Indira Gandhi, Morarji Desai, Rajiv Gandhi, Narasimha Rao and Gujral years. This coalition has had a strong voice in the Ministry of External Affairs, the Prime Minister's Office and even within the atomic energy establishment (but never in the Indian missile establishment). It has a public voice in the writings of Delhi commentators who were opposed to Indian nuclear testing, weaponization and deployment and favoured heeding American counsel so as not to upset the sole superpower. Perkovich is right in saying that the Indian military has not played a major role in the decision-making process. Partly this was the result of Nehru's antipathy for the armed forces and in part it reflected the Indian military's preoccupation with the modernization of the conventional military segment.

Perkovich argues that Indira Gandhi's aversion to nuclear weapons was based on moral considerations. In the 1960s and the 1970s—following the 1962 debacle with China, the development of the NPT system and China's nuclear testing—the Indian military did not interest itself in nuclear affairs because the priority was modernization of the army. Simultaneously, however, the relative merits of 'defence' and 'deterrence' were debated intensely. Professor Sisir Gupta even more than K. Subrahmanyam brought out convincingly the issues in this debate: the relationship between diplomacy and force, as well as the domestic and international contexts of India's strategic agenda. Gupta had his moorings in the Congress, he knew about inner-party debates and his writings showed the connection between domestic politics and international security. During the same period, respected Indian economists like Raj Krishna, J.D. Sethi and Subramaniam Swamy debated the economic and strategic aspects of the Indian bomb. Mrs. Gandhi was fully aware of these views, especially Gupta's. Realpolitik and self-interest, not morality, were in reality, the basis of her approach to Indian political and international affairs. Note her ruthlessness in the conduct of the 1971 campaign in Bangladesh. Her nuclear policy reflected the pressures of Indian and international politics, including the pressures of the US-led anti-bomb strategic enclave mentioned above.

Perkovich assumes that the Indian tests disrupted the normalization of Sino–Indian relations. This is simplistic because this process does not have much substance. During Prime Minister Rajiv Gandhi's visit to China, the Chinese leadership refused to discuss nuclear disarmament with India because it was not a nuclear power. China repeatedly refused to explain its motive in supplying nuclear and missile assistance to Pakistan. China has denied its naval activities in the Bay of Bengal, and is still ambiguous about the importance of Indian nuclear disarmament. India and China are now actively engaged in a diplomatic and military rivalry in the Himalayas, Bay of Bengal, Myanmar and southeast Asia.

The Indian tests helped the Washington establishment as well as the Chinese leadership to focus on Indian threat perceptions and interests. China's backing down from support for Kashmiri self-determination is not significant because it is linked to Indian restraint on the issue of Tibetan autonomy. In other words, Prime Minister Vajpayee did not miscalculate the effects of the tests he ordered. The aim was to expose the China-Pakistan-US nuclear nexus and China's policy of containing India through military and diplomatic means. This message is registering with major think tanks like the International Institute for Strategic Studies.

Perkovich does have a point however. Indian nuclear decision-making has been *ad hoc* and uncoordinated and it has not been presented in a credible way to domestic and international audiences. This point is also made by Admiral Raja Menon in *A Nuclear Strategy for India* (2000). Lack of co-ordination is the result of the colonial style of decision-making in India as well as the Indian bureaucracy's aversion to external scrutiny and accountability, as well as a reluctance to share power with other legitimate players. Indian policy-makers have also failed to appreciate the importance of psychological warfare, an essential part of national security strategy. Furthermore, as Admiral Menon points out, the Indian military establishment has avoided involving itself in strategic policy-making. As a result, the political establishment and the Ministry of External Affairs have marginalized the defence establishment in strategic affairs. The Indian government has thus not succeeded in pooling the experience and talent of different ministries in a coordinated manner to deal with important strategic questions. In India, issues concerning international security are dealt with by the Ministry of External Affairs, whereas arms control delegations of the USA, Russia, Israel, China and most European countries routinely consist of diplomatic, scientific, military, intelligence and political experts. Bringing about a change in the composition of Indian delegations is a good way of addressing the problem of coordination and coherence in the development of a national security policy so that a new institutional mechanism is created to achieve policy development in a proactive way. The problem however is that successive Indian Prime Ministers have lacked the determination and the vision to coordinate and share power and to engage in meaningful administrative reforms that could help the country develop a credible strategic position. Ways have to be found to significantly improve coordination and achieve greater transparency without compromising security.

Though I have not examined the details of administrative reform, I have discussed the problems of weak political leadership, the penchant for moralism and legalism in arguments about discriminatory international arrangements and the importance of nuclear disarmament and the unwillingness of the Indian government to substitute talk by actions that showcase India's strategic priorities. To be taken seriously by the world community, Indians will have to show that they take their own strategic needs seriously. Owen Lattimore pointed out in his 1949 book *The Situation in Asia*, that Asia was out of control. It still is. The USA and China mistakenly believe that the USA is the sole global superpower and China is the leader of Asia and it is for Indian policy-makers to demonstrate by action that India has a place in a multipolar Asia and is a mature non-expansionist international force. Perkovich claims that Nehru and his successors, before Vajpayee, exercised 'self-restraint' in their nuclear decisions. I call this 'weakness'. The term 'self-restraint' applies when one can inflict harm, but chooses to hold back. The new mantra should be 'negotiated not unilateral restraint' and this requires demonstration of capabilities in the conventional and nuclear spheres along with credible military, diplomatic and economic strategies.

Several post-1998 developments in the nuclear arena frame the issues I have dealt with. First, in 1999, India publicized a draft nuclear doctrine. This was in sharp contrast with the Nehruvian approach which was pitched in legalistic and moralistic terms, i.e. India opposed discriminatory international arms control arrangements and wanted global nuclear disarmament because it held the moral high ground by practising unilateral self-restraint with respect to nuclearization. The reality was that India's so-called self-restraint (1960s–1998) was a result of internal division and American/Russian pressure rather than a well thought out strategic plan or moral opposition. The 1999 draft nuclear doctrine formally accepted nuclear weaponry as a vital part of India's military plan. By pointing to the value of a security dialogue with China and others, the nuclear doctrine signalled a quest for self-reliant nuclear planning and negotiated restraints which inevitably required concessions from India's diplomatic and military rivals. The draft doctrine is consistent with my argument that the Indian political leadership, principally the Prime Minister and Cabinet, needs to take the lead in defining, explaining and projecting the Indian strategic agenda to its people and to the 'world community' in a transparent and a convincing way. It should publicize India's priorities which should reflect vital Indian interests, rather than churn out meaningless annual reports which preach the value of friendly relations with enemies like Pakistan and China. I have emphasized the need for a strategy of psychological warfare in addition to a comprehensive national security policy.

However, I should point out that the draft nuclear doctrine is just the first step. It is still just a draft. While it adopts the principle of nuclear weaponization and deployment, the debate in the Delhi press indicates that the political establishment is still divided between those who want further nuclear testing, weaponization and deployment, and those who believe that the 1998 level of nuclear testing is enough to meet India's future strategic needs (say in the 2000–2010–2020 time frame). The latter also believes that weaponization and deployment can now be delayed or that a freeze (capping) of Indian nuclear activities at the 1998 level is a tolerable price to pay (by signing the CTBT) to gain American goodwill. There is continuing tension between the two approaches. I have shown the history of competing pressures to 'go nuclear' (test, weaponize, deploy and then seek negotiated arms control restraints), or to unilaterally cap, reduce and then eliminate India's nuclear programme, or at the least, to degrade the value of India's nuclear weapons capability by freezing it at the current level. The latter was the preferred alternative in the Nehruvian era. Despite the shift in India's stance in 1998, the Vajpayee government, and the strategic analysts who write in the Delhi press, continue to send conflicting signals. This means that both lines are in play and they reflect competing pressures. Hence it is worthwhile to link my discussion about the policy positions of foreign-linked Indian constituencies on the nuclear question during the Nehruvian era (1947–98) to contemporary nuclear debates in Delhi (1998–2000).

The second set of post-1998 developments are Pakistan specific. Pakistan's decision (made by the military and intelligence services, with former Prime Minister Nawaz Sharif's approval) to challenge Indian interests in Kargil (1999) was made under the cover of Prime Minister Vajpayee's 'bus diplomacy'. It reflected Pakistan's confidence and a conscious calculation that its nuclear and missile programme (which is mostly Chinese and North Korean in origin, aided by equipment purchased from European suppliers), as well as the reactive nature of Indian decision-making which gave Pakistan the opportunity to adopt a low-risk, high-intensity warfare in the Kashmir region. The Pakistani strategists were clearheaded compared to their Indian counterparts. Pro-active military action by a tightly-organized and highly-motivated but 'smaller' counting, Pakistan, was successful in initiating an intrusion into Kargil; it caught the 'bigger' country, India, off guard. The Indian advocates of 'bus diplomacy', friendship and a diplomatic dialogue with Pakistan did not see Kargil coming. They did not appreciate that the army and the intelligence agencies in Pakistan were the centres of power, that insurgency was good business and good politics for them, and that they would not accept friendship with India even if Kashmir was given to Pakistan. To avoid future Kargils a strategic plan which integrates diplomacy, conventional warfare and nuclear activities is needed so that 'bigger' India can function as 'better' India.

The Kargil experience produced two important lessons. It undermined the theory of strategic experts like K. Subrahmanyam who thought that a nuclearized India and Pakistan dampened the prospect of conventional warfare in the region. This was a false expectation. By suggesting that it was cheaper to build nuclear bombs and missiles than aircraft and tanks, these experts missed the point that in dealing with Pakistan and China India needed nuclear as well as conventional armaments. The thinking of General Aslam Beg (former Pakistan Army chief) indicated that Pakistani nuclearization was meant in part to facilitate an intensification of insurgency and psychological warfare in Kashmir. Thus Kargil showed that India needed both a conventional and a nuclear strategy in dealing with Pakistani pressures and ambitions. The same is true *vis-à-vis* China. The second lesson was a positive one. Nuclear deterrence worked in a crisis situation because the two rivals choose not to escalate the war to the nuclear plane. Although India escalated the conflict by using air power along with ground forces to repulse the intrusion, the boundary between conventional and nuclear warfare was maintained; Kashmir was not worth a nuclear holocaust. This also undermined the widespread Western belief about the danger of an accidental nuclear war by irrational Indians and Pakistanis.

In other words, as I urge in the following pages, the problem of Pakistan and China cannot be dealt with by diplomacy of friendship and normalization as is emphasized by the Ministry of External Affairs. Coercive action with calculated risks is required but this requires coordinated planning, not *ad hoc* responses to new situations. The emphasis on Indian peace diplomacy was a recurring Nehruvian theme which failed to advance any tangible Indian strategic interest. China and Pakistan are still dangerous rivals. India's decision to cut off further political dialogue with Pakistan is sound because there is no one in Pakistan who has an incentive to negotiate a mutually satisfactory political settlement. There is no common area of negotiation; and where are the Pakistani negotiators who are in a position to deliver a deal to India anyway? The Musharraf military coup is a non-event in my narrative because real power has been in the hands of the army intelligence agencies and fundamentalists, even when democratic regimes under the two Bhuttos and Nawaz Sharif have been in place. To counter the former, the Indian political leadership needs to establish a strategic initiative by convincing military that it means business. This will entail building up psychological pressure instead of waiting time on diplomatic talk. The Indian armed forces also need to weigh in as an institution in internal strategic debates and decision-making. They should not leave regional and international security issues in the hands of diplomats who are well-meaning but nevertheless lack the professional training and experience to deal with military and scientific issues.

The third development of the post-1998 period concerns the ongoing debate within India concerning the CTBT. There are three aspects to this issue. One, there is a debate within India which is aimed at developing an internal consensus on the issue. Two, the issue is located at the Indo-US intergovernmental level in the form of the Talbott-Singh talks. But these ran out of steam during 1998-99 and exist now as a forum for discussion and for cosmetic effect. Three, even if India does not formally accept the CTBT, the ban against future testing is now an international non-proliferation norm. A norm is not a binding legal obligation but even so it creates a practical restraint against testing. In other words, the Vajpayee government is practically now in the pro-CTBT camp although its official position is that no internal consensus exists to formally accept the treaty. Moreover, the Indian debate on the CTBT is not a real and a thorough debate. It confirms a point I make, that politicised Indian nuclear scientists and missile experts give advice which they believe their political masters wish to hear. Following the 1998 tests Dr Chidambaram and Dr Kalam argued that India could join the CTBT because India's five tests were sufficient to confirm the integrity of the Indian nuclear deterrent. This is a political statement; it is not a scientific fact. It is flawed in two ways. One, doubts exist among Indian nuclear scientists about the actual yield of India's single thermonuclear test in 1998, and it is debatable whether a credible deterrent in the coming decade(s) can be based on a single test and computer simulation. Even after hundreds of tests the US Senate refused to ratify the CTBT because it felt that further testing could be needed to maintain the integrity of its nuclear arsenal. Two, the Indian armed forces need to spell out their nuclear and missile requirements after user trials have verified the reliability of the weapons concerned. The size and nature of the nuclear arsenal will also have to be tailored to meet specific and contingent military threats. Diplomats and nuclear scientists are not military experts and cannot be relied upon to spellout these requirements. Moreover, the CTBT is a non-proliferation measure, as US under-secretary of state for arms control, John Holum, has pointed out. A freeze would inevitably degrade Indian nuclear capabilities. The question then turns on the ability of Indian scientists, missile experts and military experts to manage the gap between India and Chinese and Pakistani nuclear capabilities in the coming decade. So the resolution of the CTBT debate requires a transparent interface between Indian scientists, Indian armed forces and Indian diplomats which the political leadership has to develop. My book highlights, the major role the Ministry of External Affairs played in the 1950s and the 1960s in safeguarding India's nuclear weapons option and fissile resources from falling under international controls. At that time the ministry was hard-headed. I have argued that it became soft and faction-ridden on the nuclear question from the 1970s onwards. Consequently, it now has a limited utility in developing the policies to deal with problems in India's backyard which involve conventional warfare, nuclear strategy and psychological warfare. That is, issues of defence, deterrence and coercive diplomacy require a strategy which is formed and coordinated at the highest level of the Indian government rather than in a single ministry.

After the 1998 tests, China was identified, for the first time, as being, potentially, India's most dangerous rival. This declaration by the Indian defence minister created friction between the two countries, but it also brought into the open the simmering rivalry between China and India. The tests were followed by a two-track strategy: the first was conducted at the diplomatic level and emphasized the importance of normalization and tranquillity on the Himalayan border; the second revealed a pattern of military and political engagement in India's neighbourhood. Before the 1998 tests, India's China policy, nuclear policy and Pakistan policy seemed to run on compartmentalized or unintegrated bilateral tracks. The 1998 tests signalled a need to integrate there and connect it to the issue of Indo–American relations. The nuclear and non-proliferation activities of China, Pakistan and the USA and their pressure on Indian interests brought about the awareness of the need to integrate these tracks. But to successfully integrate them into a coherent and a credible national security policy, the issues have to be dealt with at an organiza-tional level that is higher than the ministry of external affairs, which does not have the mandate to promote friendly relations with these powers. It does not have a mandate to analyse Chinese military activities in the Himalayas or the Bay of Bengal. Its disposition is to negotiate, not confront, or expose enmities or deal with them militarily.

A new Indian strategic culture is required which overcomes the present system of compartmentalized, secretive, *ad hoc* and reactive strategic decision-making. I have shown the ill-effects of the old system of decision-making. Since Nehru's time Indian decision-making has relied on personality and other unpredictable factors. Today strong impersonal forces (such as militant Islam, Hindu nationalism, Russian nationalism, Chinese expansiveness, Japanese re-thinking about the meaning of power following the failure of its reliance on economic power, ethnic violence in places like Indonesia which until recently were Western models of stability and so on) impact on a country's economic, political-diplomatic and military affairs and cultural identity. New institutional arrangements have to be developed to deal with these forces. My book is a plea to learn from the past and to move in a new pro-active strategic direction.

Acknowledgements

Although I have drawn freely on my earlier writings, the book offers an integrated and a historical view of different dimensions of Indian nuclear policy and its consequences for Indian diplomacy and military strategy. My earlier writings emphasized the Nehruvian approach to the nuclear question. Here the Nehruvian phase is outlined as an essential background and a contrast to the post-Nehruvian phase which has emerged under the direction of the BJP leadership.

I would like to thank the Social Sciences and Humanities Research Council of Canada for its support in the preparation of this volume. I am grateful to the number of specialists and practitioners for sharing their thoughts with me: former Prime Minister I.K. Gujral, Dr H.K. Kesavan (University of Waterloo), Dr M. Anandakrishnan (Vice-Chairman, State Council for Higher Education, Chennai), Mr F.C. Kohli (Tata Consultancy, Mumbai), Mr N. Ram (Editor, Frontline), Dr P.K. Ayengar (former Chairman, Atomic Energy Department), Dr R. Chidambaram (Chairman, Atomic Energy Department), Mr S.K. Singh (former Foreign Secretary of India), Vice-Admiral K.K. Nayyar (Indian Navy, retired), Brigadier V.K. Nair (Indian Army, retired), Dr Y.S. Rajan, (Confederation of Indian Industry, formerly with Indian Space Organization), Professor M.L. Sondhi (Jawaharlal Nehru University and Chairman, Indian Council of Social Sciences Research), and Ambassador Arundhati Ghose. Dr Ashok Mohan, Technical Advisor, Atomic Energy Department, Mumbai was kind enough to send me copies of official reports. I have also benefited from conversations with senior Canadian, Australian, Indian and American practitioners who spoke on conditions of anonymity. None of them bear any responsibility for the facts and interpretations in this book.

Contents

Figures and Tables

TABLES

Abbreviations

1.	ACDA	Arms Control and Disarmament Agency
2.	AEC	Atomic Energy Commission
3.	ARF	ASEAN Regional Forum
4.	ASEAN	Association of South-East Asian Nations
5.	BJP	Bharatiya Janata Party
6.	CANDU	Canada Deuterium–Uranium
7.	CIRUS	Canada–India Research Reactor
8.	CSIR	Council for Scientific and Industrial Research
9.	CTBT	Comprehensive Test Ban Treaty
10.	DAE	Department of Atomic Energy
11.	DRDO	Defence Research and Development Organization
12.	EIF	Entry into Force
13.	ENDC	Eighteen-Nation Disarmament Committee
14.	ESA	European Space Agency
15.	FBR	Fast Breeder Reactor
16.	GOI	Government of India
17.	IAEA	International Atomic Energy Agency
18.	IDSS	Institute of Defence and Strategic Studies
19.	ISRO	Indian Space Research Organization
20.	LAC	Line of Actual Control
21.	MEA	Ministry of External Affairs
22.	MOD	Ministry of Defence
23.	MTCR	Missile Technology Control Regime
24.	NAM	Non-Aligned Movement
25.	NATO	North Atlantic Treaty Organization
26.	NEE	Nuclear Explosives Engineering

27.	NGO	Non-Governmental Organization
28.	NNRMS	National Natural Resources Management System
29.	NNWS	Non-Nuclear Weapon State
30.	NPT	Non-Proliferation Treaty
31.	NWFZ	Nuclear Weapon Free Zone
32.	NWS	Nuclear Weapons State
33.	PNE	Peaceful Nuclear Explosion
34.	PRC	People's Republic of China
35.	PTBT	Partial Test Ban Treaty
36.	RAPP	Rajasthan Atomic Power Project
37.	RSS	Rashtriya Swayamsevak Sangh
38.	SALT	Strategic Arms Limitation Treaty
39.	SEATO	South-East Asia Treaty Organization
40.	SITE	Satellite Instructional Television Experiment
41.	SNEP	Subterranean Nuclear Explosion Project
42.	STEP	Satellite Telecommunication Experiments Project
43.	TAW	Tactical Atomic Weapons
44.	UN	United Nations
45.	UNSCOM	United Nations Special Commission
46.	US	United States
47.	USA	United States of America
48.	USSR	Union of Soviet Socialist Republics

1

Introduction

This book is about an evolving and a dynamic relationship between Indian science, state, and society in a changing and conflict-prone regional and international security environment. The relationships are an expression of the interplay among several variables: a changing state form between the 1930s and 1947 and the political attitudes of Indian scientific and policy elites; the foreign policy boundaries of Indian nuclear science planning in the Cold War international system; the research frontiers of India's scientific elite and the tension and interplay between the policy and the research boundaries; and the impact of regional and international politics on the attitudes and policies of attentive publics in the Indian state and society. The weight of each variable changes over time as does the pattern of relationships amongst them, but the importance of each variable is beyond doubt.

The title of this book is 'Pokhran and Beyond: India's Nuclear Behaviour', but to get to Pokhran and beyond, it is necessary to first explain the prehistory and the history of Indian nuclear decisions, its nuclear diplomacy, and its military strategy as it concerns the nuclear question. Chapters 2 to 6 provide the necessary historical perspective. Chapters 7 and 8 deal specifically with the relationship between the scientists and the state since the 1980s; and the relationship between the armed forces and the nuclear question is dealt with in Chapter 7. In unravelling India's nuclear behaviour, this work puts forward two main theses and I discuss these below.

1. The Indian Tests in May 1998 were a major event which was a response to provocative Chinese, American, and Pakistani strategic behaviour. It should be studied in the context of major changes in regional and international relationships and approaches.

The Indian series of nuclear tests in May 1998 is seen as a major event which has a continuing impact on the international non-proliferation and nuclear, as well as missile proliferation, arenas; it also has strategic implications for the emerging balance of power in Asia–Pacific or the emerging pattern of multipolarity in the region. This book considers the Indian tests not so much as a recent, *ad hoc* response, but as the culmination of a long-delayed response to what Indian policymakers saw as provocative strategic behaviour by China, the United States of America, and Pakistan, among others (such as the UK, Canada, and Australia who sought Indian nuclear disarmament), in India's strategic neighbourhood and in the international sphere. India's nuclear and diplomatic behaviour should be assessed in the context of major changes in the balance of power in Asia and at the international level over the preceding two decades. These changes highlighted the importance of the USA, the People's Republic of China (PRC), and Japan as the pillars of security in Asia–Pacific. Except for the US, its allies, and the PRC, they highlighted, as well, the importance of nuclear and missile non-proliferation for most Asian states. The changes appeared to indicate the emergence of a moderately stable or predictable pattern of international and regional security arrangements in the Asia–Pacific area and the international sphere. However, this appearance was misleading. The Indian tests will undoubtedly alter the distribution of power and the pattern of relationships in the Indian subcontinent, as well as in the Asia–Pacific and the international spheres. Most Western academics and governments had expected the prospect of Indian nuclear testing after the development of the 'global' non-proliferation norm, which is almost universal, to be merely a remote possibility. Surprisingly, there was a universal failure of diplomatic and military intelligence in all the major capitals of the world concerning the likelihood of Indian tests and the consequences of India's nuclearization. Smugness and overconfidence in the durability of the global non-proliferation norm and the Non-Proliferation Treaty (NPT) regime, not Indian deceit, explains the intelligence failure. This book will show that the Indians have continuously provided semi-opaque signals of India's nuclear intent and capability since the late 1950s, but these were not taken seriously by the world's capitals because India, and its strategic culture, have not been taken seriously. In hindsight, it is clear that the history of Indian nuclear science, as well as the impact of external changes on Indian strategic thought and behaviour, pointed to the Indian tests as a high probability and a high impact event. Given this background, the purposes of this volume are twofold: to explore the history and the factors which culminated in the 1998 tests, and to examine how the international security system might constructively deal with the emergence of India as a major player in Asian and international affairs.

Western experts judge the 1998 tests correctly to be a major international event, but the reasoning is flawed. Consider, for instance, the assessment of Harald Muller, a noted European security expert.

The events in South Asia have changed the parameters of world politics, and in particular those of nuclear non-proliferation and disarmament, fundamentally. They are as significant as the fall of the Berlin Wall nine years ago. Unfortunately, they point us in the opposite direction: away from cooperation, arms control and disarmament, towards confrontation, arms racing and eventually nuclear war. The world community must make its utmost efforts to stem this fateful tide.[1]

Such an emotional and one-sided assessment requires a thorough appraisal. It is irresponsible for an armchair strategist, who is far removed from the Indian subcontinental zone of conflict and whose judgement does not entail any risk-taking or decision-making concerning issues of war and peace in the region, to dismiss the strategic and prestige aspects of Indian nuclear behaviour. It is also illogical and simplistic to locate the issue in the party politics of the Bharatiya Janata Party (BJP) and not in Indian strategic policy when successive Indian governments since 1968 have declined to join the NPT and have insisted on keeping their nuclear weapons option open.

The Muller bias ignores the fact that the recommendation to go ahead with nuclear testing was on the desk of successive Indian prime ministers (Narasimha Rao and I.K. Gujral) and the motivation, as well as the timing of the test, was the result of several calculations:

(i) To ensure that the Indian armed forces have the means to deter a nuclear conflict with China and Pakistan, should that become necessary. This point is based on the fact that Indian military doctrine since the mid-1980s has evolved on the premise that India would have to fight a two-front war, that it would also have to manage its commercial and strategic interests in the Indian Ocean, and that it would need to rely on itself and not an outside great power such as America or Russia for its economic and military security.[2]

(ii) The non-proliferators in the international arena were also the most prominent tolerators and promoters of nuclear and missile proliferation in the Indian subcontinent. This point refers particularly to Chinese nuclear and missile supply to Pakistan and American toleration of Pakistan's nuclear weaponization since the 1980s.

(iii) The fact that almost 70 per cent of Pakistan's conventional armament is of PRC design and almost 90 per cent of its missile production is based on varied types of PRC aid makes Pakistan an extended arm of the PRC in the Indian subcontinent, in Indian estimation. For Indian strategic planners, the issue behind the decision to have a series of nuclear tests in May 1998 was to signal to Indian public opinion as well as international opinion that India possessed the conventional, as well as the nuclear means, to address direct Chinese military pressure against India through Tibet and the Himalayan border, as well as the indirect Chinese pressure through Pakistan and through Myanmar and the Bay of Bengal—the latter two function as India's strategic flanks and both play a role in China's India policy.

(iv) Indian testing was necessary to smoke out the activities and the policy responses of the major and minor players in the subcontinental scene. 'Smoking out' helps to bring the issues to the table and this was deemed to be essential before channels of discourse and negotiation could be developed.

(v) Another Indian calculation was that the Comprehensive Test Ban Treaty (CTBT) was due to 'enter into force' in September 1999. This deadline was both a danger and an opportunity. The choice or dilemma for India was to 'use it (the nuclear weapons option) or lose it'.

(vi) With increasing American and Western pressure on the weak BJP government coalition not to test, another tactical consideration was to undertake the tests before the coalition collapsed. After the BJP-led coalition government came to power, the American strategy in Indian politics was to keep the BJP off balance by encouraging criticism through the international media about the BJP as a 'Hindu militant nationalist party' and by encouraging Indian regional political parties (for example Jayalalitha's AIADMK in Tamil Nadu) and the Indian opposition parties (especially the Congress party under Sonia Gandhi) to bring down the BJP coalition. BJP's concern about the pattern of and likely consequences of US intervention in Indian domestic politics was therefore an important contextual element in BJP's nuclear behaviour. This point indicates a triangular dynamics which erodes the line or the compartmentalization between domestic politics, on the one hand, and foreign policy, nuclear policy, and interstate relations on the other. Figure 1.1 outlines the dynamics.

These reasons point to the existence of external–strategic as well as domestic–political considerations in the decision to test. They also indicate that even though mature democracies do not go to war with each other,[3] the history of the relationship between the American and Indian democracies is ridden with a pattern of US intervention, pressure, and economic as well as technological sanctions to contain and alter Indian strategic policies and behaviour and to make it consistent with US strategic interests.

(vii) Finally, prestige was also a consideration. Prestige is not vanity and as the late Professor Martin Wight pointed out:

prestige is a halo around power. Prestige reflects a reputation or a belief which others have about how someone is likely to act in a given situation.[4]

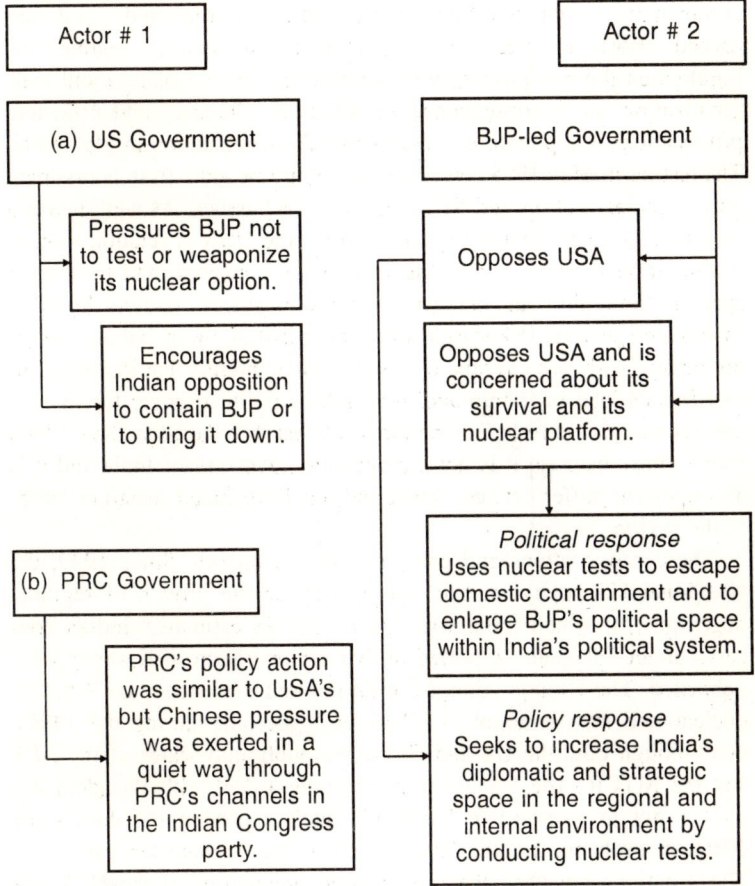

FIG. 1.1: Dynamics of Domestic Politics/Interstate Interface

The series of Indian tests shocked the world community, largely because it was unexpected and differed from earlier Indian behaviour. After the 1974 test, Indira Gandhi had insisted that the 1974 test was peaceful and that it would not be repeated. The world was shocked because world leaders expected that the BJP would behave with restraint, as Indira Gandhi had after the 1974 test. The mistake that Harald Muller and others make is to ignore the links between security, strategy, and prestige in the Indian body politic and in India's nuclear history. The recent tests can be explained as an Indian response to systemic changes since the 1970s in the distribution of military and economic power as well as the pattern of relationships at different levels—the Indian subcontinental; the regional Asia–Pacific; and the international—as it concerned efforts to create a new international security regime that highlighted the non-proliferation norm. The fear of isolation and marginalization as a consequence of Western, Chinese, and Pakistani provocations and pressures explains India's strong action in May 1998. The testing in May 1998 was a way to immunize India from harassment on the nuclear option, the NPT, and the CTBT issues. As well, it was a way to acquire negotiating space *vis-à-vis* the USA in relation to non-proliferation diplomacy and Indian security concerns, and to acquire space in the diplomatic, nuclear, and missile spheres *vis-à-vis* the PRC. In this perspective, Pakistan has become a sideshow in Indian nuclear diplomacy with two caveats: it was in India's interest that Pakistan follow India's lead in testing and give India a political cover for its test; and secondly, it is in India's national interest that Pakistan should be a stable entity because it is not a permanent adversary of India and it is an important buffer between India and the Talibanized sectarian forces in the region.

These provocations and pressures have a history. Since 1949, the traditional US policy in Asia was to oppose the growth of regional hegemons, of which India was one in the US estimate.[5] Indian concerns about Pakistani-supported military intervention in Kashmir went unheeded. The Clinton administration ignored evidence about Chinese nuclear and missile supply to Pakistan, especially during the 1990s, even though both the US and China are public advocates of the NPT and the MTCR. The US government made a deal with President Zia ul-Haq not to interfere in Pakistan's nuclear programme during the 1980s in exchange for the latter's help in the Afghanistan campaign. These actions breached the fundamental obligations of the NPT; the Indian tests in 1998 widened the breach but did not create it because the haemorrhaging had started much earlier. China too did not take Indian security concerns seriously, and Indian pleas for a strategic dialogue have gone unheeded. China has refused to explain the nature and purpose of its missile and nuclear facilities in Tibet, the purpose of its missile and nuclear supply relationship with Pakistan, and the purpose of its naval presence in the Bay of Bengal. All these activities have implications for the Sino–Indian military relationship well into the twenty-first century, and it is useless to ask India to be transparent in its nuclear work when major players in its neighbourhood decline to do so. Historically, since 1949, China has never given India a clean chit. It has complained about the danger of Indian hegemony; it refuses to accept Sikkim as a part of the Indian Union; it claims Arunachal Pradesh, a strategic province in India's north-east as its own; and it has asked India to roll-back its nuclear programme and to sign the NPT. While the Strobe Talbott–Jaswant Singh talks continue and the Indians and Americans look for channels of discourse and mutual interest, the PRC seeks unilateral Indian concessions reminiscent of its traditional Middle Kingdom attitude.

India's nuclear tests should be considered in the context of multipolarity in the Asia–Pacific. Although India emerged as the dominant military power in the subcontinent in 1971, it saw itself as a non-expansionist but activist force in the Indian subcontinent and the neighbourhood, including in the Indian Ocean area. Since the 1950s, Pakistan has tried to bridge the asymmetry in the distribution of power and influence with India and to seek bipolarity within the subcontinent by borrowing American and Chinese power through its alliance activity and by its internal military efforts. But India has continually rejected Indo–Pakistani bipolarity as the basis of stability in subcontinental international relations. Instead, it sought a position for India in a multipolar Asia; its niche would be in the areas bordering Afghanistan and Iran to the west, and the South China Seas to the east. Implicit in this quest was the belief that Pakistan was not a permanent adversary of India, that it was in the direct Indian interest to have a stable Pakistan and a buffer *vis-à-vis* religious and sectarian forces in the region (this is especially true with a Talibanized Afghanistan today), and that Indians and Pakistanis (or Hindus and Muslims) shared a common civilizational base which created points of affinity and discourse. In its eastward orientation, Indian diplomacy sought commercial, cultural, political, and strategic presence and influence for India on a non-exclusive basis. India does not accept the PRC proposition that it is a great power, and hence, the

PRC is entitled to build a submarine capability in the Bay of Bengal, in close proximity to the Indian coastline, and that the Indian Ocean should not be Indian. In this context, a doubt exists in Indian strategic planning about the meaning of PRC's push into Myanmar. It makes sense because of Yunnan's interior position and its pressing need for economic development with an access to port facilities. Here, Myanmar's ports are as desirable for Yunnan's trade as Calcutta is for Nepalese trade. However, the distinction breaks down because the PRC has great power ambitions and Nepal does not. India, according to the Central Military Commission Report of February 1993, is the 'largest threat' to the PRC.[6] Furthermore, in diplomacy which parallels Chinese attitudes about India, the Clinton administration emphasized India's future international position in the context of 'South Asia' and gave India no berth in the Asia–Pacific. American diplomacy has been preoccupied with China, Japan, and American associates in Australia, South East Asia and North East Asia, leaving the Indians feeling marginalized.

In sum, Indian policymakers viewed the world in the 1990s, especially in its neighbourhood and in Asia–Pacific generally, as a vortex of fluidity, contention, and collusion involving a number of competing players, issues, and interests. In the strategic environment of the 1990s, several hostile paired strategic relationships (the two Koreas, USA/North Korea, PRC/Taiwan, PRC/Japan, PRC/USA, PRC/Vietnam, PRC/India, India/Pakistan, USA/Iran, Iran/Saudi Arabia, and Iran/Afghanistan being the important ones) competed with a moderately stable set of inconclusive regional dialogues (ASEAN/ARF, India/Pakistan, USA/India, USA/North Korea, and PRC/USA/Taiwan) and security arrangements (bilateral security ties between the USA, Japan, South Korea, Australia, and Indonesia being the main ones). This scenario relegated India to the margin of Asia–Pacific because in the minds of Western, Japanese, and Chinese policymakers, Asia–Pacific seemed to stop at the Thai–Myanmar border. This made no sense to the Indian policymakers because even before the end of the Cold War, the traditional subregional boundaries had started to fade. In India's north-west, the Afghan campaign in the 1980s and 1990s, the policies of the Inter-Services Intelligence Organization (ISI) of Pakistan, and the Pakistani Army had thrown up the Taliban as a major force, and with its help, Pakistan had extended its ideological and strategic space westwards. A *nexus of players* (ISI–Army–Taliban–opium dealers), opposed by Iranian, Russian, select Central Asian (Tadjiks and Uzbeks), and Indian agencies, as well as a *cluster of issues* (opium, religion, oil, regime politics, and regional stability) had emerged. Likewise, the PRC's push into Myanmar and the Bay of Bengal was accompanied by a flurry of gun-running which fuelled subregional insurgencies, a proliferation of fishing boats with little fish and lots of military and intelligence gear, massive drug trade in the subregion, and the occasional Chinese submarine activity. So the moderate stability was, in reality, a situation of temporary military truces rather than substantial political settlements. It represented a condition of limited stability in the context of asymmetry in the distribution of power and influence, mixed with hostile mental make-ups of elites, a combination of religion and politics, mutual mistrust and dilemmas of 'limited peace' which required military modernization, as well as confidence-building measures. The stability was fragile. Despite the PRC's policy of peace and priority of economic modernization, the Asia–Pacific scene was engaged in military modernization, US–Japan military guidelines were being revised and enlarged, and there was no clarity about the end result of PRC's planned military modernization by AD 2010. Moreover, in Asia–Pacific, the dominant trend was that of nuclear proliferation, and not non-proliferation.

2.   *India's approach to the nuclear question was formed before independence and it reveals a preoccupation with the relationship between Science, National Development and Power, and international security. But India's nuclear behaviour is retarded; it has elements of reactivity and proactivity, as well as 'made in India' dilemmas.*

To understand the story of Pokhran and its consequences with respect to Indian policies, regional security, and international relations, it is necessary to explain the origins and subsequent development of different facets of Indian nuclear behaviour. The book adopts a historical approach, beginning with the prehistory in Chapter 2. It outlines the mental outlook and the approach of Indian political and scientific elites about the role of science in India's development. This is essential to an understanding of the post-1947 Indian nuclear policy and diplomacy since the general Indian approach to the nuclear question was formed prior to independence. The context was a changing state form—namely the expectation of Indian elites that British rule was coming to an end and independent India had to plan its future policies. With regard to nuclear affairs, the driving element in the prehistory was the belief of India's political and scientific elites that India had missed the fruits of the Industrial Revolution and post-colonial India needed to harness modern science for India's development.

The initial motive was non-military, but after 1947, as India was drawn into the Cold War international system, the nuclear programme acquired a built-in defence potential. Nehru was the secret godfather of this potential, even though Nehru was publicly for anti-war, anti-military, pro-peaceful diplomacy, and pro-nuclear disarmament. On the other hand however, Nehru authorized the organization of an Indian defence machinery as well as military expenditures and activities. This indicates the existence of two Nehrus, so to speak, in the context of a wide range of Indian social and political thought.

Before India became independent, a spectrum of Indian social and political thought had emerged. This is outlined in Figure 1.2.

This spectrum revealed tension among the different lines of Indian thinking and policy action. Post-1947 Indian nuclear attitudes and

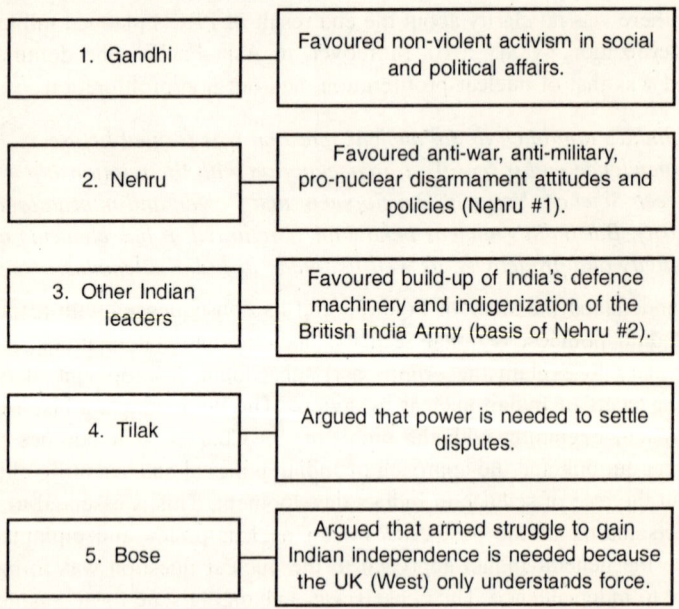

1. Gandhi	Favoured non-violent activism in social and political affairs.
2. Nehru	Favoured anti-war, anti-military, pro-nuclear disarmament attitudes and policies (Nehru #1).
3. Other Indian leaders	Favoured build-up of India's defence machinery and indigenization of the British India Army (basis of Nehru #2).
4. Tilak	Argued that power is needed to settle disputes.
5. Bose	Argued that armed struggle to gain Indian independence is needed because the UK (West) only understands force.

Fig. 1.2: Historical Spectrum of Indian Political and Social Thought, Pre-1947

Source: Compiled by author on the basis of information in S.P. Cohen, *The Indian Army* (Berkeley: University of California Press, 1971).

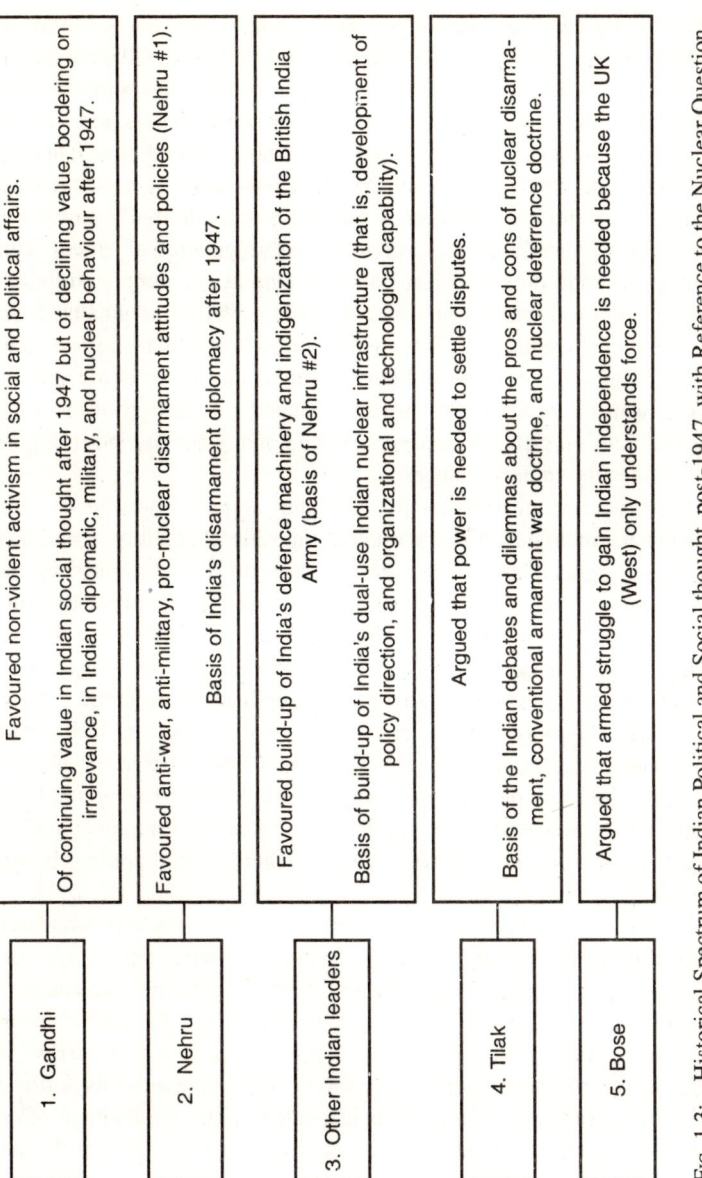

1. Gandhi

Favoured non-violent activism in social and political affairs.

Of continuing value in Indian social thought after 1947 but of declining value, bordering on irrelevance, in Indian diplomatic, military, and nuclear behaviour after 1947.

2. Nehru

Favoured anti-war, anti-military, pro-nuclear disarmament attitudes and policies (Nehru #1).

Basis of India's disarmament diplomacy after 1947.

3. Other Indian leaders

Favoured build-up of India's defence machinery and indigenization of the British India Army (basis of Nehru #2).

Basis of build-up of India's dual-use Indian nuclear infrastructure (that is, development of policy direction, and organizational and technological capability).

4. Tilak

Argued that power is needed to settle disputes.

Basis of the Indian debates and dilemmas about the pros and cons of nuclear disarmament, conventional armament war doctrine, and nuclear deterrence doctrine.

5. Bose

Argued that armed struggle to gain Indian independence is needed because the UK (West) only understands force.

Fig. 1.3: Historical Spectrum of Indian Political and Social thought, post-1947, with Reference to the Nuclear Question

Source: Compiled by author on basis of information in S.P. Cohen, *The Indian Army* (Berkeley: University of California Press, 1971).

policies originated and developed in the context of this spectrum of thought. Indian nuclear politics and policies after 1947 reflected the imperatives (compulsions and opportunities) as well as the contradictions within this spectrum. At the same time, Indian decisions and debates concerning nuclear, space, and missile affairs shaped the dialectics within the spectrum. Eventually, by the 1990s, they reduced the contradictions within the spectrum of the 1930s and the 1940s, and led to the public's rejection of some choices and acceptance of others. This book argues that India's nuclear politics and policies, along with India's military and war behaviour since the early-1970s, marginalized the Gandhian and Nehruvian (Nehru #1) impulses which stressed non-violence, anti-war, and anti-military attitudes and policies towards issues of war and peace. They instead validated and reinforced the Tilak line and built on Nehru #2's approach, and then went beyond it. Figure 1.3 outlines the radical changes.

The favoured mechanism in the Indian approach was to develop dual-use technologies. This facilitated plausible deniability of military intent and application, and yet the option to do so was created by the development of the organizational and the technological infrastructure. Between the 1950s and the 1970s, dual-use technologies were not primarily a cover for military use because the strategic necessity to convert dual-use technologies into military applications emerged only in the 1980s. This book first explores the pattern of dual-use technology development and problem of development of hardware in the nuclear and space spheres and then goes on to highlight the growing emphasis on military applications in the context of a threatening regional and international security environment which challenged Indian security and prestige.

As well, this book explains the history of India's nuclear behaviour. According to the Webster's College dictionary, 'behaviour' means 'the aggregate of responses to internal and external stimuli'; 'the action or reaction of any material under given circumstances'. To behave means 'to act or react in a particular way', it also means to act 'properly'. In India's case, nuclear behaviour refers to the development of its *political attitude* about the role of Indian nuclear science, the development of Indian science and technology *infrastructure* or *organizations*, the acquisition and enhancement of Indian nuclear *weapons and missile capability* along with conventional armament, and the development of diplomatic and military *policies* which facilitated engagement of the Indian forces in the external (regional and international) environment.

Foreign and military policy is a study of interaction between competing forces within a country and outside its borders. This book will explain this continuous interaction, and the pattern of action or reaction to internal/external stimuli. It will show that India has acted in a particular way. Whether or not it has been 'proper behaviour' is a question of political judgement.

The overall theme is that progress or development has been slow and retarded and there is still room for improvement despite the 1998 tests. This book argues that it is necessary to articulate an Indian nuclear doctrine and to integrate nuclear weapons and missile capability into the Indian defence posture if India is to be taken seriously by the international community as a nuclear power. Indians will have to take their nuclear weapons and missile delivery capability seriously and to demonstrate this publicly before it can be taken seriously by outside forces. Conversely, India will remain vulnerable to external pressures so long as there are signs of hesitation in the development of a clear nuclear doctrine and a credible nuclear deterrent. At issue is the necessity to develop a new Indian strategic culture where restraint is not viewed as weakness by regional and international forces. Restraint is restraint only if the capacity to inflict harm clearly exists, it is demonstrated, and it is not exercised; in the absence of continuous demonstration of the existence of such capacity, and unless the other side negotiates in a meaningful way, Indian restraint is likely to be perceived as Indian weakness. Deterrent strategy must be studied and practised as a mind game. It is psychological warfare where the aim is to persuade the opposition to alter its behaviour and motivation. The quality of a country's nuclear strategy depends in part on the quality of its weapons capability and in part on the quality of the deterrent messages which are conveyed to the public and secret enemies. Sun Tzu's *The Art of War* highlights the role of psychological warfare in strategy. Kenneth Waltz's work highlights the importance of deterrent messages in nuclear strategy. Here, foreign perceptions that Indians talk a lot but lack 'staying power' suggests that the nuclear question is not simply a strategic issue; it is also a cultural one.[7]

Furthermore, nuclear behaviour is either reactive, as a response to clear *public* external threats, or it is proactive action in response to an *anticipated* threat from an emergent hostile country or a hostile coalition. In the Indian case, the nuclear development shows a mix of reactive and proactive behaviour in the nuclear, space, and missile spheres. This book makes the argument that Indian policymakers have been generally slow to grasp the effect of nuclear and missile development in its strategic neighbourhood; and they have been slow to grasp the negative influence of the international non-proliferation activity of the P-5 nuclear weapon states on Indian strategic interests. Since the 1970s, the P-5 nuclear powers have come together despite the differences in their political systems and their strategic interests. There is contention as well as collusion among the P-5 states (for example, the USA and the PRC) in their strategic behaviour but on the issue of non-proliferation, there is more collusion than contention. Three of the P-5 states (the USA, the PRC, and the UK) have come together on the belief that a nuclear India is a regional and an international problem, and that it must be contained and isolated. To solve this problem, the P-5 powers have divided the world into three categories: the nuclear haves and their allies whose diplomatic and military interests must be protected and whose margin of strength must be retained because they represent the responsible core of international security; the nuclear have-nots, like India, who should be isolated and marginalized in international security affairs because they are potential regional hegemons and 'rogues' in the international security system; and the 'pigs who could not fly'—the majority of states in Africa, South America, and the South Pacific who lack the strategic necessity and the means to acquire nuclear weapons capability but who provide the votes in international non-proliferation conference diplomacy. It is argued that India's political class and diplomatic practitioners have continuously *overstated* the importance of nuclear disarmament for international and regional affairs, especially in regions of conflict; and they have continuously *understated* the importance of nuclear deterrence in Indian security and diplomacy. It took Indian policymakers close to fifty years to resolve their internal debates about the role and purpose of military and nuclear strength in modern international relations and in Indian policies. Despite the shift away from Gandhian pacifism and Nehruvian peace diplomacy in the 1950s, to the embrace of the nuclear weapons option in the 1990s, a significant gap still exists between the demonstration of Indian nuclear weapons capability and its production, deployment, and induction into the Indian armed forces. As India faces the millennium, it is at a strategic crossroad. If prospects exist to secure a political settlement with the USA, the PRC, and Pakistan—India's main rivals in the strategic sphere—then it makes sense to develop a policy of non-development and non-deployment of India's nuclear weapons capability. But on the other hand, if Indo–US, Sino–Indian, and Indo–Pakistani negotiations do not produce a political settlement, then non-production and non-deployment of nuclear weapons capability may appear as a sell-out to American, Chinese, and Pakistani pressure; it will appear as appeasement. The devil is not in the detail of an arms control agreement, but it is in the context or the framework of a political settlement.

The argument is that Indian policymakers frequently find themselves tangled up in dilemmas (that is, having to choose between unpleasant choices). More often than not, they are of their own making. The habit of creating such entangling dilemmas (rather than creating entangling alignments which create leverage with international powers) is not limited to nuclear affairs. The standard Indian diplomatic mantras emphasize the importance of non-alignment because it preserves the freedom of political choice, independence of thought, and policy action. This right, however, makes sense only if it is actually and continuously exercised by the Indian political class and if it produces effective policies.

Consider a few major examples of self-inflicted Indian dilemmas.

(i) Nehru, the architect of Indian non-alignment, managed to create a big dilemma for India in his Kashmir policy. This was Nehru's pernicious legacy to India. He referred the Kashmir issue to the United Nations (UN) under Article 35 of the UN Charter (which speaks of a threat to international peace and hence becomes an international issue of interest to the P-5 countries) rather than Article 39 of the Charter which refers to aggression. Nehru also ordered a ceasefire in Kashmir and stopped the Indian Army from recovering all of Kashmir when it appeared able to do so; all this occurred with Lord Louis Mountbatten's advice. Nehru's thinking about Kashmir affairs was neither 'independent', nor was it in India's best interests. H.V. Hodson's research of the Mountbatten papers and other British official archives establishes the determining role of Lord L. Mountbatten in the formulation of India's Kashmir policy.[8]

(ii) Similarly, the Government of India's reluctance to start nuclear testing after it acquired the capability to do so in 1957 invited international pressure. Despite the threat posed by China's nuclear testing and missile capability during the 1960s, India declined to test a nuclear device. Then again it declined to test between 1975 and 1998. This was seen as weakness on the part of India. Prime Minister Indira Gandhi chickened out after the 1974 nuclear test, claiming that it was a peaceful explosion, and disclaimed an intent to seek nuclear weapons capability.

The nuclear behaviour of Indian policymakers showed a contrast between two Indian policies: the development of a technological base of the nuclear option on the one hand; and the declared emphasis on nuclear disarmament rather than Indian nuclear weapons development on the other hand. The two policies or postures revealed a contradiction which the outside powers did not hesitate to exploit.

However, getting entangled in 'made in India' strategic dilemmas is only a part of the Indian story. Between the 1930s and the 1950s, Indian behaviour also revealed significant proactivity. This was indicated by the establishment of the infrastructure which led to the development of Indian nuclear science. Secondly, the framework of Indian diplomacy was established in the 1950s. It firmly and continuously, with some modifications, opposed international controls on Indian nuclear decision-making and its nuclear capacities. Although international and domestic pressures circumscribed Indian nuclear decision-making during the Indira Gandhi, Rajiv Gandhi, and Narasimha Rao leadership years, still, the foundation of Indian nuclear science and Indian nuclear diplomacy of the 1930s to the 1950s withstood external and internal pressures to roll-over and disarm like a defeated state. Here, the proactivity of the 1930s to the 1950s had a lingering and durable effect. It acted like a shock absorber or a buffer against mounting external and internal pressures which were meant to induce Indian nuclear disarmament.

The third major indicator of proactivity is to be found in the origins and development of Indian space capability. This is a fascinating story because India's missile programme was built on what was initially and primarily a civilian activity which nonetheless had built-in dual uses of space technology. Chapter 7 tells this story.

The fourth sign of proactivity concerned Indian diplomacy regarding the decision not to accept the CTBT. With political will and diplomatic risk-taking, and contrary to the earlier pattern of timidity since the 1974 nuclear test, the Indian government under Prime Minister I.K. Gujral blocked the CTBT against the advice of Indian specialists who proposed Indian abstention rather than a veto of the CTBT. The fifth example of proactivity was the public declaration by the Indian defence minister, George Fernandes, that China, not Pakistan was India's potential enemy number one.[9] This sent shock waves in major capitals of the world, but it also created a clear public identification with the China problem; and it shifted the focus of the attentive public within India and outside to the rivalry within China. Finally, Prime Minister Vajpayee's surprise decision to order a round of Indian nuclear tests in May 1998 was the most recent and the most dramatic evidence of Indian nuclear proactivity.

In other words, there are elements of reactivity as well as proactivity in Indian nuclear behaviour. The latter has changed the parameters of India's policies as well as the parameters of international nuclear non-proliferation and nuclear proliferation policies of a variety of players. This book argues that impact and influence have been gained by Indian proactivity, and it was temporarily lost by Indian reactive behaviour. The policy implication is that proactivity, not reactivity, is required to stay in the nuclear arms race and to participate in the international strategic discourse among major and minor powers in the world today. Of course, the nuclear engagement with China and Pakistan has to be managed and controlled. This is an argument to guard against accidental conflict. It is not an argument to avoid calculated and controlled risk-taking and escalation if it serves a strategic cause and the public good. That is, strategic activity must have a clear political purpose and a moral justification, namely that the use of nuclear arms serves as the ultimate defence of a country's survival, security, and values.

In sum, there are two Indian stories. The first one reveals bursts of proactivity by the Indian political class and the body politic; the second one reveals inertia, passivity, and timidity by the Indian political class and body politic. The first one involves calculated risk-taking and fear-lessness; the second one is intimidated by external and domestic pressures. Both types of organizational behaviour coexist in the Indian state and in Indian society. Here, 'India' may be divided into black boxes of secretive and compartmentalized worlds. These are like imperial China's Forbidden Cities. Each possesses an internal political and strategic culture, ethos, hierarchy, decision-making process, and decision rules; and career as well as institutional interests of the players are at stake. These 'worlds' or 'forbidden cities' are not self-contained or self-sufficient. Like billiard balls or like atoms, they interact and clash with other worlds or cities within and outside India, and they form temporary alliances with them. Breaking the compartmentalization and secrecy of each such world or city is a challenge which Indians face in their quest to combine the energies and talent of each such world or city and to make India into a modern, integrated, and effective presence in regional and international politics.

ENDNOTES

1. Harald Muller, 'The Death of Arms Control?', *Disarmament Diplomacy*, no. 29, London, August/September 1998, p. 2.
2. Confidential interviews, New Delhi, September 1998.
3. For the theme that liberal democracies are peaceful in their relations with each other, see M.W. Doyle, 'Kant, Liberal Legacies, and Foreign Affairs, Part I and Part II', *Philosophy and Public Affairs*, vol. 12, no. 3, Summer 1983, pp. 205–35, and vol. 12, no. 4, Fall 1983, pp. 323–53.
4. Martin Wight offers a clear insight into the relationship between 'prestige' and 'power'. To quote him:

   Closely bound up with the idea of 'honour' is the idea of 'prestige'. Honour is the halo round interests; prestige is the halo round power.

   Prestige is one of the imponderables of international politics, but it is too closely connected with power to be considered as belonging to the moral order. It is the influence derived from power. And unless the power is *present* power there can be little prestige. Deference to historical importance and gratitude for past achievement are even less apparent in international politics than in other kinds of politics.

   See Hedley Bull and C. Holbraad, eds, *Power Politics*, 2nd edition (New York: Viking Penguin Inc., 1986 edition), p. 97.
5. T.H. Etzold and J.L. Gaddis, 'The Position of the United States with Respect to Asia', NSC 48/1, (Top Secret) 23 December 1949, *Containment: Documents on American Policy and Strategy, 1945–1950* (New York: Columbia University Press, 1978), pp. 252–3.
6. India is labelled as the 'largest potential threat', in *Can the Chinese Army Win the Next War?*, A summary of conclusions in PRC's Central Military Commission, 1993.
7. Sun Tzu, *The Art of War*, Translation and Introduction by S.B. Griffith (London: Oxford University Press, 1963, 1971). Kenneth Waltz, 'Nuclear Weapons: More May be Better' in Lawrence Freedman, ed., *War* (Oxford: Oxford University Press, 1994), p. 355.
8. K.P. Saxena, 'Dialogue Considered Unlikely to Resolve Kashmir Dispute', *India Abroad*, 16 October 1998, p. 2. H.V. Hodson, *The Great Divide* (Karachi: Oxford University Press, 1959), Chapter 25.
9. J.F. Burns, 'India's New Defence Chief Sees Chinese Military Threat', *New York Times*, 5 May 1998.

2

Early History (1930s–1947) and the Structure of Nuclear Science, State, and Society

Introduction and Framework

Indian attitudes and policies concerning science in general and nuclear science in particular originated in the 1930s in the context of a changing state form; that is, there was an expectation that British colonial rule in India was coming to an end and independent India was emerging. What were the attitudes among Indian political and scientific elites about the role of science, including nuclear science, in India's social and economic development and in its external relations? What was the proposed relationship between scientists, state, and society? What were the issues in the debates and what were the results?

India's scientific establishment has emerged as one of the largest pools of scientists in the world but, strictly speaking, it is not a scientific community with a shared set of common interests and a common approach to scientific questions. Despite, or because of, its large size, many members of the Indian science pool are marginalized, depoliticized, demoralized, and not fully interactive.[1] Furthermore, the history of contemporary Indian science reveals the impact of Indian culture on the planning and management of Indian science. According to Kalam and Rajan,

We have often asked ourselves and others why India in its several thousand years of history has rarely tried to expand its territories or to assume a dominating role. Many of the experts and others with whom we had a dialogue referred to some special features of the Indian psyche which could partly explain this: greater tolerance, less discipline, the lack of a sense of retaliation, more flexibility in accepting outsiders, great adherence to hierarchy, and emphasis on personal safety over adventure. Some felt that a combination of many of these features have affected our ability to pursue a vision tenaciously.[2]

Despite these characteristics however, there is a history of extensive policy-driven interaction and power struggle between Indian scientists and Indian politicians at the upper end of the policy-making pyramid. The debates have historically been located in the upper reaches of the policy-making group(s). The decision structure consisted of a few powerful individuals; it was highly personalized. Historically, Indian strategic decision-making has been small group activity. 'Development' or 'improvement' of Indian scientific and military capabilities must be studied in this context. The individual high-powered players made decisions on the basis of personal, as well as institutional, attitudes and interests, and their respective views of the national interest or the public good. Thus, the history of Indian science reveals, on the one hand, a pattern of scientist–state–society interactions *within* India and, on the other hand, an interstate stimulus–response (reactive or proactive) that reflected the influence of regional and international relationships on India's national interests as well as the institutional and personal interests of the key players. The impact of the external environment has been critical in the Indian case. Given the culture and history of Hindu-style (also Socratic-style) debate and internal division without closure in political as well as scientific affairs, international changes have often radicalized and polarized Indian scientific and policy consciousness. In turn, the external inputs have increased pressures on Indian decision-makers. Figure 2.1 outlines the parameters of the Indian decision processes.

International Environment	
Competing Indian scientists' attitudes and policies	Indian political decision-makers and their power struggle(s)
Indian society with competing points of view about the role of the state	

FIG. 2.1: Parameters of Indian Decision-making in Science

Two types of dynamics are inherent in this process. (1) If the Indian elite structure and Indian society is secretive, compartmentalized, inattentive, passive, depoliticized, and internally divided or unintegrated, then India's science policy is vulnerable to international pressures which are meant to paralyze and retard the development of India's scientific and technological base and capacity to dominate India's strategic environment. This type of Indian dynamic is typical when the country is in a non-crisis mode. (2) On the other hand, significant changes in the international environment (that is, war(s), rise of hostile alignments that threaten India's physical security and strategic interests, and rise of external norms that challenge Indian interests) have often radicalized the Indian elite structure from its compartmentalized, inattentive, passive, depoliticized condition, and then international pressures have turned out to be counterproductive. The reason is that Indian society is still responsive to nationalism in a crisis. When aroused, Indian nationalism has emerged as a source of domestic pressure on the Indian decision-making apparatus and has sought to oppose international pressures on India.

These two different types of dynamics reveal two different types of engagement among forces within India and outside it. India's nuclear history reveals an oscillation between the two types of dynamics and the two types of engagement. But this oscillation occurred after India gained its independence, though the parameters were established before 1947. To a discussion of the early history or the 'prehistory' we now turn.

The Prehistory

The leaders of Indian science policy after independence were advocates of the importance of science in Indian debates even before 1947. This justifies the strong emphasis in this book on the attitudes and policies of scientific and political personalities in the Indian case. The story is that politically conscious, nationalist Indian scientists in pre-independent India established coalitions with Indian politicians, especially J.L. Nehru, before 1947.[3] The coalitions reflected the winners in the pre-1947 Indian debates, as well as the winning arguments about Indian science policy. After independence, the scientists in the dominant pre-1947 coalition captured high government positions in India. They set the research agenda as well as helped define the legislative and institutional framework of policy. They captured the state apparatus as it related to Indian scientific affairs and created an autonomous science empire, a state within the Indian state. J.L. Nehru, prime minister of India (1947–64), the senior political member of the pre-1947 winning and dominant coalition, became the minister in charge of atomic energy. He shaped and defined the policy agenda. He provided the political legitimacy and engineered the legislative authority for India's scientific and diplomatic endeavours which involved the different branches of the Indian government as well as the scientific organizations which were autonomous in their internal administration and organization but which were funded by the state. The scientists–politicians interaction developed a dual pattern: (1) Indian scientists pursued their research agenda without political interference; they functioned within the policy boundaries set by the political leadership; (2) After 1947, from time to time, Indian scientists inside the policy pyramid intervened and pressured the political leadership to change Indian policies. They did so by creating technological options that enabled Indian leaders to increase India's space in the international system. Furthermore, they engaged in political advocacy that went beyond politically neutral scientific activity. Combined with the options created by scientific developments, the in-house political advocacy of Indian scientists tested the policy boundaries of the state and eventually altered them significantly. In this sense, Indian scientists who occupy the policy pyramid in India have typically worn two hats: as a scientific leader in a chosen field, and as a *politicized scientist* (not to be confused with a political scientist). The following chapters will show that Indian scientists were able to increase the military content of India's nuclear activity and posture, to enable Indian diplomatic practitioners to resist international pressures to denuclearize India, to create the technological base to advance civilian as well as military applications of nuclear and space science, and generally to shift the orientation of Indian social and political thought away from a faith in non-violence and peace diplomacy (or engagement of the external environment primarily by peaceful means) towards a policy of relying on internal economic, military, and scientific/technological strength and participation in international strategic affairs through a strategy of activism and autonomy. The strategy was obviously not anticipated by Indian politicians and scientists in the 1930s–1947 era, but in hindsight it appears that the foundation was laid in the approach and the method of India's scientific development in the prehistory.

Historical Patterns: 'Happy Convergence', 'Ritualistic Confrontations', and 'Deadly Quarrels'[4]

The first pattern of state–scientists interaction crystallized in the context of a changing state form—that is, when British colonial rule in India was in the process of being replaced by independent India. Between the

1930s and the early 1950s, a pattern of 'happy convergence' and 'ritualistic confrontation' evolved around the political aims and the science strategy of the key players: Saha, Bhabha, Bhatnagar, and Mahalanobis (the scientists); and Nehru and Bose (the politicians).[5] Saha, a physicist and a contemporary of Bhabha, disagreed with the latter's approach to India's nuclear science policies and administration. Saha was politically close to Bose, a political leader who sought Indian independence through an armed struggle and who opposed the policies of Gandhi and Nehru in the Indian independence movement (see Figure 1.3 in Chapter 1). Bhabha, a close confidante of Nehru, became the czar of Indian nuclear science. His approach to the development of Indian nuclear science is still the basis of India's policy, even though Bhabha died in a mysterious aircrash in 1966. Bhatnagar enjoyed the confidence of Bhabha and Nehru and he ran India's scientific establishments during the Nehru years. Mahalanobis, a statistician, who founded the Indian Statistical Institute performed the data analysis for India's Five-Year Plans as well as Indian scientific planning. They all agreed on the need to secure power and self-reliance for India and to use science to solve national development problems. However, their aims and science strategy revealed sharp differences.

Saha emphasized the following:

(i) There must be a complete reorganization of the society and economy of India.

(ii) Planning must be on a rational and national basis with an emphasis on industrialization and the public sector.

(iii) The state must address energy problems, including nuclear power and hydroelectric resources.

(iv) The Gandhian approach to economic change (with an emphasis on village industries rather than industrialization) was backward looking.

(v) The links of the Indian Atomic Energy Commission (AEC) with private industry and foreign firms were detrimental for the national interest.

(vi) Universities should be the foundation of research in India. The approach of the Council for Scientific and Industrial Research (CSIR), to create a chain of research institutes independent of universities, was undesirable.

(vii) Science must have a social purpose.

In contrast, Bhabha's agenda emphasized the following:

(i) The need was to build specialization and to create autonomous schools.

(ii) The purpose of this approach was to support fundamental research.

(iii) Fundamental physics was the spearhead of research and practical applications in industry. The USSR was the model in this regard.

(iv) Nuclear energy was important for energy production in India.

(v) There was value in creating research groups around suitable scientists.

(vi) Government *support* for research was essential but it was to be without government *control* or political interference over scientific research or the administration of the institutes. The emphasis was on the autonomy of science.

(vii) Development of international scientific contacts and exchanges was necessary to facilitate Indian scientific activities.

Bhatnagar's agenda was linked to Bhabha's and emphasized the creation of a chain of state-funded research institutes independent of Indian universities. The encounter was between the Saha–Bose approach and that of Bhabha, Bhatnagar, and Nehru. Key scientist(s) and a key politician converged in each coalition. The struggle between the two was settled in 1947 with the victory of Bhabha and his allies. The winning strategy would determine who among the Indian scientists would guide science policy in independent India, what method would help organize India's scientific infrastructure, and what should the nature of India's nuclear policy be. By 1947, the first and the second questions were settled in favour of the Bhabha–Bhatnagar line. The third question was addressed in an ambivalent policy stance that stressed India's commitment to develop the peaceful uses of nuclear energy and India's faith in security through disarmament. However, Prime Minister Nehru's position also included a reference to 'other use of atomic energy, if India is compelled to do so'.[6] The winning coalition emphasized the need to harness science for Indian economic development, and the need to mobilize national resources and national power but downplayed the military dimension of this link. Out of these twin concerns came the strategy to develop dual-use technologies and to develop international scientific cooperation between India and the scientific leaders in the world. This strategy implied seeking technologies and materials with clear civilian applications as well as military uses or spin-offs. Along with this strategy was a policy and posture of peaceful uses only but with a built-in defence use if necessary.

The Indian case thus reveals two patterns of scientists–state relations. By 1947, a pattern of 'happy convergence' emerged in Indian scientific affairs. Following Indian independence and Nehru's rise to national power, he dominated Indian foreign and atomic energy affairs after 1947. The pre-1947 controversy between Saha and Bhabha was settled in favour of Bhabha. Bhabha's political patron, before and after 1947, was Nehru and the two had a special relationship where Bhabha addressed Nehru as *bhai* (brother) in his frequent and private meetings with the prime minister. A critical part of the Saha–Bhabha controversy concerned the role of Indian universities as primary centres of scientific work. Saha favoured the universities. Bhabha and Bhatnagar (later head of the Indian Council for Scientific Research) favoured government funding for highly specialized and functional research institutes, that depended on government funding but were nevertheless free to choose their research priorities and strategies without interference by politicians and civil servants. The Nehru government agreed to the latter approach. This created a 'happy convergence' in the form of active scientists–state collaboration through the development of research institutes that were affiliated with the government. This gave the establishment scientists a basis of political power as well as financial autonomy and a freedom to pursue their research agendas within the overall framework that sought to link science to national development.

This 'happy convergence' meant a big leap forward for India in a historical perspective. Ancient India had a tradition of quality scientific work in different branches of science followed by centuries of social, economic, and political backwardness and foreign conquest. In the first half of the twentieth century, 'Indian' scientific work was limited to a few universities and involved a few Indian scholars. However, the British India government introduced western scientific ideas and technology through its use of industrial revolution technology such as the steam engine, geological surveys, and the development of functional (sector-oriented) research institutes (see Appendix A). After independence, the Government of India, under Nehru's direction, embarked on a plan to develop India's scientific infrastructure on modern lines. This was done by developing a network of state-funded and state-directed, semi-autonomous institutes in a variety of scientific areas such as atomic energy, space, scientific and industrial research, electronics, energy, environment, ocean development, medical research, agricultural research, and biotechnology. Today, there are about two hundred research laboratories in these areas. More recently, the aims of scientific activities were outlined in the Science Policy Resolution adopted by the Indian parliament in March 1958, and the Technology Policy Statement released in January 1983. These stressed the importance of state intervention in securing the benefits of science and technology for the Indian people. They stress the importance of self-reliance and social and economic development as national goals.[7]

This collaboration also created a two-tiered research infrastructure in India. The government-affiliated research institutes were the primary beneficiaries of government funding and they had decision-making autonomy regarding scientific affairs, subject to nominal supervision by the Prime Minister who also held the atomic and science portfolios. The scientists heading these institutes formed the inner circle of Indian science administration. The second tier consisted of isolated and politically weak universities and research centres that received limited government support but were marginal in the decision-making process; they were outsiders. There was a 'happy convergence' between the state (the dominant political leadership) and the inner circle of scientists but there was also growing tension between the inner and the outer circle of scientists. The 'inner' circle refers to scientists who had captured important scientific posts after 1947 inside the policy making pyramid; the 'outer circle' refers to those scientists, like Saha, who did not do so after 1947. Another kind of 'inner–outer' circle of scientists was to emerge later. Since the mid-1960s, Indian scientists who are located within the policy pyramid have been divided on the pros and cons of the development of Indian nuclear weapons and the conversion of the nuclear weapons option (established in 1974) into nuclear weapons capability, which was revealed publicly by the May 1998 Indian nuclear tests. This debate is discussed in Chapters 5, 6, and 7. The inner circle enjoyed political power (and access to the prime minister and the relevant government departments) and they controlled the national scientific establishment. So the inner circle was able to manage the tension.

The second pattern was one of emerging encounters over nuclear policy matters between the inner and outer circle of scientists (as outlined above). They can be divided into two categories: encounters that produced 'ritualistic confrontations' between say, the advocates of the peaceful atom, nuclear disarmament, and non-nuclear India on the one hand, and advocates of a nuclear India on the other. We call them 'ritualistic' because these are like oft-repeated mantras which lack impact in the policy sphere. They do not reflect the internal Indian governmental debates about the costs and benefits of decisions, and about governmental needs and requirements in the context of internal and external compulsions, opportunities, and dilemmas. The latter are labelled as 'deadly quarrels' because they produce policy choices as well as winners and losers in Indian bureaucratic and political circles. 'Deadly quarrels' involve small group activity among governmental policymakers. The ritualistic encounters had little impact on the 'happy convergence' between scientists and the state because scientists were tenured once appointed to government posts and to research institutes. They could not be removed. Ritualistic differences lacked policy impact, and policy differences inside the Indian governments remained mostly secret because of India's stringent Official Secrets Act. The 'deadly quarrels', on the other hand, had an impact on Indian public policy but the Indian experience did not reveal their existence in the 1940s–50s period.

The pattern of 'deadly quarrels' between Indian scientists and the state's political leadership emerged in the mid-1960s when the NPT was debated and the role of nuclear weapons in Indian foreign policy came to the foreground. A multipolar pattern of frequent interactions emerged between nationalist Indian scientists and political leaders (who held government positions) on the one hand, and ambivalent political leaders, 'foreign linked' sections of India's foreign policy establishment,[8] and the scientific bureaucracy on the other. These encounters dampened the search for autonomy and nuclear weapons development in Indian diplomatic and military affairs during the mid-1960s and 1970s, but they did not eliminate it at the same time. The main effect of these encounters was to create ambivalence (oscillation) and internal controversies about the military applications of Indian science. However, by the 1980s, the nationalist sector of the Indian scientific community and civil bureaucracy gained the upper hand, and other sectors of the Indian bureaucracy and science administration lost the struggle to denuclearize India. As a result, Indian scientists decisively changed the orientation of Nehru's disarmament diplomacy and his peaceful (non-military) nuclear policy. By the 1980s, Indian nuclear and space activities acquired military content, but still the debate about the value of Indian nuclear tests, acquiring nuclear weapons, and embracing nuclear deterrence doctrine as a basis of Indian security continued into the 1990s.

These 'nationalist' versus 'foreign-linked internationalist' confrontations point to the existence of two competitive subcultures in the upper echelons of Indian decision-making since 1947. The first one was nationalistic, and was represented by Dr Homi J. Bhabha and his allies. Its political drive was shaped by attitudes formed prior to Indian independence in 1947, and its influence after 1947 was evident in India's fears of international arrangements, that were dominated by a superpower, in nuclear and disarmament affairs. This approach was expressed in the following positions: (i) November 1948: India supported the Baruch Plan but opposed international ownership of uranium and thorium. India possessed thorium and recognized it as an economic asset; (ii) May 1954: in commenting on President Eisenhower's 'atoms for peace' plan, Nehru expressed his opposition to participation in an organization dominated by the great powers; (iii) 1957: India accepted the International Atomic Energy Agency (IAEA) Statute but argued against a safeguard regime that applied only to importing countries; and (iv) 1950s: India sought participation and representation in international organizations because it distrusted meetings that were dominated by the great powers. This distrust went beyond nuclear and disarmament meetings and was expressed in policies concerning Korea and the Indo–China conferences as well.[9]

The second approach was shaped by some of Bhabha's successors, who were active in *Indian bureaucratic politics* and were mostly oriented towards the American ideas about a US-dominated international and regional security order and about India's limited role in international affairs. The outcomes of these confrontations depended on the relative strength of the competitive subcultures in India's nuclear history. Generally, when the nationalist subculture prevailed, scientists–state interactions reveal 'happy convergence'; but when the 'internationalist' faction gained the upper hand, scientists–state interactions evolved into ritual confrontations and deadly quarrels. Both subcultures work within a politically sheltered, secretive, closed politics (that is, without continuous public scrutiny), and a financially autonomous base. The two subcultures allowed successive Indian scientific elites to intervene repeatedly, and often successfully, in policy debates concerning a variety of Indian policies, such as the development of resources (for example thorium), nuclear weapons, disarmament, space, energy, and environmental issues. We believe Indian scientific elites have used their scientific knowledge and political skills to advance their respective world views and conceptions of Indian destiny as well as their personal scientific and institutional interests. They have done so by mobilizing India's political system and social attitudes in support of scientific as well as military, political, and developmental objectives. This pattern of behaviour was established in the prehistory and it continued after India's independence.

The ability to define the national research agenda, to draw on budgetary support for their research activities, to organize state-funded institutes and laboratories, and to participate in international scientific meetings, while defining India's position in these meetings, strengthened the domestic political power of these elites. As a consequence, there were no effective mechanisms of political and social control over scientific activities. As to science policy, it reflected the balance of power within the government of India in different historical periods.

Structural Influences

So far, personality and ideological factors, such as the close personal relationship between Nehru and Bhabha, have been addressed in this chapter. Yet structural factors, such as the influence of regional crisis and international developments, significantly increased the need for such personalized interactions. Frequent involvement in regional conflicts (the 1962, 1965, and 1971 wars), India's continuous attention to a hostile international environment, and the perception that the great powers were intrusive actors, led to significant levels of investment in dual-use atomic and space technological developments. This dual-use commitment also required extensive international contacts. The nature and level of contacts with the outside world was driven by a search for scientific partners who shared Indian scientific priorities. These contacts were driven by a quest for autonomy, not dependence. The rationale for a strategy to rely on dual-use technologies in Indian nuclear and space activities was two-fold: (1) Dual-use technology facilitated a plausible deniability of military intent; (2) At the same time, it enabled the development of a weapons option should adverse contingencies require such a policy shift in the future. Here the interactions between the Indian state and the international system were triggered by threats; and they facilitated Indian scientific activities through scientific exchanges.

There are two important historical periods in the analysis of structural influences on India's political economy of science:

Pre-1947

The ideology of using state-supported science to develop national power emerged during the 1930s and 1940s in a unique colonial, historical context. Three points are important in this period: (1) The British India government had created an infrastructure of industrial and scientific activity in the form of railways, roads, irrigation, post and telegraph communications network, and a variety of scientific and functional institutes, as noted earlier. Though this infrastructure was set up by the British mainly to serve their own objectives in India, still it served as a useful building block for India after 1947. The exposure of Indians to British education and science stimulated the rise of a Western educated Indian scientific elite. (2) Among Indian scientists and politicians, there was an expectation of an impending change in the nature of the Indian state (from a colony to an independent state) and of the required changes in the scientific tasks of the new state. (3) There was also an expectation of a fusion between science and national development objectives and massive socio-economic change to promote the public good. This meant a centrally-planned system to use science to take India into the twentieth century, to escape the backwardness of the past, and to avoid scientific imperialism and dependency.

The origins of independent Indian science therefore, lay in changing historical state forms and in the political attitudes of India's scientific and political elites. Before 1947, as argued, the function of British military and industrial science and technology was to serve the aims of British imperial domination over India, and not to facilitate Indian economic development or political autonomy. The aim was, in other words, to make India a dependent part of the British global economy. British investment in India's military and industrial research was limited. The main structural influence was that of British colonial domination of India which nonetheless allowed the rise of an indigenized Indian scientific elite. The colonial experience aroused Indian nationalism and the need to mobilize Indian political will and resources to build Indian strength. A related structural element lay in the importance of knowledge and science in Indian history and society. These structural influences stimulated the quest for Indian science to develop India's place in the world. Note that the quest for indigenous scientific development was a consequence of interaction of international (British) and indigenous forces. In this case, the indigenous response, 'that of Indian political and scientific elites', was to use science and development to *increase* the space for Indians in the new India and the space for India in the international system.

Post-1947

After 1947, the state form and its aims changed radically as did the global and national boundaries of Indian science; a new political (attitudinal, organizational, and policy) framework of science–state relations emerged. The shared anti-colonial experience among pre-independence Indian scientists and political leaders shaped the political consciousness regarding the socio–economic and political functions of science; it also highlighted the importance of national autonomy. Here, a shared political history led to a 'happy convergence' between scientists and Indian political leaders.

The main emphasis of the post-1947 political economy of science was on:

(i) The quality of the 'Indian mind' and a tradition of devotion to the study of science *and* political statecraft;[10]

(ii) India's material backwardness and the need to use science for economic development;

(iii) India's weak international economic and military position and the ambition of Indian political and scientific elites to establish the material base of Indian power in scientific, defence, and foreign affairs. Here, state requirements and the perceptions of the elites inside and outside the Government of India (1940s and 1950s) rather than market forces defined the demand to produce and to organize scientific knowledge and its practical applications. The primary producers and consumers of scientific knowledge and its applications were state-sponsored scientific and technical establishments and the government itself.

In the early stages of development of Indian science policy and scientists–state interactions, state interventions in the definition of research priorities was practically nil. In the years before Indian independence, 'Indian' market forces were linked to British imperial requirements. In the early years after Indian independence, Indian market forces were not strong enough to define the demand of production of scientific knowledge. The political consciousness of Indian scientists and the attitudes of leaders like Nehru and Bose, rather than market forces, established the basis of scientists–state interactions.

Despite the varied impact of structural influences, the origins and history of Indian scientists–state interactions have always been political. Market focus has always been secondary. In the Indian case, 'politicization' has three aspects. First, political values and political goals of Indian political and scientific elites drove Indian scientific activities. Secondly, scientists used scientific knowledge to engage in internal political debates. Here, the Indian scientist played a political role behind closed doors and was not simply working at the cutting edge of science; their advocacy had political consequence(s). This observation has a caveat: because the decision process was secretive and elitist, it was not open to critical public scrutiny; if 'politicization' means participation in a public debate, the majority of Indian scientists usually were not political. Finally, Indian scientific activity became politicized in a complex way from the 1960s as a result of American (and other western) intervention *vis-à-vis* the Indian government, the growth of foreign-linked Indian bureaucratic politics on questions such as signing the NPT and staying non-nuclear, and finally, because of the negative impact of military crises with China and Pakistan and the growth of China's nuclear power. From the 1960s, the main structural influences came from three sources: first, the US philosophy of containing 'further nuclear proliferation' but not containing 'vertical' proliferation. This structural influence emerged in the form of the Non-Proliferation regime and the threat it posed to Indian security interests. Secondly, the emergence of a pro-US, anti-nuclear Indian bureaucratic–scientist–societal coalition sought to curb India's nuclear weapons and missile development and deployment. Thirdly, military crises with China and Pakistan created a military necessity to go nuclear.

The triggers for political mobilization, the membership in the dominant coalition, and the results of scientists-state interactions varied during the 1947–80s period. Table 2.1 outlines the changing pattern of scientists–state interactions in the nuclear sphere. This Table provides an overview to contrast the pattern of scientists–state interactions in the prehistory and in the post-1947 periods. It reveals the increasing complexity of structural influences after 1947. This outline ·is not comprehensive; the hard information is buried in secret government files. It should therefore be treated as a suggestive, rather than a definitive, framework.

Summing up this section on the relationships between external and internal factors, the 'prehistory' is critical to understanding Indian scientists–state interactions. The pre-1947 debates shaped policy and re-

Table 2.1

Scientists–State Interactions, 1947–80s: An Overview

Period	Triggers of Action	Dominant Coalition	Results
1947–50s	Changing historic state form; US policies after 1947.	(i) Nehru–Bhabha. The political centre is strong and the bureaucracy is strong.	(i) Policy of nuclear autonomy and double track nuclear development. (ii) Development of technical infrastructure.
1960–66	India–China and India–Pakistan tensions and wars occur.	(i) Nehru–Bhabha up to 1964. (ii) Shastri–Bhabha up to 1966. The political centre is weakened by internal and external developments.	(i) Scientists intervene against Nehru's policy injunction against Indian nuclear arms. The intervention is not public. Tension between the policy and the research agenda is apparent.
1966–71	India's internal political situation is volatile. Mrs Gandhi is engaged in a power struggle, but there are opportunities for bureaucracies to influence India's nuclear and military policies.	(i) Mrs Gandhi and changing set of political and science advisers, depending on issues. The political centre is weak, the bureaucracy is divided and politicized, and it is vulnerable to vetoes by foreign-linked (US) internal bureaucratic controversies. Foreign (US) constituencies affect, by issue (ii) Mrs Gandhi-centric dominant coalition activity.	(i) Deadly confrontations occur on NPT, IAEA, and nuclear supply issues. (ii) Indian policy oscillates between 'autonomy' and 'dependence' on NPT/IAEA regime, foreign governments, and nuclear supply issues.
1971–80s	International and regional resistance to development of India's power, including nuclear power, emerges.	(i) Mrs Gandhi–Sarabhai–Sethna–Ramana. (ii) Foreign (US) constituencies, as before. (iii) Rajiv Gandhi–Srinivasan after Mrs Gandhi's death in 1984. (iv) Rajiv Gandhi–Iyengar in late 1980s.	(i) Space development is activated by Sarabhai with strong support from Mrs Gandhi. In 1974, India explodes a nuclear device. (ii) After some oscillation in nuclear and NPT affairs, 'autonomy' is restored. As a result of missile developments, the policy prescription against Indian nuclear weapons is undermined significantly.

Source: Compiled by author.

search priorities and produced winners and losers. The big loser was Saha. The big winners were Bhabha, Bhatnagar, and Mahalanobis. Both winners and losers had important international scientific links since the 1930s and 1940s. Thus, it was natural for foreign influences to have a bearing on Indian scientific affairs after 1947, with new policy challenges and opportunities. The foreign inputs into Indian scientific affairs were exclusively western because Indian scientific elites had gained their advanced training in European research organizations. Contacts with communist countries did not exist. After independence, Nehru defined India's nuclear and science policies because he was one of the few politicians interested in scientific affairs. The period 1947 to 1960 was one of 'happy convergence' between the scientists and the state. The policy boundaries were broad enough to accommodate multiple Indian scientific and political interests. Indian scientists fell into two categories. The 'doves' wanted Indian nuclear disarmament and atomic energy work for peaceful uses only. The 'hawks' wanted an Indian weapons programme and, as an intermediate step, the development of the nuclear weapons option. Dovish scientists justified their world view by working on peaceful uses of atomic energy, and the hawks expressed themselves by pushing Indian reprocessing activities. But regional, international, and domestic events from 1960 onwards put pressure on Nehru and the Indian political system to make difficult choices and to redefine the policy.[11] This process started in the Nehru years, but it crystallized after his death in 1964. The wars with China (1962) and Pakistan (1965, 1971), China's emergence as a nuclear power (1964), the development of the NPT (1964–8) and IAEA safeguards regime (1960s), the emergence of a US–USSR détente in atomic affairs after the Cuban Missile Crisis (1962), the emergence of bilateral pressures from the US and Canada on India in the nuclear sphere (1970s), and the growth of clandestine foreign influences in Indian nuclear decision-making triggered confrontations among scientists, and between scientists and their political masters.

The process and the pattern varied. The 1947–50s period was one of political passivity and 'happy convergence' because there was agreement about policy and research priorities. From 1960 onwards, the process of scientists' intervention in the policy boundaries emerged in the context of external pressures and the growth of Indian nuclear capability. By 1957, India developed a technical capability, to make an atomic device, and, according to a US government estimate of 1964,

'The Indians are now in a position to begin nuclear weapons development if they choose to do so.'[12]

The scientists' position was led by Bhabha and was targeted against Nehru, the prime minister. Very secretively, Bhabha sought permission to make a nuclear bomb using plutonium. Nehru resisted but kept the option open. The debate was not settled when Nehru died in 1964.

The 1966–71 period was one of high ambivalence and polarization in scientists–state interactions regarding Indian nuclear affairs. There was an oscillation between a political (public and bureaucratic) tendency to seek autonomy in nuclear and space affairs, on the one hand, and a tendency to increase interdependence between a US-dominated international security regime and Indian nuclear and space activities on the other. The setting for this intense struggle about the future direction of India's nuclear programme lay in a changed internal political context. Indian Congress Party politics were polarized and there was an intense struggle for power between Mrs Indira Gandhi and her internal political enemies. Mrs Gandhi's political preoccupations and inexperience in nuclear affairs created opportunities for US-linked or influenced Indian scientists and bureaucrats to assert the case for interdependence and Indian denuclearization.

The 1971–80s period saw a return to the policy of technological autonomy in nuclear and space affairs, and an intensified development of space and missile programmes. The 1974 test of a nuclear device, India's first, was an expression of this quest. But the parallel track of foreign-linked Indian bureaucratic politics also existed. Its influence was reflected in Indira Gandhi's declaration that the 1974 test was peaceful, that the government did not intend to go nuclear, and that India sought security through global nuclear disarmament. On one hand, these research and policy developments reflected the influence of nationalistic Indian scientists in scientific and political affairs, but on the other hand, they showed the influence of foreign-linked Indian bureaucratic politics that opposed Indian nuclearization and missile development. In the 1930s, before Hiroshima, Indians had recognized the importance of the Atom. By the 1980s, India possessed nuclear weapons and missile capabilities. Throughout this period, 'happy convergence' was followed by 'ritualistic confrontations' and 'deadly quarrels' which, in turn, led to a new three-track pattern of coexistence among the three types of relationships. However, overall, the tilt towards nuclear arms and ballistic missiles appeared irreversible.

Research Design Implications

The nationalist orientation shaped by the colonial period and the post-1947 history of interactions between Indian scientific and political leaders requires an emphasis. US studies emphasize the nature of the state and the political economy of science as key structural influences. Further, it is implied that state interventions define the policy and the research framework of a country's science policy. In India's case, the political thinking of Indian scientists had its origins in British India's colonial context. The first sign of the influence of Indian scientists was that the nature of the Indian state and Indian administration after 1947 was based on the priorities of Indian scientists and Indian political leaders prior to 1947. These required heavy state intervention in economic, science, and military planning. The science policy planners were Indian scientists who had been key players in the pre-1947 history and who later became key players in the formulation and management of Indian scientific activities. In both eras, the attitude of Indian scientists and Indian leaders was that India missed the first industrial revolution and should not miss the second. The colonial context was decisive in defining the political thinking of Indian scientists as well as the science-oriented thinking of key Indian political leaders. They shared the belief that India needed twentieth-century science and technology to solve current socio-economic problems. In our account, there are no Indian or non-Indian institutional buffers, mediators, or umpires between the state and the scientists. The relationship is intimate and continuously so. The political ethos of important Indian government scientists did not conflict with the political goals of India as set out by Indian leaders such as Nehru. Indeed, the political ethos of important Indian political, bureaucratic, and scientific groups was indigenous and nationalistic in its origin. The ritualistic confrontations and deadly quarrels concerned attempts by sections of India's scientific and foreign policy bureaucracy and elements in its political leadership to rely on foreign solutions for Indian problems and to dilute the nationalistic role of Indian science in an adverse diplomatic and military environment.

In India's case, the 'socio-economic characteristics of the scientific community' are not relevant in defining the scientists–state interactions. Before 1947, the number was small but the scientists were internationally recognized. After 1947, this group was divided into 'insiders' and 'outsiders'. Both were in contact with influential scientific elites in India and abroad. However, the 'insiders' were Indian scientists who participated in the policy process and who defined the research priorities and strategies of Indian science. This group also had some weight in international scientific and political circles. In contrast, the 'outsiders' had weight in scientific circles, and enjoyed limited budgetary support from the Indian government (for example Saha). The state's political leaders, bureaucratic administrators, and 'insider' scientific administrators controlled the political and budgetary allocations to 'outsiders'. This distinction, rather than the socio-economic characteristics of the scientific community, is the relevant consideration in this case. In pre-independent and post-independent India, the political and scientific ethos emphasized scientific and political elitism so as to capture and develop pockets of excellence that could aid Indian developmental and security aims. The feeling was/is that it did not really matter whether the scientist was a rich Bhabha or a poor Saha. Both were important and both types were committed to the development of Indian science, Indian economic, social, and military development, and the making of a new India.

Our focus here is on *intervention strategies of Indian scientists vis-à-vis the state* (the Government of India) and the development of *scientist–politician coalitions* that had an authoritative role in developing national plans and Indian science policy. We emphasize the activities of scientists *vis-à-vis* a *generally passive state apparatus* in scientific affairs. The rationale for this emphasis is that political elites played a prominent role in the withdrawal of British power from India and in the organization of Indian political power and institutions after independence but were mostly (with the exception of Nehru) passive in their attitude to scientific affairs.

Indian Science under Nehru: General Comment

Nehru and important Indian scientists defined two relationships: (1) between science, technology, and economic development; and (2) between peaceful development of Indian atomic energy and nuclear weapons capability. Nehru was the sole formal decision-maker in Indian foreign and scientific affairs up to 1962 because he directed the Foreign Office and held the atomic energy and planning portfolios. He emphasized the importance of secrecy in atomic affairs, and thus immunized himself and his government from public scrutiny.[13] The scientists–Nehru coalition defined the nature of the state, the policy framework concerning science, the administrative method of scientific policy making, the budgetary support for scientific activity, the role of science in national planning, and the importance of a mixed economy and the public sector. Nehru's writings reveal his faith in the role of modern science for national development and as a source of Indian military power. He stressed the importance of central planning and of a strong administrative and political centre in the Indian Union taking an all-India view of national interests. Nehru's romantic view of the Bolshevik revolution (in contrast with Nehru's horror regarding Stalinist terror) and his Fabian socialist leanings led him to stress the need to change backward societies through a planned economy. At the same time, Nehru's policy actions revealed the realpolitik basis of his atomic energy policy. By 1946, the dual-track atomic energy programme emphasized the peaceful uses of atomic energy while leaving the military option open. Thus, under Nehru, scientists–state interactions occurred always in the context of two permanent imperatives in Indian policy regarding development and security. Nehru's nuclear behaviour is discussed further in Chapter 3.

Different scientific fields played important roles in defining the nature of the state and its scientific priorities since 1947. The need for planning machinery with a scientific basis was advocated and organized largely by Professor P.C. Mahalanobis, a statistician. All planning for the first Indian Five-Year Plan took place in Calcutta at the Indian Statistical Institute. Here statisticians played the greater role in defining the normative value of planning and in creating the database for it. The work of Indian physicists took place in this context.

In India, control in public affairs comes from three different sources: (1) from the right to issue orders through a high administrative post; (2) from an ability to develop an exchange relationship, that is, by using pressure, compromise, and compensation, to accommodate key players' interests. Here 'policy' is the result of such accommodation. In India, two kinds of exchange relationships exist: between purely domestic constituencies; and between domestic constituencies who are involved in domestic controversies and who are simultaneously aligned with foreign constituencies where the US government is the key external player; (3) finally, control is gained from an ability to persuade, to achieve a meeting of minds via discussion. All three types of control emanate from the state.

Of these methods of control, the first two are more important but the third is the most democratic. The third requires a high level of tolerance of pluralism and consensus. The first approach is the least democratic.

The second one, with two variants, is neither democratic nor authoritarian. The first control approach is deeply embedded in India's administrative culture. The Government of India works on the imperial principle that the office-holder at the top possesses responsibility and, hence, also the right to command. This was the basis of administration in British India, Mughal India, and ancient India and remains the basis of modern Indian administration as well. However, though it formed the formal basis of Nehru's science policy administration, the 'ritualistic' and 'deadly' encounters in Indian science point to the central importance of the second control method.

Whether the first or the second method was prominent in the history of Indian science decision-making after 1947, the administrative structure was such that high-level decisions filtered down; lower-level debates did not filter upwards towards the decision centre. The policy debates were among equals in a small decision group at the top. Nehru was not an umpire among competing scientific schools within the Government of India. Umpiring was not necessary because the decision-making process was collegial and secretive and the deviants had been marginalized. The system was not developed, if the term implies the existence of publicly competing political and scientific cultures, competing institutional interests, role differentiation, adversarial societal relationships, competing social purposes, mass mobilization, and public confrontations. Such development reveals continuous and organized elite–mass and inter-elite interactions as well as pluralism, coalition activity, and infighting in scientific and political affairs on a massive, societal scale. Instead, the scientists–Nehru coalition captured the state apparatus early on. It established its command of the key instruments of state power concerning scientific and foreign affairs. It defined the boundaries of national policy and scientific activity. To the scientists, the state was important because the foremost member of the power elite, Nehru, possessed and provided the political will and the financial resources to support scientific activities. To Nehru, the scientists were important because their work enabled his government to refashion India in the image of Nehru's thinking. The coalition was stable in the 1950s because the political and the scientific priorities were compatible and mutually advantageous to the two groups. This discussion reveals the existence of an autonomous coalition, a directorate of Indian scientific affairs in the 1940s and 1950s.

What were the determinants in Indian scientists–state interactions during the Nehru years? This book proposes a distinction between *pre-*

crisis (1930s–1962) and *post-crisis* (post-1962) relations. The anticipation of India's independence and its upward mobility in the international system produced an anticipation of the need to restructure India's internal economic, institutional, and military strength, and to restructure India's power relations with the outside world by making India an autonomous force in the world. These attitudes led to a high level of political commitment and state support for the development of dual-use science and technology. Despite the official secrecy, the system was open. For instance, Nehru was willing to rely on foreign scientific advisers (for example Professor P.M.S. Blackett). Nuclear science cooperation flourished between scientists in India, Canada, the US, the UK, and France during the 1950s and the mid-1970s. This indicated a high level of tolerance of international scientific exchanges and external, non-Indian scientific advice. Bhabha was also open in declaring his ambition to take India into the nuclear club. But on the other hand, the system was highly secretive. Nehru was committed to the 'built-in defence use if compelled' view of Indian nuclear science but did not advertise his commitment publicly. The internal Nehru–Bhabha debate in the 1960s about the importance of nuclear arms for India was secret; it still lies buried in government files. The pattern of Indian technical activities in the nuclear, space, and missile areas is generally known, but the relationship between the technical activities and policy is buried in secret files and in orally communicated decisions of the political leadership on a need-to-know basis. The method was not to record major decisions in official minutes because of the presumption that Indian government departments were penetrated by spies.

Despite the secrecy, the autonomy of the dominant scientists–state coalition of the Nehru era was fractured as a result of increasing political pressures in Indian politics and the rise of bureaucratic politics since the 1960s. External developments effected these changes. Table 2.1 shows the circumstances in which the scientists–Nehru coalition started to lose its closed, secretive, and totally autonomous character. External developments (the India–China war, the India–Pakistan war, China's nuclear testing, and the NPT) put pressure on Indian policy positions and rhetoric and, as a result, a public debate followed. These pressures became entrenched in India's political system and were irreversible. The present Indian nuclear policies are radically different to those of the Nehru years. For Nehru, nuclear disarmament was an urgent question; for his successors, it is a distant goal. For Nehru, the public commitment against Indian nuclear arms and for peaceful uses of atomic energy was firm; for his successors, the emphasis is on acquiring nuclear weapons and missile capability. This position is the result of the confrontations of the 1960s, 1970s, and the 1980s that started in the last phase of the Nehru era, although the debates took shape after Nehru's death in 1964, which culminated in the series of tests in May 1998.

Indian Science: Post-Nehru

The ethos of the scientific, political, security, economic, and non-governmental (public/academic/press) constituencies started to diverge. The autonomy of the scientist–political coalition came under attack. Public debates reflected and reinforced internal bureaucratic debates about India's nuclear and disarmament policies that involved Bhabha, Nehru, and the civil servants. Two new elements shaped these confrontations. First, following the India–China war of 1962 and China's nuclear test in 1964, there was an increased public, parliamentary, non-governmental opposition to the Nehru posture that stressed a primary reliance on peaceful uses of nuclear energy. Out of this public opposition came additional pressure to move towards the development of an Indian nuclear weapons programme. Second, by the mid-1960s, the US government was actively involved in internal bureaucratic battles in India pushing aggressively for Indian denuclearization. (Declassified US government cable traffic shows heightened US awareness of India's nuclear ambitions at this time.) Three lines of nuclear thinking emerged in India at the time. The US-linked bureaucratic coalition in India, which was located in the Indian Ministry of External Affairs (MEA) and in the Indian Atomic Energy Department, favoured the elimination of Indian nuclear autonomy as well as submission to the international non-proliferation regime. The second line sought to maintain a semi-opaque Indian nuclear weapons option. The third line wanted a declared nuclear weapons programme. The third approach was expressed by Indian diplomatic and strategic planners who opposed the pro-US approach. The second approach was meant to keep the US happy because a threshold status did not breach the NPT line against further horizontal nuclear proliferation; it did not attack the non-proliferation regime. It enabled the US and other NPT parties to accept Indian denial of nuclear weapons intent positively; a threshold status created plausible deniability.

Between the early 1960s and the 1990s (up to 1996), Indian governmental nuclear decision-making and its posture in international conference diplomacy oscillated between the first and the second policy lines. Both lines coexisted inside the Indian government and in public debate, but the third line also appeared to maintain its position in the decision process even though India's declared policy up to May 1998 favoured the second policy line. The controversy led to an intensified growth in dual-use technologies. Out of the 1962–71 controversies came Vikram Sarabhai's space programme and the preparations for a nuclear test which occurred in 1974. Military applications of Indian nuclear science were investigated secretly and the costs of a weapons programme were checked. Internal controversy and external pressure to join the NPT regime led to an intensified development, under dual-use cover, of the military content of Indian nuclear and space activities. This pattern continued in the 1980s when the decision to develop missiles led to acquisition of intermediate range missile technology.

In sum, as a result of external pressures on India and internal controversy about nuclear policy, three patterns of behaviour are revealed: First, Indian scientists have been politically active in scientific and policy spheres, but after 1947, the nature of the activism depended on whether or not the scientist had foreign links. Secondly, Indian policies have oscillated as a result of scientists–state interactions. For example, Prime Minister Shastri moved towards a bomb test in 1965; Mrs Gandhi's first draft in 1967 favoured the NPT but she backed away from signing the Treaty in view of internal bureaucratic and Cabinet opposition. Mrs Gandhi opposed Indian nuclear testing in 1966, but approved it in the early 1970s. Mrs Gandhi opposed a weapons programme, but she supported the development of an Indian space infrastructure and weapons-related research and development. Prime Minister Rajiv Gandhi wanted India to join the NPT, but eventually accepted scientific and military advice to promote Indian missile development. Prime Minister Narasimha Rao refused to sign the NPT and kept the nuclear weapons option open in a declaratory way, but accepted US pressure to curb the testing of AGNI, an intermediate range missile, and appeared to be on the verge of signing the CTBT. Prime Minister I.K. Gujral, however, declined to accept the CTBT. He blocked it against the advice of some so-called Indian nuclear hawks but declined to authorize Indian nuclear testing. Prime Minister Vajpayee, on the other hand, authorized the nuclear tests in May 1998 and then went on to signal a willingness to join the CTBT regime in the context of the on-going Indo–US negotiations. Despite the oscillations and the twists and turns in Indian nuclear decision-making, the story is one of incremental growth of Indian nuclear weapons capability.

ENDNOTES

1. For problems in Indian science planning, see V. Shiva and J. Bandyopadhyay, 'The Large and Fragile Community of Scientists in India', *Minerva*, vol. 18, no. 4, 1980, pp. 575–94.

2. A.P.J. Abdul Kalam and Y.S. Rajan, *India 2020* (New Delhi: Viking Penguin India, 1998), pp. 23–4.

3. R.S. Anderson, *Building Scientific Institutions in India: Saha and Bhabha*, Centre for Developing Area Studies, McGill University, Occasional Papers, Series no. 11, 1975.

4. I am indebted to Etel Solingen for these distinctions.

5. See notes 3 and 10.

6. See Chapter 3 for a full discussion of the nuances of Nehru's nuclear policy.

7. For details, see *India, 1988–89*, Publications Division, Ministry of Information and Broadcasting, Government of India, 1989.

8. I have spelled out this idea in A. Kapur, *International Nuclear Proliferation* (New York: Praeger, 1979), pp. 211–13. Also see the discussion in P. Gummett's chapter in J. Simpson, ed., *Nuclear Non-Proliferation: An Agenda for the 1990s* (Cambridge: Cambridge University Press, 1987), pp. 142–4.

9. For these attitudes, see S. Bhatia, *India's Nuclear Bomb* (Vikas: U.P. Publishing House, 1979), pp. 43, 50, 51, and 55 respectively.

10. See D. Chattopadhyaya, ed., *Studies in the History of Science in India*, 2 vols. (New Delhi: Editorial Enterprises, 1982) for Indian scientific activities extending to ancient times. Kautilya's work represents India's realpolitik tradition in ancient India.

11. I have discussed this in my paper, 'Nehru's Nuclear Policy', Nehru Centennial Conference, University of Toronto, October 1989. See also Chapter 3.

12. Research memorandum, INR-16, 14 May 1964, on Indian nuclear weapons development, prepared by Director of Intelligence and Research, Department of State, USA.

13. Nehru publicly emphasized the importance of secrecy in atomic energy on 6 April 1948 when he introduced the Atomic Energy Bill to the Indian Parliament.

3

The Nehru–Bhabha Years, 1947–64

Introduction

The years 1947 to 1964 are of critical importance in the study of India's nuclear history. Indian attitudes and policies were formed at this time and they shaped the parameters of India's nuclear behaviour in the coming decades. They revealed the dominant role of India's political class (expressed by J.L. Nehru) and of India's scientific class (expressed by Homi J. Bhabha) in defining the Indian approach to the nuclear question. The role of global or Indian market forces or of pacifist Indian social and political thought was insignificant in the formulation of the Nehru–Bhabha approach, except that a connection existed between the Gandhian tradition of non-violence and the belief that a suitable basis of conflict resolution in interstate relations lay in Nehruvian peace diplomacy. The views and policies about nuclear affairs were a response to the Indian assessment of the nature of the post-colonial international security system, India's dependent position in the Cold War international system, the danger posed for Indian security and diplomatic interests by the American policy to control the Atom, and the perceived necessity to harness atomic energy for India's developmental and strategic aims. Although India at the time publicly projected and highlighted its faith in the peaceful uses of atomic energy and the Indian government insisted on the central importance of nuclear disarmament as the basis of international security, the Nehru–Bhabha attitudes revealed an appreciation as well of the importance of the military potential of Indian atomic capability, especially in the context of a nuclearized China. Thus, the Nehru–Bhabha approach to the nuclear question revealed responses to three levels: (1) to the international environment, where

US policy sought to control the Atom in line with US strategic interests; (2) to the Indian domestic environment where the nuclear question was located in the context of the importance of science in Indian development; and (3) in the regional strategic context where China's nuclear activity created a potential challenge for Indian security in the context of Sino–Indian rivalry in Asia.

What were the parameters and the *intellectual context* of India's nuclear policy during the period? What was done internally and externally to establish the *organizational infrastructure* for India's nuclear development? What was the scope and thrust of India's nuclear research strategy? What were the *policy boundaries and principles* in Indian diplomacy *vis-à-vis* the nuclear question in international conferences and *vis-à-vis* the major powers? What was the scope, the circumstances, and the dynamics in the *internal governmental debate* about the military uses of atomic energy in the Indian case? To a discussion of these questions we now turn.

Pattern of India's Nuclear Development in the Nehru–Bhabha Years: Overview

India's nuclear history has three interwoven strands that originated in the Nehru–Bhabha years. The first strand is 'diplomatic'. Its framework was established and well defined in 1947, even though Indian attitudes and policies on other aspects of defence and foreign affairs crystallized (for example Kashmir policy; relations with Pakistan, USA, and USSR; defence requirements) later. Indian diplomatic activity in nuclear affairs was proactive. It had good internal logic and consistently revealed Indian interests and values. It had a national, interparty consensus and expressed India's nuclear ideology. Ideology, generally speaking, has multiple functions: (1) It is a set of principles, beliefs, values, or attitudes that serve as a filter to evaluate information and activity in the external environment. Ideology filters, records, and measures the external stimuli. It creates an *attitudinal prism* to define reality that has policy or operational relevance. (2) Ideology offers an *intellectual justification* for policy action, either in anticipation that a particular line of state action may emerge, or *ex post facto*. (3) Ideology can also be a *guide* to radical action. (4) Finally, ideology enables a policymaker to *engage* other players in the international sphere at the academic and policy levels. Ideology is the *basis of ideological or psychological warfare* or pressure on the rival(s). In our study, all these functions are relevant, but the weight of each is a subject for debate.

The second strand is labelled 'scientific/technological activity'. It too took shape in 1947 as a quick follow-up to the scientists–politician interactions of the prehistory noted in Chapter 2. This strand also revealed proactivity and, in hindsight, a phasal development. But in the Nehru–Bhabha years, the diplomatic and the scientific/technological spheres were autonomous in relation to each other. The diplomatic projections and the scientific activity were both meant to maintain and increase India's independence or *option(s)* in the international sphere. They were not meant to make India a nuclear weapon power. India's nuclear ideology in the Nehru–Bhabha years was not a guide to the development of Indian nuclear arms; the Nehru–Bhabha years expressed a posture of conscious *self-restraint*. In this sense, the Nehru–Bhabha years had two aims, viz., to establish India's independence in the nuclear sphere and to avoid a bomb programme.

During this period, India's nuclear ideology established the attitudinal prisms which facilitated diplomatic engagement with the international environment, but it was not a preparation at the time for India's bomb programme. Although Nehru articulated the intention to go nuclear if compelled, there was no such expectation at that time. So there was a disconnection at the time between the public attitude, expectation, and policy of the Indian political leadership (Nehru) and India's scientific/technological activity. The former indicated a movement towards an Indian bomb programme; the latter indicated a movement against it.

Because of this gap, it is essential to note the crucial importance of the third strand. This is labelled 'Indian nuclear decision-making about the role of nuclear armament'. The contention is that neither the first nor the second strands by themselves help explain or predict Indian nuclear behaviour. According to a 'technological determinism' view, India should have proceeded into nuclear weaponization when it could. It could have done so any time after 1957, but it did not. Since the Nehru–Bhabha years, a pattern of *ad hoc*, reactive, competitive, bureaucratic, and foreign-linked domestic politics has affected Indian nuclear decision-making.

Unlike the first and the second strands, the third is reactive and heavily politicized with cross-currents. It reacts to external and internal compulsions and incentives that require decision-making in conditions of crisis. The first and second strands have developed in a non-crisis mode. 'Crisis' implies that policymakers feel compelled to make policy choices under pressure and with deadlines. Hence the reactivity. The first strand does not explain or predict India's nuclear weapons decisions or the dynamics of the decision-process during the major decision-points (discussed later in this chapter). The first strand is a necessary condition because it creates the legal and political foundation for Indian bomb activity. But it is not a sufficient condition in the absence of the political decision to do so. This is true as well of the second strand except that the second strand reveals the development of the technical capacity to make the political choice in favour of Indian nuclear weaponization. Table 3.1 sets out the pattern of the three-dimensional Indian nuclear development.

TABLE 3.1
General Pattern of India's Nuclear Activities, 1947–64

Period	Technical Activities	Diplomatic Activites	Indian Nuclear Decision-making
1940s–1964	India developed its civilian and dual-use nuclear programme: it acquired an unsafeguarded research reactor; it sought fuel cycle independence.	India rejected international atomic controls but accepted partial safeguards on foreign supplies.	The internal debate was within the Government of India; it was secret, not public. It revealed a tension between advocacy in favour of the bomb, advocacy in favour of global and Indian nuclear disarmament, and advocacy in favour of diplomatic and technical activity to develop a nuclear weapons option.
1964	India started reprocessing. Indian technical moves revealed a commitment to incrementally develop a nuclear weapons option.		

The three strands point to the existence of two kinds of 'Indias' at play in nuclear affairs. The first and the second strand reveal an India that has been willing to develop its scientific prowess in the nuclear field and engage the world through its nuclear diplomacy. This is the confident India which sought space for itself in nuclear-diplomatic and nuclear-science affairs. This was the proactive, forward-looking India. The second kind of India is revealed by the third strand. It shows that the Indian policy and decision-making process oscillated between advocacy for global and Indian nuclear disarmament, advocacy for a crash Indian bomb programme to meet China's strategic challenge, and advocacy to develop a nuclear weapons option instead of a crash bomb programme. This was a picture of ambivalence, not ambiguity. Prime Minister Nehru had a foot in two different camps: he advocated global nuclear disarmament and implied the value of Indian nuclear disarmament in that context; and he authorized and supported the development of an Indian nuclear option 'if compelled'. So the Nehru–Bhabha years revealed a fluidity and oscillation in policy thinking within the Indian government. Table 3.2 outlines the structure of the debate and the wide space for the oscillation in Indian policy. This is discussed in a subsequent section.

In other words, the Nehru–Bhabha years point to two critical aspects in the study of India's nuclear behaviour. These aspects emerged during 1947–64 but continued in subsequent eras up to May 1998. The first aspect stresses the following: India's external diplomatic activity in questions concerning international safeguards; the attitude towards the NPT; the search for peaceful uses of atoms for India; negotiating transfers of atomic equipment, materials, and technology from Canada and the United States; and generally protecting India's nuclear option for possible conversion in a weapons programme against China if necessary. The second aspect stresses the nature, problem, and style of Indian nuclear decision-making, focusing on the relationship between domestic politics and foreign policy. In the latter case, a stress on interpersonal relations between highly politicized members of the Indian elites is indicated, and the study is devoted to an examination of the external diplomatic behaviour as well as the dynamics of nuclear decision-making. The message is that there is a success story to be found in India's nuclear diplomacy, but such success must be seen in the light of the external as well as internal constraints that the diplomacy operates under. As to the 'internal' constraints, the study directs attention to the *ad hoc* nature of Indian nuclear decision-making. '*Ad hoc*' in this study means the following. India's diplomatic behaviour refers to the following problem areas: superpower imperialism; discrimination in international nuclear law making; discriminatory stress on controlling peaceful rather than military nuclear activities; superpowers' stressing controls over potential horizontal proliferators rather than on the existing vertical ones; and, a China armed with nuclear weapons and a submarine capability. But whereas India's verbal stance expresses a principled stance and one that is hard to refute in scholarly terms, it is not clear if India's nuclear decision-making in Delhi is also based on perceptions of principles rather than perceptions of the political fortunes of the domestic political players (including civil servants and scientists). *Adhocism* can mean Charles Lindblom's 'incremental change', conveying a sense of a logical, linear, and an inevitable connection between 'attitude', 'means', and 'political decision'. India's decision to produce a peaceful nuclear test in May 1974 may appear to be such an incremental change, a step towards Indian nuclear weapons. India's May 1998 test elevates India's nuclear stance from the ambiguity of India's nuclear weapons option (1974–98) to the clarity of a declared Indian nuclear weapons status. So, there is a phasal shift from a 'peaceful uses only' stance (1956–74), to a peaceful use/nuclear weapons options stance (1974–May 1998), to a declared nuclear weapons status (May 1998 onwards). The data shows incremental change, but it does not reveal a linear progression towards an Indian nuclear weapons programme that leads to production and deployment. An emphasis on the study of Indian nuclear decisions is critical because invariably there is an obvious Indian nuclear decision as well as a significant one; and often there are two simultaneous decisions that appear to be contradictory. For example, in the 1960s, India made two decisions: to keep the bomb option open and to develop the necessary technical means to go nuclear if necessary, and to refrain from building the bomb at present. Thus, methodologically, to establish a linear connection between declared stance and actual nuclear behaviour, it is essential to organize the data in terms of 'decision points', the set of obvious and significant decisions made, and the vulnerability of the decision process to inputs from different and competitive governmental (prime minister and prime minister's office [PMO], science and defence organizations of the government, and others) and nongovernmental agencies.

To understand how nuclear issues are defined and pursued in Indian decision processes, it is important to recognize that the Indian government is not monolithic, rational in the Western essence, or a fully institutionalized entity. Rather, the decision structures are often highly personalized (where the attitude of the head of government and a small coterie of advisers prevails), small in size (where the impact/role of societal forces is generally marginal but it can be significant at times of external and internal crisis), and decision making is a mix of bureaucratic politics and small group activity among competing definitions of the problem and solutions. That is, the decision process neither follows the lines of authority laid out in the organization charts, nor is it truly dictatorial, nor is it truly open or public in the Western meaning of democracy. It is mostly secretive and competitive. It is democratic in the sense that a variety of interests and points of view are in continuous play in the inner circles of both governments, they are responsive to external and internal pressures and inputs, and the process responds to a cross section of opinions and interests of competing players. It may be fruitful to visualize the decision process as a process of interaction among a number of 'forbidden cities', where each such organization has a base in the state and possesses compartmentalized, internally integrated decision structures with defined values and strategic cultures. The task for the outside analyst is to discover the identity, nature, and domestic power of each such city/organization in the proliferation and the non-proliferation sphere in particular, and its attitudes, policies, and roles in relation to alliance politics and security politics in general. In other words, the inner realities that drive the relationship between domestic structures and issues of nuclear proliferation and non-proliferation must be understood in the Indian case.

As noted earlier, Indian scientists and politicians started to think actively about atomic energy, science, and development in the 1930s and 1940s. A changing state form rather than a military crisis formed the context of the Indian debate. Science and atomic energy were seen to play a vital role in Indian development and, furthermore, by the mid-1940s atomic energy was seen to have a defence potential as well. The pre-independence debate was shaped by H.J. Bhabha and J.L. Nehru, and both emerged as the principal players in Indian atomic affairs after 1947. They stressed several themes: the importance of science and technology for national economic development; the need to create an independent infrastructure to promote atomic energy work in India; the desirability of nuclear disarmament and peaceful use of atomic energy in India and worldwide; and finally, the defence potential of Indian atomic energy in adverse circumstances. The approach was driven by a concern with Indian political independence in international and atomic energy affairs. This political value was widely shared. There was no internal dissent in India from the atomic energy establishment, from the political side, or from the Indian society. This attitude was the basis of Indian policy towards international safeguards and technology transfers. Two policy streams emerged. On the one hand, partial safeguards were accepted as a matter of necessity to acquire desired technology from advanced foreign sources. But on the other hand, the international preference for general curbs on Indian atomic industry was opposed.

Table 3.2 outlines the steps taken to implement the methodology to develop India's atomic energy programme given in Figure 3.1, during the Nehru–Bhabha era.

TABLE 3.2
Pattern of Indian Nuclear Technical Indigenization

Activity	Year	Weapons Capability	Safeguards Status	Foreign Collaborator
Policy position to go nuclear if compelled was announced by Nehru.	1946–48	Nil	Nil	Nil
Indian atomic energy research committee was established.	1946	Nil	Nil	Nil
Atomic energy cooperation with foreign governments was established.	1955 onwards	Nil	Nil	Canada, USA, UK, France
Research reactor APSARA — light water, medium enriched uranium, went critical. (This was the first research reactor in Asia.)	1956	Potential	Nil	UK
Fuel fabrication uranium metal plant produced nuclear-grade uranium.	1959	Potential	Nil	Nil
CIRUS research reactor — heavy water, natural uranium, was critical	1960	Yes	Nil	Canada, US governments*
Zerlina—heavy water, variable fuel, went critical.	1961	Nil	Nil	Nil
Heavy water production started.	1962	Nil	Nil	West German company
Plutonium was separated at Trombay	1965	Yes	Nil	Nil

*Canada supplied the research reactor and the heavy water. The US too subsequently provided heavy water.

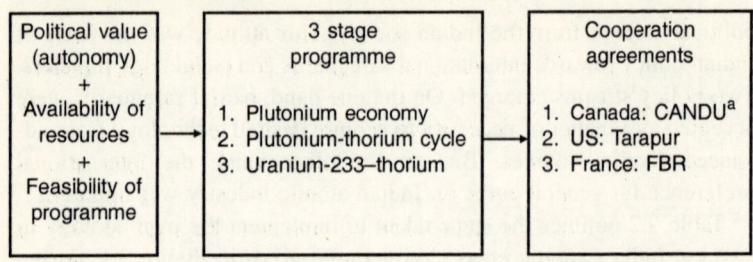

FIG. 3.1:   Methodology to Develop India's Atomic Energy Programme,
Pre-Crisis, 1940s–1962/64[b]

Notes: [a]Canada Deuterium–Uranium
[b]1962 is a dividing line because the 1962 war with China increased India's
commitment to find solutions to defence problems. 1964 is a dividing line because China's first nuclear test opened up the Indian debate about nuclear issues.

The Attitudinal and Policy Framework of
Nehru's Nuclear Policy

Nehru's and India's nuclear policy (1940s–64) reveals three themes:

(i) Nehru's policy was ambivalent about the peaceful and defence uses
of atomic energy in India. His known commitment to nuclear disarmament was driven by a combination of idealistic and practical considerations rather than strictly ethical ones. Nehru was not a naive utopian.
He was not indecisive about the importance of nuclear science in India.
He was fascinated by the necessity to plan and to leapfrog into the
twentieth-century and to move into the second industrial revolution
rather than to catch up with the first one that India had missed. In his
romance with science and planning, atomic energy had an important
place. Micheal Brecher sees Nehru as indecisive.[1] Eric Stokes sees
Nehru as driven by contradictory impulses.[2] There is a better fit between the view of Stokes and Nehru's nuclear policy than between
Brecher's view and Nehru's policy.

(ii) Nehru, a one-man foreign office, saw himself as the maker of Indian
foreign policy. He also held the atomic energy portfolio. He set the
policy boundaries of different facets of India's atomic energy affairs.
But India's scientific elite, especially H.J. Bhabha, set the *research
boundaries* which drove India's atomic energy activities in the technical

sphere. There was continuous tension between the policy and the research boundaries because (i) Bhabha, 'nationalist' members of Indian bureaucratic and scientific elites, and 'nationalist' academic and public opinion favoured Indian Bomb development but Nehru was ambivalent on the subject; and (ii) Indian atomic energy activities had a built-in defence use. As India's nuclear infrastructure and technical capability to make a bomb grew, and India's external and internal circumstances changed between 1947 and 1964, the *tension* between the no-bomb and nuclear disarmament stance and the bomb advocacy also grew.

(iii) As a consequence of internal and external developments (especially the 1962 China war, 1964 Chinese nuclear testing, NPT debate, internal bureaucratic politics in India, and the pressure of Indian public, parliamentary, and academic opinion), a process of *erosion* of the anti-bomb, anti-nuclear testing policy boundaries set by Nehru developed. These developments encouraged domestic controversies in India and produced oscillatory pressures in the Indian decision processes connected with atomic energy work (especially start-up of reprocessing, and international conference diplomacy concerning the NPT). So the decision-making system opened up in the sense that secret intra-governmental and public Indian debates took place, and an interface between the two layers of foreign policy/atomic energy debates crystallized. During Nehru's lifetime, the oscillatory pressures and the controversies persisted in the decision-making and in the public spheres because the policy framework was ambivalent, and the scope of the ambivalent nuclear policy was wide enough to accommodate diverse points of view and competing definitions of security. The controversies and oscillatory pressures were to develop and persist after Nehru's death. They led to major shifts in Indian atomic energy activities and postures under Shastri, Indira Gandhi, and Rajiv Gandhi.

To understand Nehru's atomic energy policy, it is necessary to understand the duality and ambivalence in his declaratory policy as well as in the civil/military potential of Indian technical activities in the atomic field in the Nehru era. The duality in Nehru's/India's political thinking and its Indian technical activities is revealed in the following chronology of declarations and events, and in Figure 3.2.

13 November 1945, Statement by Nehru: 'The revolution caused by discoveries having to do with atomic energy can either destroy human civilisation, or take it up to unheard of levels.'[3]

Peaceful uses only	Potential military uses	No Indian testing; no Indian atomic arms
• Constructive uses only' (E) • faith in nuclear disarmament (E) [Nehru; Menon; Bhabha] • civil applications of atomic energy [Bhabha and colleagues]	• 'built-in defence use if compelled' (R) [Nehru; Bhabha; parts of Foreign Office] • unsafeguarded plutonium and reprocessing work (R) [Bhabha and colleagues]	

Fig. 3.2: India's Dual Policy Framework in Atomic Affairs: The Nehru Years

Notes: (E) means 'erosion' over time
(R) means 'reinforcement' over time
☐ Secret side of India's posture and scientific activity
▨ Public side of India's posture and scientific activity

26 June 1946, Statement by Nehru: 'As long as the world is constituted as it is, every country will have to devise and use the latest scientific devices for its protection. I have no doubt India will develop her scientific researches and I hope Indian scientists will use the atomic force for constructive purposes. But if India is threatened she will inevitably try to defend herself by all means at her disposal. I hope India in common with other countries will prevent the use of atomic bombs.'[4]

1946: India's Atomic Energy Research Committee was established.[5]

1948: Indian Atomic Energy Commission was established.[6]

6 April 1948: Nehru justified atomic energy development in India and explained the Atomic Energy Bill. He emphasized (a) the importance of secrecy, (b) his preference for peaceful use of nuclear energy, (c) its potential for use for 'other purposes' if India is 'compelled', and (d) the need to remain abreast of modern technology and developments.[7]

1955: India signed important atomic energy agreements with the UK, USA, and Canada.[8]

1956: APSARA went critical.

1958: Bhabha told P.M.S. Blackett of his intention to develop nuclear arms and to keep the nuclear weapons option open.[9]

1959:   Fuel fabrication facility was due to start up.[10]

1959:   Decision was taken to build plutonium extraction plan and heavy water reconcentration unit.[11]

1961:   CIRUS went critical.[12]

1963:   Indian members of Parliament sought Indian nuclear arms.

January 1964:   Pilot chemical separation and reprocessing plant was commissioned.[13]

1964:   Plutonium separation plant was due for completion in the year.

1964:   Nehru died.

Fig. 3.2 shows the distribution of the dual civil/military aspects in Nehru's/India's declaratory nuclear posture and its technical activities in the nuclear field.

The 1962–4 phase of the Nehru years was remarkable in several ways: (1) The intra-governmental debate about Indian atomic affairs became radicalized as a consequence of external developments. Table 3.3 outlines the debate in the non-crisis and near-crisis/crisis mode. 'Near-crisis/crisis' refers to the crisis of India's defeat in the 1962 Sino–Indian war and the 'near-crisis' situation as a result of China's first nuclear test and its impact on Indian public opinion. (2) For the first time in independent India's history, the Government of India lost its exclusive right to debate and decide on a sensitive issue like the defence implications of atomic energy; Indian society in the form of public and parliamentary opinion and non-governmental experts, academics, and journalists became involved. (3) The US government, along with its western allies, also became active in the Indian nuclear debate, albeit in a private and secretive manner. (4) Finally, the triggering events in the Indian debate were external. The result of these events and processes was that India's nuclear debate now reflected an interaction between forces within and outside India. The Nehru–Bhabha years are therefore important for laying the groundwork for India's nuclear development as well as witnessing the origin of the process of domestic–external engagement in nuclear policy-making. One cannot think of another country whose nuclear debate was subject to such multiple and intense cross currents and pressures over a prolonged period of time.

The dynamics of Table 3.3 may be expressed also by Figure 3.3. In the non-crisis mode, decision-making strength lay exclusively with the dominant scientists–politician coalition and the second circle. The other

TABLE 3.3

Structure and Process of India's Nuclear Debate, 1946–64

Theme	Nuclear Disarmament for World	Nuclear Abstention for India	Global Arms Control (CTBT/PTBT), etc.	Development of Indian Weapons Capability
Decision-maker(s)	• Nehru • Krishna Menon • Bhabha • MEA	• Gandhians • Krishna Menon (representing Indian leftists) • Sections of MEA	• Nehru • MEA	• Nehru (under certain conditions) • Bhabha • Sections of MEA
Level of Debate	Interstate: • India/West • India/USSR	• Indian society and intellectual opinion • Indian bureaucracy	Interstate: • India/West • India/USSR	• Inner circles of Indian government/ bureaucratic policies • Academic/societal

Note: Three events intensified the debate in the first half of the 1960s, that is, the last four years of the Nehru era. India's military defeat in the Sino–Indian war (1962) showed the insufficiency of Nehru's peace diplomacy and the importance of defence preparedness. However, it did not change India's stance with regard to nuclear disarmament and nuclear weapons. The NPT negotiations had a negative fallout in Indian policy and academic circles and it reinforced the polarization among the four sides of the Indian debate. But it did not alter the uneasy coexistence and balance among the four sides of the debate. The first Chinese test (1964) also had a negative fallout in Indian policy and academic and social thinking. It strengthened the weight of the Indian Bomb lobby but overall, it did not change the pattern of uneasy coexistence and balance among the four sides of the debate.

FIG. 3.3:   India's Nuclear Science Policy Decision Process

sources of input were not influential in the decision-process. In a near-crisis/crisis mode however, (1962–4 in the Nehru–Bhabha years), the inputs from the outer or third circle became important because they were public and they dealt with an issue of public importance in the democratic set-up of India.

At the same time, the debate was taking shape in the context of a paradigm which had been shaped by the Nehru–Bhabha leadership. This is outlined in Figure 3.4.

Theoretical Considerations

The structure of the Nehru–Bhabha nuclear thinking and behaviour challenged the validity of the dominant intellectual tradition in North American scholarship concerning the role and influence of weaker states/powers in the modern international system in comparison to that of the great powers. American and Americanized western scholarship relied primarily on the 'dominant–subordinate states system' paradigm.[14] Steven

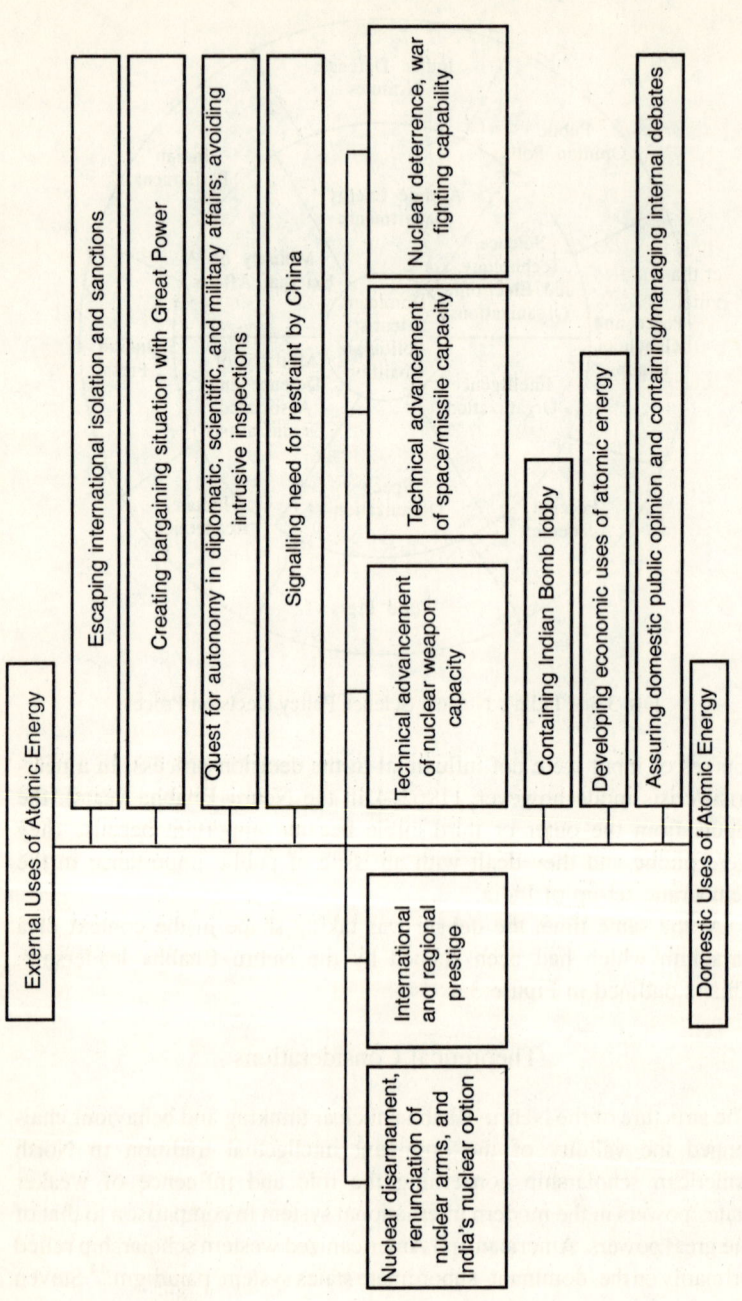

FIG. 3.4: Paradigm of Indian Nuclear Decision-making

External Uses of Atomic Energy

Escaping international isolation and sanctions

Creating bargaining situation with Great Power

Quest for autonomy in diplomatic, scientific, and military affairs; avoiding intrusive inspections

Signalling need for restraint by China

Nuclear deterrence, war fighting capability

Technical advancement of space/missile capacity

Technical advancement of nuclear weapon capacity

Containing Indian Bomb lobby

Developing economic uses of atomic energy

Assuring domestic public opinion and containing/managing internal debates

International and regional prestige

Nuclear disarmament, renunciation of nuclear arms, and India's nuclear option

Domestic Uses of Atomic Energy

Spiegel, among others, reflected the dominant American scholarly orientation and bias:

The gap between the most powerful and the weakest of states has been widened by technological developments which aided those already most powerful.

It is the position of each state in the international hierarchy which determines in large measures the way in which it acts and the way in which it is treated by other governments.

While medium-range nations may be able to influence countries with less power than their own, only primary powers are able to influence and even direct the policies of countries of all sizes and strengths.[15]

R.L. Rothstein sharpened the great power/small power dichotomy further in the following observation:

Small Powers are not simply weaker Great Powers and that they must be defined in terms of something other than their relative power status. Any new definition should also take account of the fact that there is a psychological, as well as a material, distinction between Great and Small Powers. The latter earn their titles not only by being weak but by recognising the implications of that condition. Thus, a Small Power is a state which recognises that it cannot obtain security primarily by use of its own capabilities, and that it must rely fundamentally on the aid of other states, institutions, processes, or developments to do so; the Small Power's belief in its inability to rely on its own means must also be recognised by the other states involved in international politics.[16]

India's diplomatic, military, and nuclear behaviour has falsified the dominant tradition or approach in North American scholarship of the 1950s and the 1960s. The groundwork of the intellectual challenge was laid by Indian practitioners when the Cold War was at its peak, and the international system *appeared* to be bipolar. Before we explain the theoretical base of Nehru's approach to external affairs and nuclear affairs, it is important to note that the Nehru–Bhabha approach in hindsight had an affinity with the approach of the late British Professor Martin Wight. He distinguished between major and minor powers and recognized that 'power', like 'prestige', was 'present power':

Prestige is one of the imponderables of international politics, but it is too closely connected with power to be considered as belonging to the moral order. It is the influence derived from power. And unless the power is present power there can be little prestige. Deference to historical importance and gratitude for past achievement are even less apparent international politics than in other kinds of politics.[17]

One might add that 'power' is an 'effect' as K. Knorr pointed out:

The phenomenon of power lends itself to two sharply different conceptions . . . Since coercive influence limits the conduct of an actor subjected to it, power can be seen to reside in the capabilities that permit the power-wielder to make effective threats. But it can also be seen as identical with, and limited to, the influence on the actually achieved behavior of the threatened actor. On the first view, power is something that powerful states have and can accumulate; power is a means. On the second view, power is an effect that is the influence actually enjoyed. It is generated in an interaction which is an encounter. On the first view, power is something that an actor can hope to bring into play in a range of future situations. On the second, power comes into being, is shaped, and enjoyed only in a specific situation; its measure is the amount of influence actually achieved.[18]

Thus defined, 'power' is situational and relational rather than a reflection of the international hierarchy and/or historical circumstance. In this context, for example, the claim that the US is the 'sole military superpower' because the USSR collapsed is meaningless by the definitions given by Wight and Knorr.

Although Wight's writings dealt with the western experience, his insights are relevant to the post-1947 Indian nuclear experience. Wight's work dealt with the relationships between independent powers. He distinguished between 'power' and 'influence' arguing that 'influence is not power. It is concrete power in the end that settles great international issues'. There are different kinds of powers. A 'dominant power' (or a universal empire) is one that possesses power and purpose 'to measure its strength against all its rivals combined'. Wight points out that a dominant power is not an accepted category in international thinking, and the 'only distinction in informal diplomatic intercourse is that between great powers and other powers'. 'Great powers' have 'general [system wide] interests' and it can 'confidently contemplate war against other existing single power'. 'Minor powers', on the other hand, have limited interests and limited power to protect or advance them by force. (Wight also discusses 'world powers', but this is not relevant for our purpose here.)

Wight is among the few who takes the category of minor powers seriously. There are two kinds of minor powers: regional great powers and middle powers. The former is a state 'with general interests relative to the limited region and a capacity to act alone'. Such a regional great power is a candidate, in the states system at large, for the rank of 'middle power'. A middle power was accepted as a category of power in 1815 among the German states but unlike great powers they did not find a place in UN arrangements. It has distinctive characteristics and appeal in the states system. It possesses 'such military strength, resources and strategic position that in peacetime the great powers bid for its support, and in wartime, while it has no hope of winning a war against a great power, it can inflict cost on a great power out of proportion to what the great power can hope to gain by attacking it'. According to Wight, middle powers appear when 'the qualifications for great power status are being revised', and the 'number of middle powers varies inversely with the number of great'. Still there is a great gulf between the middle and the great powers. The former cannot unify continents, or rule the seas, or control the international market. They have disputes with their neighbours and they possess limited interests and limited power. Wight recognizes the durability of middle powers because their ambitions are limited compared to great powers, and they appear to possess adequate power and influence to protect and manage their interests without risking the danger of overreach as in the case of dominant and great powers.[19]

By relying on the Wight approach and by rejecting the fashionable but analytically weak hierarchical approach, we can now appreciate the influence of international politics and the international system on the Nehru–Bhabha approach.

Several events influenced India's arms-control policy and nuclear-diplomacy in the 1950s and 1960s. Substantial US military aid to Pakistan in the mid-1950s, China's takeover of Tibet in 1950 and the subsequent problems in India–China relations, and the willingness of the Soviet Union to invest in Indian economic development in the mid-1950s and thereafter were three developments that shaped India's political and military responses in the 1950s. The US policy of keeping India off balance through a strategy of supplying military equipment on a grant or concessional basis to Pakistan evoked strong Indian protests. Apart from the danger that the Pakistani military posed to India's position in Kashmir and its lines of communication in India's north-west, the US strategy from the Indian perspective appeared to have broader implications. The broader focus was felt to reflect US hostility for India's position as a non-aligned force in world politics. This focus became a contextual feature in the arms-control and disarmament negotiations—that is, whenever India and the United States faced each other in arms-control and disarmament negotiations. For example, India's attitude against President Dwight D. Eisenhower's 'Atoms for Peace' proposal of 1953–4 appeared to be shaped by general Indian perceptions about the nature of US foreign policy in the Indian subcontinent.

China's behaviour on the Tibet issue during the early 1950s had implications for the future of Tibet itself, the future of Tibet as a buffer between India and China, and the future of Indian–Chinese relations. From 1949 (when the People's Republic of China was established) to 1961 (when the Zorin–McCloy Principles[20] [Soviet Union–US Statement of Agreed Principles] on Collateral Arms Control were defined), China did not seem to be the central factor in India's arms-control and disarmament diplomacy.[21] India's enthusiasm for the partial test ban agreement symbolized India's acceptance of the idea of Soviet–US détente as a basis of arms control. This enthusiasm in part recognized the importance of *moderating the superpower rivalry*. Conceivably, in part, it also recognized the importance of *shaping an agreement that excluded China* and was, therefore, political in nature—that is, it had an implication that was more than that of reducing superpower rivalry.

While US policy in the Indian subcontinent caused India to suspect US intentions generally, and China's behaviour during 1954–9 caused India to find comfort in its relationship with the Soviet Union, Moscow's willingness to invest substantially in India's economic and political future after 1954–5 encouraged India to structure its arms-control and disarmament policy in terms of its general political relationship with Moscow. Two events—Soviet opposition to the Baruch plan, and the US plan to establish an international regime to control the peaceful uses of atomic energy—encouraged Indo–Soviet cooperation in the field of disarmament. This cooperation reflected a similarity of Indo–Soviet arguments—that is, between Soviet arguments *vis-à-vis* the United States on the Baruch plan and Indian arguments *vis-à-vis* the United States on the safeguards issue in the IAEA deliberations. This cooperation did not actually entail sharing of Soviet atomic technology with India. In March 1960, Moscow offered atomic energy assistance to India on terms similar to those of its other aid projects.[22] This assistance involved the establishment of a power plant. However, the Indo–Soviet agreement that was reached in October 1961 referred to research, not to a power plant.

Despite the shifts in India's relations with the United States, the Soviet Union, and China, India's nuclear policy remained constant from the 1950s to May 1974. Nehru's hopes for the peaceful use of atomic energy dated back to 1946. According to Kavic, 'Nehru stated his hope that India would develop atomic power for peaceful uses but warned that, so long as the world was constituted as it was, every country would have to develop and use the latest scientific devices for its protection'.[23] In the 1950s and the 1960s, Canada was the principal supplier of atomic fuel and reactor technology to India. At this time, India's opposition to controls over the peaceful uses of atomic energy applied principally and publicly to US proposals to have rigid controls and, to a lesser extent—albeit privately—to Canadian suggestions to strengthen safeguards in Indo–Canadian atomic energy agreements. India's opposition related to the view that peaceful rather than military uses needed to be safeguarded. India did not oppose the principle of safeguards, only that the system should be universal, not discriminatory. (See Chapter 4 for details.)

This discussion has a major theoretical/paradigmatic implication. Weaker powers are not simply the helpless objects of great powers' competition and dominance—as is predicted in the 'dominant–subordinate' states' system approach. In Wight's sense, weaker powers are regional or middle powers and the effect of their power is a product of the skill they demonstrate in exploiting the contradictions or the fault lines in the external environment, and in guarding against danger and pressure. Indian foreign and nuclear policies under Nehru and Bhabha were bargaining strategies with twin aims: to *mediate* international rivalries and to *intervene* in their context so that Indian interests could be advanced.

There was a greater emphasis on international mediation than on military intervention in the Nehru years. Post-Nehruvian Indian policies, however, revealed an increased faith in interventionism—be it in the form of war behaviour in 1965 and 1971, crisis behaviour in Brasstacks (1987) and in subsequent crises (1990), or in the form of nuclear testing in 1974 and 1998.[24] That is, a sharp change in India's diplomatic, nuclear and military behaviour is indicated in the post-Nehruvian eras. The interventionist acts were directed against US efforts to dominate international and South Asian regional security systems. The basis of Indian intervention was established by the Nehru–Bhabha–MEA combination, although its full expression occurred later.

The second theoretical consideration concerns the western view of Nehru's diplomacy: it is seen to be driven by pacifist, reformist, and ethical considerations. Thus, the late Leonard Beaton noted:

[India's] proposals took the form of protests against any notion of a power system and reinforced the emotions that had given rise to the doctrine of non-alignment. This tradition has been continued by the non-aligned powers in the

Geneva disarmament committee. No doubt this activity helps to give countries which feel excluded from the central direction of world affairs a sense of participation in world order. A posture of moral superiority is available to those who find this a satisfying compensation for their lack of influence. Countries availing themselves of this option are usually those in which a reputation for being men of peace is a valuable domestic political asset to prime ministers or foreign ministers.[25]

Our assessment, however, emphasizes the geopolitical and realpolitik basis of the Nehru–Bhabha–MEA approach to the nuclear question. Consider the following elements of realpolitik in Nehru's statecraft.

Assessing Indian attitudes and behaviour in foreign policy is hard because much official Indian thinking is usually garbed in moral and utopian terms. Yet beneath the rhetoric lies much hard thinking. Our task in the following pages, therefore, is to uncover the 'hard' strategic calculations, using Nehru's views on war and peace, non-alignment, military force, power politics and balance of power, and peaceful coexistence as a basis of analysis. The point is made that a careful reading of Nehru's speeches reveals a basic honesty in signalling intentions, provided the 'ifs and buts'—the nuances—of his views are closely studied in relation to Indian policy contexts. The discussion indicates that 'security' is a major, if not a master, framework for the study and practice of Indian foreign policies.

During 1950–54, Nehru sensed a significant underlying tension or divergence in the Sino–Soviet bloc. In 1954, India and China signed an agreement reiterating the importance of the five principles of peaceful coexistence; this followed the death of Stalin and preceded the visit of N.A. Bulganin and Nikita Khrushchev to India. In 1957, the United Nations passed a resolution accepting peaceful coexistence. In 1972, the spirit of peaceful coexistence seemed to underlie the US–Soviet and US–Chinese summitry. The usage of 'peaceful coexistence', of course, has evolved over time, and the meanings and strategies vary from actor to actor.

This study does not chart India–China or Indo–Soviet relations. It is not important to discuss the precise meanings of peaceful coexistence in bilateral relations; clearly the term is ambiguous. To Nehru, it meant a rejection of the military approach to world affairs; it meant that states ought to avoid war; it meant a search for peace. These themes are sufficiently ambiguous to be almost meaningless, particularly since Nehru's views did not exclude the use of military power and nuclear power in influence building. The following section describes these views. The discussion is general, but it is sufficient to show that despite Nehru's protest against power politics, his view of peaceful coexistence—war avoidance and peace—was instrumental in orientation. It was ideological, or appeared as such, but 'peaceful coexistence' as a strategy was not simply an exercise in idealism. It was based on national interest and opportunism. In retrospect, it appears to be a transitional phase in Indian foreign relations—that is, until India's economic and military strength was sufficient to defend Indian interests. The theme that emerges from a crude content analysis of Nehru's speeches is that there was a mistrust of negotiating from strength—where strength implied absolute levels of military power—and a belief in the functionality of relative power and of a diplomatic strategy until India could defend itself through material means. This chapter, therefore, identifies the parameters of Nehru's approach to security without attempting to trace the exact influence or exact relationships between these factors.

As an ethical principle, 'peaceful coexistence' derives its legitimacy as an alternative to the military approach to national security. However, it is difficult to assess whether 'peaceful coexistence' was entirely based on an ethical concern in India's behaviour. Nehru argued against the military approach, but he also rejected the Gandhian approach in foreign and defence matters. In fact, even Gandhi himself was not unequivocally against the use of force. As Werner Levi notes, 'Gandhi held that when the choice is between cowardice and violence, violence should be preferred'.[26] He 'tolerated violent defence' that produced 'just ends'. He knew that 'a modern state could not resist external aggression by nonviolent means'. Finally, Gandhi 'admired the bravery of the Indian army in Kashmir'. Therefore, 'peaceful coexistence' was and is an ethical principle inasmuch as it is meant to be a substitute for war. But at the same time, it is a rule of expediency inasmuch as its articulation was accompanied by efforts to increase India's power.

To elaborate: While Nehru preferred that security policies be pursued through the development of proper policies and diplomatic means, a connection between diplomacy and military force was also made. The use of force as a last resort was permissible particularly if force was used to alter discrimination against the have-nots and to protect Indian interests. In this connection, the difference between Nehru's and Gandhi's thinking was carefully explained. To quote Nehru:

We were moved by these arguments, but for us and for the National Congress as a whole, the non-violent method was not, and could not be a religion or an unchallengeable creed or dogma. It could only be a policy and a method promising certain results, and by these results it would have to be finally judged.[27]

In other words, it was not because of its righteousness that non-violence could be justified. Rather, the justification centred on the utility of a particular method in relation to national policy goals. Nevertheless, Nehru made a distinction between joining a military pact, reserving the right of self-defence under Article 51 of the UN Charter, and accepting foreign military assistance for self-defence. He rejected military pacts because these invigorated a psychology of negotiating from a position of military strength, which prejudiced the position of weaker states like India, and which tended to 'serve the particular interests of the big powers'. The Soviet Union was hostile during 1945–53 to negotiations from a position of strength. In this respect, India has followed the Soviet diplomatic strategy. Yet there are substantial differences between the Indian and the Soviet approaches. While Moscow argued against 'negotiation by strength', it actually went on to do precisely that. Secondly, India's argument has been against medium or small powers serving big-power interests. The Soviets could hardly be expected to make this argument, or to accept Indian criticism on this point.

The aforesaid perspective indicates that peaceful coexistence was a strategy that appealed to India for two reasons: (1) India was economically and militarily weak, and peaceful coexistence gave it valuable time to find security through diplomacy with two communist giants who were involved in zero-sum activity with the United States and who would, logically speaking, have reacted strongly against India if it joined the Dullesian scheme of military containment. (2) Since Nehru held during 1950–4 that there was significant tension or divergence within the Sino–Soviet bloc, peaceful coexistence helped India to disassociate the one from the other, to reduce Indian dependence on one or the other, and, finally, to induce Chinese and Soviet involvement on India's behalf against US intervention in subcontinental affairs.

The strategy of peaceful coexistence was based on policy premises that differed from Western premises. It included an assessment of the role of military power in the nuclear age and the limited utility of military alliances between small states and the great powers. These points are expanded below.

The picture Nehru painted about national and international security was somewhat as follows: (1) India could not avoid being involved in world politics because of its geographical and political position and given its material resources and size. (2) India had some actual influence and even more potential influence. (3) The influence of the great powers ought not to be overestimated because the foreign policies of the major powers had not been successful. (4) India need not be frightened by the military might of the military blocs. (5) Of course, strength was needed for interference to be effective. (6) India needed to strengthen itself economically and militarily to defend itself against external attack, but not with a view to becoming an imperialist power. (7) The idea that security was obtained by military power was only partly true; it is equally true that security is protected by policies. A deliberate policy of friendship with other countries goes further in gaining security than almost anything else. (8) Possession of great economic and military power did not necessarily imply that policies of the great powers were correct. Here a need for a 'correct view' appears vital along with military and economic power.

In his far-ranging speech to the Indian Parliament on 25 February 1955, Nehru reflected on the international power structure, indicating a familiarity with Western deterrence theory and the limitations of military alliance politics. He made several points, as follows:

(i) The need for India's economic and military strength. To quote Nehru:

I am a little afraid that this House in its enthusiasm might perhaps imagine that we are doing more than we are really doing . . . We feel, in so far as international policy is concerned, that right or wrong counts. But it is not the rightness of a proposition that makes it listened to but rather the person or the country which says so and the strength behind that country.

(ii) The disadvantage of military alliances between great powers and small powers. To quote Nehru:

In this nuclear age the only countries that count, from the point of view of nuclear war, are those countries which are, unfortunately, in a position to use these bombs. But to attach small countries to themselves in alliance really means—and I say so with all respect to those countries—that they are becoming very much dependent on these countries. Such associates do not add to their defensive power, for they have little or no military value.

(iii) The dysfunctionality of overkill nuclear capacity. To quote Nehru:

The fact that one country has a few more bombs than the other is of no great relevance. The point is that even the country that has less has reached the saturation point, that is, it has enough to cause infinite damage to the other country. There is no real defence against nuclear weapons; you can at best damage or ruin the other country. When you have arrived at the saturation point, you have arrived at the stage of mutual extermination. Then the only way out is to prevent war, to avoid it. There is no other way.

(iv) The instability of the existing global balance and the danger of altering it by war. To quote Nehru:

As things are today, we have reached a certain balance—it may be a very unstable balance, but it is still some kind of balance—when any kind of major aggression is likely to lead to a world war. That itself is a restraining factor. Whether aggression takes place in a small country or a big one, it tends to upset the unstable balance in the world and is, therefore, likely to lead to war . . . If you extend the argument, you will see that the only way to avoid conflicts is to accept things more or less as they are. No doubt, many things require to be changed, but you must not think of changing them by war. War does not do what you want to do; it does something much worse. Further, by enlarging the area of peace, that is of countries which are not aligned to this group or that, but which are friendly to both, you reduce the chance of war.

(v) Western confusion about Asia. To quote Nehru:

Then there is the school of—shall I say—learned confusion. It talks very learnedly about international affairs, delivers speeches, writes articles, but never gets out of a confused state of mind. There is a fourth school, equally prominent, of ignorant confusion. So that, between all these various schools it is a little difficult to get to know where we are and what we are, more especially when the problem relates to Asia, because most of the currents of thought today in international affairs come from Europe and America. They are great countries, to be respected, but the greatness of a country does not necessarily endow it with greater understanding of some other country; and the fact that Asia has changed and is changing has not wholly been grasped by many people in other continents. Therefore, their confusion is the greater when thinking of Asia.[28]

The final theoretical consideration concerns the role of internal policy and politics, including bureaucratic politics (including the question of economic costs of a bomb programme), in the Nehru–Bhabha years. In a memorandum that Nehru wrote to K.P.S. Menon (then Indian Ambassador to the USSR), he noted that India's foreign policy 'will ultimately be governed by our internal policy'.[29] Appadorai also notes the need to examine the impact of domestic developments on foreign policy, to demonstrate the basic connection between the two. He cites Nehru to the effect that 'any attempt on our part, i.e., the Government of the day here, to go too far in one direction would create difficulties in our own country'.[30] These assessments imply the need to examine the effect of domestic politics on foreign policy making.

Our discussion of the Nehru–Bhabha years, however, indicates that international imperatives (events, compulsions, and opportunities) provided the main inputs into the formulation of Indian nuclear diplomacy; domestic politics were unimportant. *But* there is an important caveat. The parameters of the Indian bureaucratic and domestic debate were established in the Nehru–Bhabha years. These concerned the issue of an Indian bomb programme, the defence requirements of its China policy, and the policy requirements to deal with the problem of US–USSR condominium in nuclear non-proliferation affairs. China's first nuclear test in 1964 simply reinforced the ongoing internal debates.

Table 3.3 and Figure 3.4 outline the parameters of the debate and decision making that emerged in the Nehru–Bhabha years. Chapter 4 explains the ambiguities and tensions in Nehru's thinking and behaviour concerning Indian interests in relation to military power, civilian nuclear power, nuclear disarmament, and India's nuclear option. When Nehru died in 1964, the ambiguities and tensions had not been resolved. The points of tension had become radicalized in Indian bureaucratic and domestic politics as a consequence of the failure of Indian defence against China in 1962, and as a result of international developments, (that is, primarily the emergence of Western and Soviet policies against horizontal proliferation and the rise of nuclear China). The tensions had not been resolved in the Indian decision process and in Indian public debates during the Nehru years. The effect of the external developments on internal policy debates from the early 1960s onwards, however, gave credence to the Nehru view (quoted earlier) about the importance of internal policy in external affairs.

To sum up, international hierarchy and the 'dominant–subordinate state system' paradigm in North American scholarly and policy thinking was irrelevant in containing India's nuclear development in the Nehru–Bhabha years. An argument can be made that the unequal distribution of power and the assertion of special international nuclear rights for the strong stimulated India's quest to reform the world order and to acquire Indian strength.

The second conclusion is that Nehru–Bhabha placed India's approach to the nuclear question on a geopolitical and realpolitik basis and this approach was maintained generally by Nehru's successors. However, thirdly and finally, the geopolitical and realpolitik basis of the Nehru–Bhabha–MEA approach was vulnerable to internal policy (economics of national development and of the bomb) and politics— bureaucratic and societal. In our judgement, the evidence indicates that the international environment (USA, Pakistan, China) sought to contain Indian power by military and diplomatic means; this was a constant element since the early 1950s in the policies of these powers. Here the external imperatives reflected the primacy of geopolitical and realpolitik considerations in the behaviour of the USA (a democracy), Pakistan (a theocracy and a military dictatorship for most of its political history since 1947), and China (a communist system). Another constant was that leaving aside the Nehruvian foreign policy to reform and to pacify the world system, the Nehruvian behaviour was driven by Nehru's assessment of Indian interests; these were defined in terms of realpolitik and geopolitical considerations. Finally, however, the scope, intensity, timing, and effect of the domestic and bureaucratic debate on India's nuclear decision process has been the variable element in India's nuclear history since the Nehru years. India's traditional approach to the question of international nuclear controls and international security was formed in the Nehru years. This set of Indian norms have become a part of the two constant and the one variable elements. To a discussion of this we now turn because these Indian norms have shaped India's opposition to a two-tiered nuclear order as well as India's nuclear weapons programme and strategy.

ENDNOTES

1. M. Brecher, *Nehru, A Political Biography* (London: Oxford University Press, 1959), p. 627.
2. E. Stokes, 'Jawaharlal Nehru in the Making' (Review), *Modern Asian Studies*, vol. 2, no. 2, 1977, p. 295.
3. Dorothy Norman, ed., *Nehru: The First 60 Years* (London: Bodley Head, 1965), p. 186.
4. Ibid.
5. S. Bhatia, *India's Nuclear Bomb* (Delhi: Vikas, 1979), p. 82.
6. Ibid., p. 83.
7. Ibid., pp. 83–4.
8. Ibid., pp. 91–2.
9. Ibid., p. 114.
10. Ibid., p. 99.
11. Ibid., p. 101.
12. Ibid., p. 105.
13. Ibid., p. 105.
14. See, for example, Leonard Binder, 'The Middle East Subordinate International System', *World Politics*, vol. 10, April 1958, pp. 408–29; George Modelski, 'International Relations and Area Studies', *International Rela-*

tions, vol. 2, London, April 1961, pp. 143–55; Michael Brecher, 'International Relations and Asian Studies: The Subordinate State System of Asia', *World Politics*, vol. 15, January 1963, pp. 213–35; also his *The New States of Asia* (London: Oxford University Press, 1963), chapters III and VI; Larry W. Bowman, 'The Subordinate State System of Southern Africa', *International Studies Quarterly*, vol. 12, September 1968, pp. 231–62; Louis J. Cantori and Stephen L. Spiegel, 'The International Relations of Regions', *Polity*, vol. 2, Summer 1970, pp. 397–425.

15. S.L. Spiegel, *Dominance and Diversity: The International Hierarchy* (Boston: Little Brown, 1972), pp. 10, 40, and 19, for this theme.

16. R.L. Rothstein, *Alliances and Small Powers* (New York: Columbia University Press, 1968), p. 29.

17. Martin Wight, *Power Politics*, 2nd edn., edited by Hedley Bull and C. Holbraad (New York: Viking Penguin, 1986), p. 97.

18. K. Knorr, *Power and Wealth* (New York: Basic Books, 1973), pp. 13–14.

19. Wight, *Power Politics*, especially pp. 63–6 and 299–300.

20. For details of these principles, see *The United Nations and Disarmament, 1945–70* (New York: United Nations, 1970), pp. 87–8.

21. Of course, one can argue that since Nehru first mooted the idea of a test ban in 1954, it was then that India sought to isolate China in the disarmament arena. The Chinese argued in 1963 that as early as 1956, 'the Soviet leaders divorced the cessation of nuclear tests from the question of disarmament'. Cited in W.C. Clemens, Jr, *The Arms Race and Sino-Soviet Relations* (Stanford, CA: Hoover Institute Publications, 1968), p. 35. This idea may also explain India's disarmament behaviour, although Nehru could not have decided that the India–China relationship was irreparable in 1954 because it was only in 1959–61 that Chinese and Indian diplomatic positions started to freeze, although they had started to harden during 1954–9.

22. 'Russia to build Indian Atom Plant', *New York Times*, 8 March 1960 and Arnold Kramish, *The Peaceful Atom in Foreign Policy* (New York: Harper and Row, 1963), pp. 194–5.

23. See L.J. Kavic, *India's Quest for Security* (Berkeley and Los Angeles: University of California Press, 1967), p. 28.

24. For details, see A. Kapur with A.J. Wilson, *Foreign Policies of India and Her Neighbours* (London: Macmillan, 1997).

25. Leonard Beaton, *The Reform of Power* (New York: Viking Press, 1972), p. 132.

26. Werner Levi, 'Gandhi and Indian Foreign Policy', in Paul F. Power, ed.,

The Meanings of Gandhi (Honolulu: University Press of Hawaii, 1971), pp. 119 and 124.

27. Cited in M.N. Das, *The Political Philosophy of Jawaharlal Nehru* (London: George Allen and Unwin, 1961), p. 59.

28. This section draws on A. Kapur, *India's Nuclear Option* (New York: Praeger, 1976), pp. 51–6.

29. Cited in Peter Lyon, 'The Foreign Policy of India', in F.S. Northedge, ed., *The Foreign Policies of the Powers* (London: Faber and Faber, 1968), p. 255.

30. A. Appadorai, *Essays in Indian Politics and Foreign Policy* (Delhi: Vikas, 1971), p. 115.

4

The Diplomatic Base of India's Nuclear Strategy

Introduction

The diplomatic base of India's nuclear strategy was established in the Nehru years. It has served India well as the foundation of its approach to international nuclear and disarmament conference diplomacy. This diplomatic base can be judged to be intellectually or philosophically logical, durable in Indian domestic politics as well as in international politics, and a serious challenge to American authority in the non-proliferation sphere as well as to the PRC's quest to be a domineering force in Asia. This base must be studied for several reasons: (a) it laid the basis for Indian engagement of the US nuclear agenda by diplomatic means; (b) it created a framework for India's technical and organizational work in the nuclear sphere; and finally, (c) it provided an important input into Indian nuclear decision making. Figure 4.1 outlines the impact of the Nehru nuclear diplomatic agenda.

This chapter outlines a particular aspect of India's diplomatic behaviour. Traditionally, Indian diplomacy emphasized the importance of peace diplomacy (where the emphasis was on peaceful rather than military methods), or international negotiations (where the principle of compromise was central), and socio-economic development (where security was more than just military security; it included economic security, but at the same time, economic activity had to be mediated by social and political compulsions and expectations in a post-colonial state and society). Contextually, traditional Indian diplomacy did not accept the US–Soviet view that Third World countries had to choose between the US and the Soviet worlds and that the choice was limited to two paradigms.

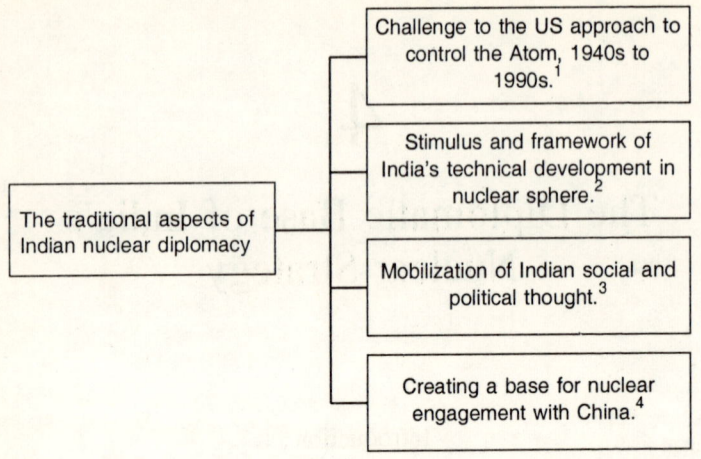

FIG. 4.1: Nehru's Nuclear Agenda

Notes: [1]Here the Government of India (GOI) participated in global conference diplomacy with a view to develop global norms and policies concerning atomic controls; and it was interfering against the US approach on the subject.
[2]Here the GOI was building India's internal strength in the nuclear sphere.
[3]Here the GOI was organizing Indian bureaucratic and societal thinking and domestic support for its approach to the nuclear question.
[4]Here the GOI was creating the nuclear dimension of regional geopolitics. This became relevant in the 1960s.

Traditionally, Indian diplomacy always functioned in the context of multipolarity in the international relations of the Indian subcontinent in Asia, and in the international system. Multipolarity was the reality because of the participation of the USA, the USSR, the PRC, India, Pakistan, and the 'smaller' South Asian states in the organization of alignments (friendly and/or conflictual) in the Indian subcontinent. In Asia, multipolarity existed in the pattern of interactions among multiple players (for example the USA, the PRC, the USSR, and the two Koreas in the Korean War).

In sum, even though Indian politics and society shared an abiding affinity with Western liberal and internationalist values, the thought processes and policies of post-colonial India revealed major fault lines between India and the West. These are summarized below.

These differing ideas are important, as a context to the current controversies between India and the West and, to some extent, with Pakistan. One is that when the world was dominated by the Cold War and bipolarity, policymakers in the Indian subcontinent were essentially functioning in a multipolar world. At that time, there were three outside powers—the United States, the Soviet Union, China; two regional ones—India, Pakistan; and a number of smaller states. Thus, the mental framework from the very beginning was multipolar, and Indians never bought into the notion of bipolarity. It is important to recognize that this belief was maintained throughout and after the Cold War.

The second point is that the Indian elite believed that weaker powers such as India could develop niches in the international system and they could develop a regional sphere of influence. The Indian subcontinent has constantly seen traditional conflicts for power and autonomy between various states. This of course created a desire in India to become a regional hegemon. The dictionary indicates both a benign view of a hegemon (a leader) and a malign view (domineering). Indians' self-image took the benign view. The policymakers in the US–UK have often taken a malign view of Indian hegemony. Consequently, the Indian quest for regional hegemony has often bumped straight into American policy. Declassified Department of Defence documents written in 1949 indicate that the US government is on record, saying that they are very uncomfortable with the idea of regional powers who are not friendly to them. This argument was framed in terms of containing the Russians, but a few other states were mentioned—China, Japan, India. Thus, the Indian notion of benign hegemony has constantly bumped into American disquiet over regional hegemons in Asia.

A third point of additional divergence can be found in conversations between former Indian Prime Minister Nehru and American ambassadors. This was the belief that nationalism was a more elemental force than communism in Asia. In the early 1950s, Nehru wanted to discover the cracks in the Sino–Soviet system. The point here was to find and to exploit contradictions in the communist world. This approach expressed a faith in nationalism as a driving element in diplomatic and military affairs in Asia.

The fourth point of disagreement was the standard Western belief that the choice for India and other developing countries was between Western capitalism and democracy or Soviet socialism. This was no real choice for the Indian policymakers who preferred a third way—the Indian one. Another belief, the fifth, was that the West was superior because of its mastery over nature and technology, and the innovation and vitality of its market-place; and that Western values and methods were generally better. This crass message did not sit well with the Indians. It stoked nationalism; the role of nationalism in India should be remembered when discussing Western initiatives in the international system, such as non-proliferation and arms control. Nationalism has been a significant basis of Indian response to Western policy proposals in the nuclear and missile spheres.

The final belief that was widely held among Western policymakers was that development primarily means economic growth. The Indians rejected most of these beliefs. They thought that the last one was important but too narrow, that there is more to development than just economic change, and that it must be defined in political and social terms. Thus, we can see how the nuclear and other controversies are stimulated by differences in thinking and approach, as well as by competing policy interests.

India's nuclear diplomacy was embedded in these attitudes about Western (especially the US) policies, and about the bipolarized Cold War international system. The latter made the USA and the USSR into both temporary international leaders (colluders) and contenders in Indian policy thinking. The dominant theme in Indian diplomatic thought was the pattern of temporary contention and temporary collusion between the major powers. The contention created an opportunity for Indian policymakers to exploit the differences among the Powers; the collusion created a danger of Indian isolation and marginalization in world and regional affairs. Because nationalism was viewed by India's political elite as the more elemental force than communism, the Indian diplomatic strategy was to build Indian nationalism, to find space for it in the international sphere, to exploit the contradictions between the US and Russia as well as Russian and Chinese nationalism and their competitive national interests, and to challenge the US tendency to denationalize third world politics while it developed US patriotism (nationalism) and hegemony in the international security sphere. India's nuclear diplomacy was developed in this context by the Nehru government and the successors.

This chapter deals with the challenge of post-war US disarmament strategy to Indian security. The challenge was both doctrinal and material. India's response to America's strategy of controlling the peaceful uses of atomic energy was to view it as a dangerous precedent—an exercise in imperialism—where the superpowers, or at least one superpower, gained the right to decide world-order questions simply because they, or it, had enormous military power and glorified US military and economic strength.

This chapter assesses India's interest in nuclear affairs in the context of India's early interest in the growth of its own nuclear power capability by developing its peaceful nuclear applications. It shows that India's mistrust of the 'big-power' orientation of US strategy in the Cold War era was reinforced by India's fear of the philosophy of control of the Baruch plan. Both these aspects were reinforced by Indian perceptions of the militaristic nature of US involvement in the Indian subcontinent when the US–Pakistani alliance was created in 1953–4.

This chapter does not focus directly on Indian responses to the US–British–Canadian declaration of November 1945 on the future of atomic energy. Neither is there evidence of a detailed and a sustained response to the Acheson–Lilienthal report of 1946 and the Baruch plan of the same year. This chapter is concerned with Indian reactions after President Eisenhower's 'Atoms for Peace' plan was outlined.[1]

Two purposes are served by referring to the 1950s. First, it demonstrates that India's objections to the NPT of 1968 and to the subsequent development of the different aspects of the NPT regime (export controls, sanctions, Nuclear Weapon Free Zones (NWFZs), CTBT, and MTCR) referred to objections made during the 1950s. This focus suggests a continuity, blended with an evolution, in India's nuclear policy to gain security, in part, via nuclear disarmament. Secondly, India's nuclear behaviour in the 1950s sheds light on India's alliance behaviour and alliance politics. In subcontinental regional geopolitics, external enmities (with Pakistan, USA, and China) shaped India's quest for an alignment with the USSR. The principle—'the enemy (that is, the USSR) of my enemy (that is, the USA, Pakistan, and China) is my potential friend'—was at work in regional affairs. In nuclear affairs, the USSR was engaged in a pattern of both contention and collusion with the USA, and the USSR therefore was not India's main nuclear partner. Instead, because of the diplomatic and nuclear activities and the characteristics of Canada and India in the 1950s, the two became the main nuclear partners. Both saw themselves, and each other, as middle powers. Both were uneasy about the Great Powers' dominance (or its danger) of the international system. Canada saw India as the main avenue for the development of its Canadian Asia policy and policies in relation to the Commonwealth of Nations and the Third World. In the scientific–technological sphere, Canada saw India as the global window for its unique CANDU nuclear reactor system and India saw the

CANDU system as an alternative to the dependence on US light water, enriched uranium system; the latter raised a problem of US control over India's nuclear planning and infrastructure. In other words, India reached out to the USSR as an ally in the regional diplomatic–strategic sphere, and to Canada as an ally in the nuclear and the diplomatic-economic sphere. Both had a subtle anti-US orientation or at least one that showed scepticism about US strategic motives. The Canada–India nuclear alignment was unusual given the geographical distance and the ethnic, economic, and political differences between the two countries. But, whatever the reasons, it is clear that the two countries were not and are not strategic adversaries.

The Indo–Canadian atomic energy arrangements of the 1950s were unique in the history of any kind of foreign aid to India and were probably also unique in comparison to US and Soviet atomic energy assistance to their allies. The aid terms favoured India, but Canada also gained politically and commercially from the relationship. Despite the inequality of functions, with Canada as the donor and India as the receiver, there was no inequality in the conditions of the aid during the 1950s. This point merits emphasis because the bilateral atomic and political relationship was shaped in the context of US opposition to Indian political and strategic efforts in general and also in the context of the Baruch plan.

The international setting in which India's nuclear policy developed was one of a war of arguments between the superpowers. The superpower controversy and the Indo–US controversy concerned the merits of the Baruch plan. The 15 November 1945 declaration by the United States, Great Britain, and Canada made two points, and these underlay the Baruch plan. First, that there could be 'no adequate military defense' against atomic weapons. Second, that the powers favoured exchange and transmission of basic scientific information but not information related to practical industrial applications of atomic energy. To quote:

The military exploitation of atomic energy depends, in large part, upon the same methods and processes as would be required for industrial uses. We are not convinced that the spreading of the specialized information regarding the practical application of atomic energy, before it is possible to devise effective, reciprocal enforceable safeguards acceptable to all nations, would contribute to a constructive solution of the problem of the atomic bomb. On the contrary we think it might have the opposite effect.[2]

Overall, there were two major qualifications in the Baruch plan approach to control the Atom. The first was to share information about practical applications of atomic technology 'just as soon as effective safeguards against its use for destructive purposes can be devised'. This itself was problematic. The second was even more problematic. This stated that no safeguards system that could be devised would 'of itself provide an effective guarantee against production of atomic weapons by a nation bent on aggression'. That is, even with safeguards, there was no guarantee against diversion from peaceful to military uses of the Atom. The suggested solution was to consolidate and extend the authority of the United Nations. In other words, the proposal was so ambitious that it required a stringent safeguards system and a radical reform of the states' system, which would make the United Nations the source of political legitimacy and military power in world politics.[3]

Generally speaking, the setting and the style of India's nuclear behaviour in the Cold War era was markedly different from that of a medium power like Great Britain. As George Quester points out,

Rather than bargaining closely on the exchange of uranium for nuclear technology the British chose instead to acknowledge a 'public interest' for the West that the American stockpile be augmented as expeditiously as possible for the protection of all Western powers. By assuming such a posture, the British not only fortified their own claim to an ultimate nuclear capability, but reinforced the sense that the United States was already reciprocally committed to the defence of Britain and Western Europe.[4]

By contrast, India's behaviour differed on several counts. A response to the problem of nuclear war was seen to lie in disarmament and not in alliance politics. In addition, India chose not to define the 'public interest' in terms of the security needs of the Western states. Instead, it defined public interest as a problem of lessening the danger of a hot war, of achieving balanced disarmament, and of avoiding the growth of international security regimes led by the superpowers. This approach seemed equitable since it appeared to take into account the security interests of the superpowers as well as the world-order concerns of third parties. Also, rather than bargain closely on the exchange of Indian thorium (of which India has a near monopoly of the world supply) for advanced nuclear technology, India chose instead to structure its atomic energy programme by seeking to increase the peaceful uses of atomic energy. Such a bargain was possible because the Acheson–Lilienthal report and the Baruch plan required international control of thorium and uranium deposits, among other things. A corollary of this policy was to insist on safeguards against military rather than peaceful uses of atomic energy.

Finally, in contrast with British diplomacy, India did not and could not seek a reciprocal Western commitment on India's behalf. Such a visible commitment would have violated India's non-aligned stance. Another reason lay in Nehru's confidence (up to the late 1950s) that India's geopolitical and military position could be protected by a policy of peaceful coexistence, or 'defense through friendship'.

Nehru on Military Power, Nuclear Weapons, Disarmament, and Nuclear Power

Nehru's thinking on nuclear matters was ambiguous. He mistrusted the US strategy of military containment of the communist powers and the strategy of controlling the peaceful atom. On the other hand, however, he recognized the importance of relative military power as well as the importance of building India's nuclear power. The ambiguity centred on two points. His rejection of 'absolute power' and his acceptance of 'relative power' left unanswered the exact meaning, or the nature, of the latter. It indicated that Nehru was not a 'peacenik', as is sometimes imagined. Yet no precise mix of the nuclear and conventional military ingredients of 'relative power' is indicated clearly in the public records of Nehru. Secondly, there is an ambiguity between Nehru's mistrust of nuclear weapons and his policy of promoting the peaceful applications of atomic energy. What, in Nehru's thinking, was the boundary between peaceful uses and military uses? Did 'sophisticated' peaceful uses mesh into the realm of military uses, as Western critics of India's 'peaceful use only' doctrine claim? Or was there really a definite military–political–psychological, if not a technological–scientific, difference between the two? Thus, a Western reader, familiar with his/her country's culture-bound analyses, is cautioned against assuming as a given, that since Nehru explicitly favoured civilian nuclear power he favoured Indian nuclear weapons implicitly.

In probing the ambiguities in Nehru's strategies in security matters, it is useful to explore three types of relationships in his 'view of the world' or his perceptions of the structure of international society. The first is between nuclear weapons and the balance of power; the second is between military power and the ability to negotiate; and, finally, the third is between India's disarmament policy and its nuclear policy. At best, Nehru's views on these points are sketchy. They lack the sophistication of several articulate Western strategic writers. Yet Nehru offered a glimpse of a strategy that questioned the superpowers', and particularly the US, approach to influence building and conflict management through a position of 'strength'.[5] To quote him:

Then there is the School which talks about negotiations through strength. It is true that nobody will listen to you if you are weak. But, as you develop your strength to negotiate, unfortunately the other party also goes on developing its strength.[6]

The meaning is not absolutely clear. It is not clear whether Nehru meant that differences in absolute power did not matter or small differences in relative power did not matter.

Overall, it is hard to be definitive about Nehru's meaning of 'relative power' in the Indian policy context. Whatever it meant, one can be certain of two points. He rejected the view that absolute military power counted, and this seemed to underlie his view of India's position—actual and potential—*vis-à-vis* the superpowers and China. He never took the view that the superpowers could perform better, to satisfy their foreign policy and security interests, just because of their superior strategic capabilities. *The balance of power seemed to be a function of the policies of states and not simply their nuclear and military capabilities.* His views of the world focus on at least four major powers: the United Sates, the Soviet Union, China, and India. However, at the same time, he did not regard influence-building activity as simply a product of 'talk'—of expressing moral concerns—unless this was accompanied by material strength. This point is explicit in his statement that '*nobody will listen to you if you are weak*'. On 8 March 1948, he noted that India was 'not, frankly speaking, influential enough to affect international events very much'.[7] But then he prefaced his remarks by stating that the other powers had not succeeded in satisfying their interests.[8]

So far, our discussion shows that Nehru was attentive to the need to have strength to negotiate, to be listened to. He did not believe that overkill nuclear capacity was needed to negotiate. This point was apparently directed against the arms race between the superpowers, but it also had a meaning for India's security policy. On the one hand, he seemed to think that India was protected by the balance of power. Furthermore, he thought that India was a pivot in western, southern, and South Asia and was convinced that it would inevitably play a role because of its potential resources and its geographical location.[9] Yet he also felt that India needed at least '15 years of peace in order to be able to develop its resources'.[10] The domestic sources of foreign policy were emphasized: Foreign policy was seen as an outcome of economic policy;[11] external affairs were seen to follow internal affairs;[12] Indian non-aligned policy was defined as a 'part of a policy' whose objective was to promote Indian national interest.[13] Finally, a dual method for analysing world problems was indicated: First, one had to analyse a particular issue in terms of Indian interests, and then in terms of its merits.[14]

The views that an Indian strategist needed to give priority to Indian national interests (and secondly to 'merit') and the suggestion that non-alignment was only a 'part' of a policy are significant in the context of yet another statement. Although Nehru tried to reduce the importance of military power as well as the role of dominant military powers of the time (that is, the USA and the USSR) as the basis to resolve political disputes, he was concerned more with the need to transform the nature of the international system. According to him, 'The status quo has to go throughout the world before war goes and the causes of war'.[15] In other words, eliminating discrimination between the haves and the have-nots had priority over the question of restraining the use of military force in international relations. Herein lies one of the fundamental differences between Indian and US policy views on the question of controlling the use of force. Nehru argued that democracy was both political and economic,[16] and suggested that the need was to maximize the economic and political security of many, rather than a few, nations. This approach seemed to be a key political value in Nehru's thinking. His argument about internationalism was an argument against the 'narrow' economic and military nationalism and imperialism of the great powers.[17]

The *anti-status* quo and anti-superpower orientation in Nehru's policy suggests convincingly that Nehru's prime consideration was not to disarm India; the role of force was not excluded from the policy framework. This point is obvious in India's strategy of military intervention towards Pakistan and its strategy of managing its military confrontation with China after 1962. It remains, however, for us to assess the relationship between India's disarmament policy and its nuclear policy during the 1950s.

India's early interest in nuclear policy[18] is not usually emphasized by Indians because Nehru, like many other statesmen, spoke the language of disarmament. Beaton makes the point that disarmament negotiators frequently use the language of disarmament 'rather than security'.[19] During the 1950s, Nehru and his disarmament representatives seemed to take this route. But Beaton also states that disarmament negotiators 'have no particular knowledge either of security problems or of security policy in the main powers', and that 'they have had no incentive to gain such knowledge'.[20] This generalization seems excessive, and at least it does not apply always to the experience or behaviour of Indian disarmament negotiators, from Ambassador Arthur Lall to Ambassador V.C. Trivedi. In the latter case, in particular, it is plainly evident that *the Indian language was that of disarmament and security*, and the disarmament negotiators had detailed knowledge about security matters. (It is hardly a secret that Mr Trivedi had served as the chairman of the Indian intelligence board in the MEA before going to Switzerland as ambassador to that country and as the head of the Indian delegation to the Eighteen-Nations Disarmament Committee (ENDC) Indian arguments on the safeguards doctrine, like earlier Soviet arguments on the Baruch plan, had obvious security motives, even though the security aspects were developed by 'hard-line' civilian diplomats rather than a military general.

The security motives related to three Indian policy issues in the 1950s. The first was to oppose the growth of a legal precedent that allowed a superpower to decide the rules and norms of an evolving international law. This argument concerned the right of great powers to decide exclusively. India's reservation dealt with the style of superpower decision-making, namely, decision-making by concert between the superpowers rather than a concert that took into account the security of all countries, as noted in principle five of the Zorin–McCloy principles. This objection dealt with the question of international safeguards. It also concerned the danger of collusion between or among the Great Powers.

The second issue was to keep India's nuclear option open—that is, free of restrictive and irrevocable safeguards. Clearly, this option was directed to the future and based on international developments, for example China's future behaviour towards India and the Indian Ocean littoral, which the disarmament speakers of the 1950s and the 1960s or the makers of the NPT could hardly predict with any precision beyond a year or two. Clearly, the option related to possible military activities in the nuclear field and not simply to continue existing civilian activities. Given this, it is arguable if the term 'peaceful uses only' conveys a precise meaning. Even 'aggressive' states claim to act in the name of peace. 'Peace' and 'aggression' are policy-oriented words, and ultimately the issue is one of assessing intent. On 24 July 1957, Nehru declared, 'India will in no event use atomic energy for destructive purposes but only for peaceful purposes. I am confident that this would be the policy of all future governments in the country.'[21]

Beyond the semantics of the term 'peaceful uses', however, lies a key point in India's disarmament and nuclear behaviour. India's nuclear option was implicit in India's peaceful nuclear programme of the 1950s, in its disarmament strategy, and in its opposition to international safeguards. It was not to deceive the world community that India talked about the peaceful uses of atomic energy. The fact was that India did not know in the 1950s or the 1960s when China would become a nuclear threat for India and what sort of a nuclear response this contingency might require. Opposition to international safeguards was not a signal that India would produce the Bomb. It was a signal that it reserved the right to do so if China developed a weapons programme and targeting doctrine that threatened India directly and if no external support was available to India.

The link between India's disarmament strategy and its nuclear policy appears to be explicit at least from 1960 on, if not earlier. In a speech, entitled 'Point of No Return', to the Parliament of India on 22 November 1960, Nehru stated,

If nothing effective is done in regard to disarmament in the course of the next three or four years, it may perhaps become too late to deal with it; it may become almost impossible to control the situation.[22]

The Chinese started testing in 1964—that is, four years after Nehru's speech. One can infer that Nehru was referring to the Chinese nuclear programme, and India's atomic intelligence was accurate about China's atomic progress.[23] From this, one can argue that even in the mid-1950s, Nehru's disarmament diplomacy was not guided simply by an altruistic concern to save humanity from war. Rather, the concern was to secure a purposive disarmament agreement that could contain China's programme, and, failing that, to retain India's nuclear option.

The third issue in Indian perceptions was to create an Indo–Canadian 'North American–South Asian' focus that bypassed US opposition to India's nuclear programme. In Indo–US arguments, India's verbal strategy was borrowed from Moscow's opposition to the Baruch plan. Yet this identity did not necessarily represent an Indian tilt towards Moscow in the nuclear field. In the 1950s, there was little or no activity between India and the communist bloc. On 6 October 1961, India and the USSR signed an 'Agreement on Peaceful Utilisation of Atomic Energy'. This stipulated cooperation in research connected with reactors using natural uranium (like the Canadian reactors) and for breeder reactors using plutonium as well as the thorium–uranium-233 cycle.[24] This agreement, however, seems to have remained inactive.[25]

Thus, there was no tilt in India's nuclear policy towards Moscow but a superficial similarity between Indian and Soviet disarmament strategies. This was an important diplomatic choice. It allowed India to use Soviet jargon against the Baruch plan approach even though Indian and Soviet interests did not necessarily, or always, coincide. The verbal strategy was nevertheless purposive. It helped India to negotiate atomic energy deals on favourable conditions with Canada. As Beaton notes, the Indian undertakings to Canada about peaceful uses were 'weak'.[26]

However, did this mean that India deceived Canada by agreeing to the 'peaceful uses only' clause? Evidence indicates that this is not so. (Thus Mitchell Sharp, Canada's Secretary of State for External Affairs, noted, in a press conference in Ottawa on 22 May 1974, that there was no violation of Indo–Canadian agreements.) Indian reservations about safeguards, particularly IAEA safeguards, were publicly known at the time the Indo–Canadian agreements were negotiated. Moreover, several Canadian attempts to strengthen the bilateral safeguards were firmly rejected by Indian officials from the time Chester Ronning was Canada's High Commissioner in New Delhi.[27] Furthermore, inasmuch as nuclear power stations are not necessarily economical—Beaton argued that they were not,[28] but the Canadian authorities thought they were[29]—an intelligent observer can infer security and political motives in a poor nation's search for participating in an internationally visible activity.

Setting and Premises of India's Disarmament and Nuclear Policy

The foregoing discussion suggests that there was some connection, albeit not an explicit one, between India's nuclear policy and its disarmament policy during the 1950s. One should briefly refer to Nehru's and Krishna Menon's views on disarmament and to trace the evolution of India's disarmament strategy. India's traditional disarmament diplomacy, as articulated by Krishna Menon in the 1950s, regarded disarmament as a realistic rather than a utopian possibility. In this focus, there was a need to eliminate superpowers' arms rather than merely to reduce or limit them. According to this view, arms reduction and limitation could be a first step towards disarmament, but unless there was disarmament, war could not be outlawed.[30] On the other hand, Nehru cautiously emphasized that disarmament was important as a strategy if it did not destabilize the global environment—that is, if it was balanced in its implementation.[31]

India's disarmament and arms-control diplomacy, since it was conceived, has had two faces. In the 1950s, India's role in part was that of a great power helper. This face was symbolized by India's call for nuclear disarmament. Nehru called for a test ban in 1954, and such a ban was in fact concluded in 1963.[32] The second Indian face was less visible but equally, if not more, salient. It reflected India's opposition to US-sponsored and, subsequently, Soviet-sponsored proposals for international control of atomic energy—a control, in effect, of peaceful rather than military uses of atomic energy.[33]

India's opposition to international safeguards originated as a response to America's challenge but became a challenge to America's right to decide security policies for the 'free world'. 'Safeguards' are defined as 'those measures designed to guard against the diversion of material, such as source and special nuclear material, from uses permitted by law or international agreement, and to give timely indication of possible diversion or assurance that diversion has not occurred'.[34] It is frequently asserted by Western critics that Soviet arms-control policies are a part of the Soviet Union's fundamental interests. Western criticisms of Soviet disarmament behaviour have not usually impressed Indian disarmament negotiators for two reasons: Indian negotiators find that US arms-control policies are also a part of the US fundamental interests; and Indian arms-control problems with the superpowers are rooted more in Indo–US relations than in Indo–Soviet relations. This has been the case because the US commitment to prevent diversion of atomic energy from 'peaceful' to 'military' uses is more entrenched than a Soviet commitment on that issue. A comparison between the US and Soviet proposals on this point, from the Baruch plan to the various plans on general and complete disarmament, makes this clear.[35]

The foregoing discussion shows India's suspicion about the US attitudes and behaviour in the disarmament field in the 1950s. This was highlighted by a contrast between the Canadian and the US approaches to peaceful uses of atomic energy. The nature of Canada's political and economic involvement in Indian subcontinental affairs during the 1950s was substantially different, in comparison to the US attitudes and behaviour during the Truman–Acheson–Dulles period. In America's behaviour, the demand to control atomic energy exceeded an offer of gain to the other side, and there was no identity of political values. In contrast, Canada's behaviour accented the reward rather than the punishment.

One fundamental difference in the behaviour of the two North

American countries towards South Asian problems during the 1950s was that Canadian disarmament and arms-control diplomacy, like the US diplomacy, was used to support Canadian diplomatic and commercial objectives, but, unlike the US policy, Canada was not preoccupied with the problem of developing its margin of military safety against potential adversaries.

A contrast between Canadian and the US approaches to the problem of controlling atomic energy in India is useful. The Quebec Agreement of 1943 between the United States, Britain, and Canada[36] provided the original framework of atomic energy cooperation between these pioneers of atomic weapons. According to James Eayrs, in this agreement, the three parties agreed not to use atomic weapons against each other, or against third parties without the others' consent; also they agreed not to communicate information about atomic energy to third parties without the others' consent and to reserve for negotiations the question of post-World War II industrial and commercial applications of atomic energy.[37]

The difficulties that Britain and Canada experienced in the post-War period with regard to this cooperative agreement have been attributed to the security consciousness of America's post-War managers of atomic energy such as General Leslie Groves.[38] The 1946 Acheson–Lilienthal report on international control was based on the view that the US atomic monopoly was a temporary one. The Baruch plan (1946) was intended as a mechanism to translate the Acheson–Lilienthal recommendations into a policy. America's approach to this problem has been adequately discussed in the literature.[39] Less noted in the US literature is Canada's contribution—as reflected in then Ambassador Lester Pearson's contribution of a draft dated 8 November 1945. As Eayrs rightly emphasizes, this must surely be one of the most significant documents of the century. The principal premises in the Pearson proposal to control the atom were as follows:

(i) The atom bomb was not the last word in the development of military technology.

(ii) American monopoly of the atom bomb was not eternal.

(iii) International rather than national solution to control the atom was necessary and desirable.

(iv) 'The knowledge now possessed by the United States, the United Kingdom, and Canada could be traded advantageously for a system of international control under the United Nations'.[40]

The joint Declaration on Atomic Energy produced by the US President Harry S. Truman, British Prime Minister Clement Atlee, and Canadian Prime Minister Mackenzie King on 11 November 1945 (to which the Pearson draft proposal apparently contributed ideas) outlined two main ideas: (1) there ought to be exchange of information for peaceful ends on a reciprocal basis; and (2) there ought to be effective and enforceable safeguards against the use of specialized atomic energy information for destructive purposes.[41]

At this time, Canadian arms-control and disarmament diplomacy was based on two ideas: First, irrespective of the difference of opinion between the United States and Canada with regard to Canada's position in the atomic business, Canada's diplomatic objective was not to aid the communist adversary. This was central to Canadian Prime Minister Mackenzie King's diplomacy. Second, Canada sought to restrain the US Cold War diplomacy during the 1950s and particularly to moderate the harsh military overtone of the containment doctrine. This was a mark of Canadian Prime Minister Louis St. Laurent's diplomacy and underlay External Affairs Minister Pearson's open disagreement with John Foster Dulles's notion of massive retaliation.

In this setting, Indo–Canadian relations developed into a unique[42] model of East–West, middle powers, and North American–South Asian collaboration in an age of ideological and military bipolarity. The Canadian approach to Asia in general and India in particular was different from America's approach at that time. As Pearson pointed out, 'the main avenue of approach for Canada to the problems of Asia has been by way of the Indian subcontinent'.[43] This remarkably candid statement provided an enormous contrast with the US strategy. The latter tried to bypass New Delhi and instead pursued military solutions against the communist states. Against this, the underlying Canadian and Indian approach was to moderate the Cold War, to establish intercontinental bridges between the East and the West, and, in the words of the Canadian Governor General, Vincent Massey, to develop a 'grouping of friendly nations making widely differing responses to the Cold War, thus cutting across the frozen configuration of international politics . . .'[44] Thus, the common Canadian and Indian approach to foreign policy was to guide an intercontinental and multiracial Commonwealth of Nations and to arrest the danger of a globalized or overextended Cold War in Asia.

A major premise in Canadian diplomacy at that time was that nothing should be done to upset the stability of the Indian subcontinent and that, as a corollary, India needed to be helped in its economic development so that its democratic framework and security could be strengthened.[45] With regard to at least three major issues, Canada's position was compatible with Indian aspirations: The Cold War ought not to be globalized; East–West competition should not be resolved through military means; and there ought to be local–regional solutions to local–regional problems. These views represented points of departure between the US views and Indo–Canadian views. It was in the context of this kind of thinking that Canada declined to mediate the Kashmir dispute and failed to support the South East Asia Treaty Organisation (SEATO) system of security in South East Asia.

Canadian interest in fostering a bilateral Indo–Canadian relationship in the 1950s in part moderated the impact of the US policy views about Indian non-alignment and in part offered an alternative mechanism to pave the way for a North American–South Asian relationship. The nature of Canadian political assumptions and the kinds of activities that Canada promoted in India rather than the extent of Canadian commitments were the salient elements in the relationship. There are two ways of studying the basis of this relationship during the 1950s. The first is simply to regard Canadian material involvement as a price that Canada paid for sharing India as an important listening post in Asia, as an avenue for structuring Canada's Asia policy, and as a means for advancing Canada's commercial interests in the field of atomic energy. The second way is to treat the Indo–Canadian dyad as a unique alternative for India and Canada, given the difficulties that Nehru experienced *vis-à-vis* the United States during his visit in 1949, and given St. Laurent's mistrust of the US stance in the Cold War. The two perspectives are not mutually exclusive, and it is in both senses that the following analysis focuses on the Indo–Canadian and Indo–US atomic arrangements.

Indo–Canadian and Indo–US Atomic Energy Arrangements

The foundation of India's atomic programme was laid in 1944 with the establishment of the Tata Institute of Fundamental Research under the guidance of Dr Homi Bhabha, subsequently the first head of the Indian Atomic Energy Commission. India entered the 'peaceful' atomic club in 1956, when the first experimental research reactor became critical in August 1956. APSARA was the first research reactor in Asia and was indigenously built. The enriched fuel element came from Britain, and a bilateral agreement ensured its peaceful use. The second research reactor (CIRUS) as well as subsequent Canadian reactors were introduced into India under a Canadian version of the 'Atoms for Peace' concept. The Indo–Canadian agreements centred on the principle of peaceful uses.[46] But there was no agreement about the specific meaning of the term, even though both sides reiterated from time to time the need to promote the peaceful uses of atomic energy. Specific disagreements between the two sides were papered over in bilateral negotiations. It was around 1966 that a serious controversy emerged in Indo–Canadian atomic relations.[47]

India's atomic relationship with Canada developed in a political framework of bilateralism and in terms of a search for scientific cooperation with the West.[48] During 1954–8, the interesting and personal relationship between Indian Prime Minister Nehru and the Canadian Premier St. Laurent enabled the two sides to seek bilateral methods for solving problems that often had a multilateral angle. The pattern of political relations in South Asia and the problem of disarmament were issues where the bilateral approach appealed to Indian and Canadian leaders. In this context, Canada adopted the position that nothing should be done to disturb the Indian subcontinent, and that cooperation in atomic energy was a type of exchange that helped strengthen the Indian economy and, indirectly, India's security.

At the time, the principles of Indo–Canadian cooperation in atomic energy were under consideration, President Eisenhower announced the 'Atoms for Peace' concept, and Britain had launched itself into a nuclear energy programme. These developments, as well as the mutual respect that existed between Canadian and Indian leaders and officials, facilitated the development of favoured-nation treatment of India by Canada. In the context of the US, Pakistani, and British objections about India's nuclear intentions and the need to have rigid inspection procedures, in retrospect it seems that the Canadian terms for setting up India's atomic energy programme were quite favourable to India and unique in the post-1956 transfers of atomic energy technology, materials, and equipment from an industrially advanced state to a developing state. Through its atomic assistance to India, Canada practically gave Indian scientists the basic means to develop the Indian nuclear Bomb.

Two policy concerns dominated India's attitudes on atomic energy and arms control during the 1950s. The most obvious was the need to harness atomic energy for industrial requirements. In 1948, Vijaya

Lakshmi Pandit, Nehru's sister, pointed out to the United Nations General Assembly that

Atomic energy could be of enormous importance in raising living standards to some reasonable parity with those in the West . . . The underdeveloped countries cannot, therefore, forego an opportunity to develop atomic energy for industrial purposes, nor can they allow any international organisation dominated by the industrially advanced countries to control their activities in regard to the development of atomic energy'.[49]

Subsequently, Bhabha argued that India's energy needs could not be met through the use of coal and hydroelectric resources only. In 1958, he explained that the decisive factor was 'not the relative cost of power stations, but the relative total cost to the economy as a whole of providing progressively larger amounts of new power'.[50]

The other concern, less obvious but salient, reflected a desire to avoid international safeguards against India, so that India's military option could be developed if the need arose to start a weapons programme. This concern underlay Bhabha's approach to nuclear disarmament and atomic energy. It is arguable if it was central in Nehru's thinking, though it clearly was not absent from his view. Such policy views showed a loose link between the 'peace' and 'security' uses of disarmament and atomic energy. Bhabha's primary interest in the 1950s was to use atomic energy to modernize India, but his commitment to 'peaceful uses' and his enthusiasm for disarmament were not absolute. Neither Nehru nor Bhabha lost sight of the potential military uses of atomic power. From the very beginning, India's nuclear programme was more broad-based than that of China. There was no specific coupling between the peaceful and military uses of atomic energy, yet there was a built-in scope for such a linkage.[51] As Arthur Lall, a former Indian ambassador in Geneva and New York, points out, 'Nehru's willingness to keep the option open did not mean that he favoured development of the bomb by India. He was against it. But he knew the political value of keeping the option open'.[52]

Nehru's strong reaction in the Indian Parliament against President Eisenhower's December 1953 'Atoms for Peace' proposal provided a glimpse of the nature of Nehru's commitment to disarmament. It is useful to quote him at length (see below) to show that he wanted a peaceful world, but he was not interested in promoting those disarmament proposals that tied India's hands. Neither was he interested in supporting proposals that helped strengthen superpower elitism in international security affairs. Nehru sought global disarmament—which would have lessened the importance of great powers in world politics—but he also supported partial arms-control measures. This was significant. In about 1956, Moscow decided to accept partial arms control—a move that signalled Soviet interest in a détente with the West even though this hurt China's interests.[53]

Three nuances underlay India's atomic interests, and these are outlined in Nehru's statements made during the period 1954–60. First, Nehru was against international control of atomic energy. In a landmark statement to the Indian Parliament (10 May 1954), he responded negatively to Eisenhower's 'Atoms for Peace' proposal. He asked, which are the nations that are going to control atomic energy internationally? To quote him:

Either you make the body of control as big as the United Nations with all the countries represented, or it will be some relatively small body with the great powers sitting in it and lording it over... We are prepared in this, as in any other matter, even to *limit*, in common with other countries, our *independence of action* for the common good of the world. We are prepared to do that, provided we are assured that it is *for the common good* of the world and not exercised in a partial way, and not dominated over by certain countries, however good their motives.[54]

Second, Nehru focused on the essentially political nature of disarmament. In a speech to the United Nations General Assembly on 5 October 1960, he emphasized that 'Most of the people sitting here have practically nothing to disarm although we are greatly interested in the disarmament of others so that war may not break out and destroy the world.'[55] He was against the management of international relations by the big powers. He argued that it was right for these powers to discuss world affairs, but he would not agree to 'finalization' of world affairs by a select group of states. Thus, he linked the need for nuclear disarmament with the need to solve the political problem of discrimination between the militarily powerful states and the lesser states.

Third, his interest in nuclear disarmament was closely guided by his appreciation of technological changes in the atomic field. In a speech to the Indian Parliament on 22 November 1960, he emphasized,

If nothing effective is done in regard to disarmament in the course of the next three or four years [that is, about the time China exploded its first atomic device] it may perhaps become too late to deal with it. . . . Once this spreads to many countries, it will become exceedingly difficult to have any effective disarmament or any effective machinery of control.[56]

These attitudes reflected India's strenuous objections to the creation of the IAEA, but once the agency was formed, India fought from within it against the development of an extensive safeguards system. Prior to 1963, the USSR had also viewed the IAEA with suspicion, and it supported India's position.[57] In 1963, the USSR moved towards the US position, namely arguing that transfer of fissile materials to any country ought to be accompanied by IAEA inspection. The new Soviet position exempted nuclear powers from international inspection. India, however, continued to argue that inspection of the atomic 'have-nots' represented a form of atomic colonialism.

Canada supported India's atomic energy plans in this setting. Despite India's resistance to international safeguards, Canada, generally speaking, continued to have faith in India's atomic programme. But Canadian agreements with India from 1956 to 1968 also indicated that a process of tough tightening of the restrictions through tough bargaining, to ensure peaceful use of atomic energy, was under way.

Two points were significant in these agreements. First, India accepted Canadian inspection related to first-generation use of Canadian-supplied nuclear materials but rejected inspection of all nuclear equipment in a reactor and of all peaceful nuclear projects. Second, the 'peaceful uses only' clause appeared in every Indo–Canadian agreement, but the definition of the term was always ambiguous. For instance, Article III of the 1956 agreement specified only that the 'Government of India will ensure that the reactor and any products resulting from its use will be employed for peaceful purposes only'. In subsequent agreements, in response to the US, British, and Pakistani pressure, India and Canada recognized the need to reiterate their 'common interest' to use fissionable materials for peaceful uses only. This entailed mutual inspection of India's Rajasthan reactor and Canada's Douglas Point reactor. But the common usage of the term 'peaceful uses' camouflaged the difference of opinion between India and Canada. Various attempts by Canadian officials in New Delhi, from the mid-1950s onward, to tighten the scope of inspection were rejected by the Indians; India was more interested in controlling the military, rather than the peaceful, uses of atomic energy. Moreover, in the context of declarations that India proposed to use atomic energy for peaceful purposes, and in the absence of an international agreement to control the military uses of atomic energy, the question of preventing diversion from peaceful to military uses seemed to be academic from India's point of view. The policy premises on both sides were diverse, but there seemed to be no particular reason to force the issue other than to make statements for the record in private conversations and in international conferences.

The 'peaceful uses only' clause became increasingly controversial in Indo–Canadian relations following India's performance in the NPT debate after 1965. The difference of opinion was intergovernmental and intragovernmental. The Atomic Energy Commission of Canada did not 'want arrangements for assisting India with CANDU (Canada Deuterium–Uranium) type reactor interfered with because of India's resistance to IAEA inspection. There was a conflict of policy in this matter between [Canadian] External [Department of External Affairs] and Canadian [Atomic Energy] Commission'.[58]

This disagreement did not arise for the first time during the NPT negotiations but had existed earlier.[59] All along, India permitted Canadian inspection of the first-generation use of nuclear fuel provided by Canada, but, significantly, the inspection dealt only with items supplied by Canada to India and not to all Indian nuclear facilities. This point should be noted because India refused to accept IAEA inspection when the latter dealt with all types of nuclear facilities, even those where foreign assistance had not been given. In other words, Indians accepted, as a compromise, at best an extension of a proprietary right to inspect those items that were 'given' (as aid) or 'sold' (at below commercial prices). Excluded from this formula was inspection of items not supplied by a foreign donor. For example, in Indo–Canadian agreements, there was no inspection of India's plutonium-separation plant. Therefore, one needs to take a closer look at some of the important Canadian official statements and to probe their ambiguities.

On 2 November 1964, Paul Martin, then Secretary of State for External Affairs, noted the following in the House of Commons:

Prior to the Chinese explosion, and subsequently in the face of the event, the prime minister of India stated that India is maintaining its policy of not manufacturing atomic weapons. I regard this declaration as a positive contribution to world peace. In so far as the Canada–India reactor is concerned, under an agreement concluded with India in April, 1956 and tabled in this house on May 9, 1956, the government of India gave an *unconditional* undertaking to use [the reactor] for peaceful uses only.[60]

The second part of the statement was incorrect. True, India gave an undertaking that it would use the CANDU reactor for peaceful uses only. However, the undertaking was not unconditional. It related to items supplied by Canada only. Inasmuch as there could only be effective control over the first-generation use of the atomic materials (according to the agreement), the irradiated material could be reprocessed in the plutonium-separation plant set up in 1960 indigenously by India. Hypothetically speaking, the reprocessed material could be used and justified by Indians as a peaceful use. This kind of use becomes problematic because there was, at the time, no legal definition of the term 'peaceful use'.

There was another reason why the Indian agreement to the 'peaceful uses only' clause was conditional. The 1956 agreement was signed in the context of India's well-known opposition to the philosophy of discriminatory international safeguards. In 1954, Nehru had pointedly questioned the elitist basis of President Eisenhower's 'Atoms for Peace' proposal. In other words, the impression left by Martin's observations in the House of Commons failed to convey the exact sense of the setting, in which, the Indo–Canadian relationship had evolved up to that time.

A subsequent statement, by the then Secretary of State for External Affairs, Mitchell Sharp, seemed to be closer to the Indian undertaking and India's understanding of the nature of the Indo–Canadian agreement, but even this statement was not free of ambiguity. Take the following points made on 4 December 1968:

Canada is a member of the International Atomic Energy Agency and therefore subscribes to the principles of the statute of the organisation. The IAEA had not established a convention on the safeguarding of fissionable materials. However, the sale of plutonium to France has been made in accordance with the Canadian government's long standing policy of 'peaceful uses' of atomic energy which is wholly consistent with the principles underlying the IAEA.

The agreement between Canada and India providing for Canadian assistance in the construction of the Canada-Indian reactor was signed on April 28, 1956 before the establishment of the International Atomic Energy Agency.

The agreements between Canada and India dated December 16, 1963 [and] December 16, 1966 providing for Canadian assistance in the construction of the two reactors of the Rajasthan atomic power project (RAPP) stipulate that bilateral safeguards will be applied on the Rajasthan atomic power station and on the Douglas Point nuclear generating station in Canada, of which RAPP is a copy. The two governments have further agreed that the International Atomic Energy Agency shall be asked to administer the safeguards responsibilities of the agreement . . .[61]

Essentially there were two problems with Sharp's formulations. First, what is the meaning of the statement that Canada's policy on 'peaceful uses' was 'wholly consistent' with the IAEA principles when

Sharp himself admitted that the IAEA did not have a safeguards convention? In 1968, Canada had joined the NPT, and presumably its policy on peaceful uses was consistent with the NPT. Yet, a comparison between the NPT safeguards and the IAEA statute shows that there is a substantial difference between the two. In one sense, the NPT safeguards are narrower in scope than the IAEA statute. In another sense, the NPT focus is broader. Paul Szasz, an authority on the IAEA, has pointed out the differences. To quote him:

The principal prohibition of the [NPT] is generally much narrower than that expressed in the Statute, since the former relates explicitly only to 'nuclear weapons or other nuclear explosive devices' and not to the other potential military uses of atomic energy. The Agency might thus be required to observe, without being able to object, that safeguarded nuclear items are 'diverted' from peaceful pursuits to military ones not prohibited by the Treaty. . .

In at least one significant way, the prohibitions of the Treaty reach beyond those of the Statute, since they ban, for non-nuclear-weapon States, the acquisition in any way of even non-weapon nuclear explosive devices—i.e., including those designed solely for civil purposes. Thus the Agency will be obliged to use its control system to prevent an activity legitimate under its Statute, indeed one that it might otherwise further as an Agency project.[62]

This example reveals a substantial difference between the scope and philosophy of the IAEA statute and NPT safeguards. As such, the statement that Canada's policy on peaceful uses was 'wholly consistent' with the IAEA statute clouds the issue. It is unclear if Sharp's statement referred to one, or the other, or both the IAEA statute and the NPT safeguards. In at least the case of Indo–Canadian negotiations, Canada's insistence on safeguards—as it was understood in the 1960s—stems from its adherence to the NPT. In this case, the IAEA administers the NPT safeguards, but it does not administer all the principles of the IAEA statute.

(To speak of a 'wholly consistent' policy is to imply a continuity in policy; or the phrase may refer to one or more agreements that are consistent with a changing policy context. The second view more accurately describes Sharp's statement because, for example, there was more flexibility in Indo–Canadian atomic arrangements than, say in Canadian–Pakistani and Canadian–French nuclear relations. Overall, however, the hypothesis of 'continuity in policy' does not accurately describe the differences over time in Canada's behaviour towards India and/or other states seeking Canadian nuclear aid.)

The third part of Sharp's statement was correct because Indo–

Canadian agreements provided for a transfer of bilateral safeguards obligations to the IAEA. One should be careful, however, in assessing the scope and meaning of this change. Theoretically, a transfer can mean two things. First, instead of the 'weak' Indo–Canadian bilateral safeguards—as noted by Beaton and as implied in the 1956 agreement—India would accept the tougher NPT safeguards or the IAEA statute. This would imply a change in the nature and scope of the obligations. The second type of change is essentially procedural. In this case, the nature of India's obligation would remain unchanged, but, instead of the inspections being administered by Canada on a bilateral basis (that is, Canada and India had a reciprocal right to inspect each other's facilities), the inspecting agency would be the IAEA. Sharp's statement referred to the second rather than the first type of change. In other words, although the IAEA was asked to administer the 'safeguards responsibilities of the agreement', these responsibilities did not necessarily conform entirely to the IAEA statute or the requirements of the NPT. And in fact, they did not. The 1956 India–Canada agreement was made before the IAEA statute or the NPT safeguards were developed. In effect, India's commitment to accept partially the safeguards concept bypassed the stringent requirements of subsequent arrangements.

Without trying to belabour the point, it is useful to note one final example of ambiguity in Canada's stance on the 'peaceful uses only' idea. On 20 January 1971, the following question was posed to Sharp in the House of Commons:

Is he now in a position to reply to my question of last Thursday, January 14, when I asked for an assurance that India has not produced weapon-grade plutonium since the Canada-India reactor was supplied in 1960?

The response by Sharp was as follows:

Yes, Mr. Speaker. In the 1956 Canada-India agreement for the provision of a nuclear research reactor the Indian government pledged that the reactor and the products resulting from its use would be used for peaceful purposes only. We have no evidence to suggest that the Indian government is not standing firm on the assurance it has given to Canada.[63]

This response bypassed the thrust of the inquiry; it missed the point about the nature of India's undertaking and it said nothing about India's plutonium-separation plant. It did not direct attention to the ambiguity of the term 'peaceful uses'. It correctly claimed that India's programme was peaceful (that is, the programme excluded nuclear weapons), but it did not specify that India had argued publicly since 1965, and privately since 1956, that a nuclear explosion was peaceful and that India intended to explode a peaceful device. Therefore, the real issue was that if India produced weapons-grade material, it would do so by processing irradiated materials in its plutonium-separation facilities, which were outside the safeguards system.

A contrast between India's nuclear behaviour *vis-à-vis* Canada and the United States is interesting. In the latter case, India revealed a willingness to make a concession if it suited its purposes. Yet it showed how it was also willing to suffer economic–technological costs to protect its national political interests. For instance, a concession was made in the 1963 Indo–American agreement for the 'Civil Uses' of atomic energy.[64] This led to the establishment of an enriched uranium-fuelled reactor at Tarapur, near Bombay, and the access to enriched uranium technology provided valuable experience for Indian scientists. Article VI of the agreement emphasized that the common interest of the two countries was to use 'any material, equipment or device made available to the Government of India' for the Tarapur station 'solely for peaceful purposes'. In addition, Article VII stipulated that the material, equipment, or devices provided by the United States would not be 'used for atomic weapons or for research on or development of atomic weapons or for any other military purpose'. Provision was made to transfer the US safeguard arrangements to the IAEA.

In Indo–Canadian views on peaceful uses, the differences were papered over. The Indo–US agreement, through Article VI, stipulated a 'contrast' between the Indian and the US positions on safeguards. The government of India reiterated that acceptance of US safeguards was 'in consideration of the fact that . . . the Tarapur Atomic Power Station will be operated on no other special nuclear material' (that is, enriched uranium) than that the United Sates was to provide. Thus, the 'contrast' served a dual purpose: It made publicly explicit an Indo–US difference over safeguards, and it enabled India to trade its opposition to safeguards for an enriched uranium nuclear reactor.

In 1964, Dr Bhabha emphasized that 'everything in this world can be used both for good or for ill',[65] and that the question of motive applied to both the nuclear and the non-nuclear weapons states (the NWSs and the NNWSs). India's positions resulted in a toughening of the Canadian stance in the negotiations that produced the 1966 Agreement. But despite the pressure in bilateral negotiations, India continued to emphasize that the need was to regulate military–nuclear programmes, and not programmes meant for peaceful purposes.

Such Indian objections outlined Indian interventions against the institutionalization of rules that discriminated between the NWSs and the NNWSs. These rules sought inspection of 'peaceful' rather than 'military' activities. The impact of India's argumentation, however, came with the appointment of Ambassador V.C. Trivedi to the Geneva-based ENDC. Unlike many previous Indian envoys, Trivedi was an expert on nuclear energy, security, and disarmament matters. He escalated India's arguments in a manner that was logically and politically relevant. The points he developed clarified the reasoning of India's political and nuclear strategy, but at the same time, Indian nuclear attitudes during the L.B. Shastri and Indira Gandhi eras developed a volatility that revealed the impact of international and domestic politics on Indian nuclear decision-making.

ENDNOTES

1. In 1949, India rejected atomic weapons and emphasized peaceful uses of atomic energy. For early Indian attitudes, see R.N. Berkes and M.S. Bedi, *The Diplomacy of India* (Stanford, CA: Stanford University Press, 1958), pp. 62–70.

2. Cited in J.P. Morray, *From Yalta to Disarmament: Cold War Debate* (New York: Monthly Review Press, 1961), p. 67.

3. This paragraph is based mostly on ibid., p. 68.

4. G.H. Quester, *Nuclear Diplomacy: The First Twenty-Five Years* (New York: Dunellen Co., 1970), p. 86.

5. There is no attempt in this study to define strength, either with reference to Indian policy or the policies of the superpowers. Coral Bell has prepared a useful study that probes the idea and the policy (policies) in US behaviour. Bell, *Negotiation from Strength* (New York: Alfred A. Knopf, 1963).

6. Jawaharlal Nehru, *Indian Foreign Policy, Select Speeches, Sept. 1946–April 1961* (New Delhi: Government of India, 1961), p. 68.

7. Ibid., p. 29.

8. Ibid.

9. Ibid., pp. 3, 8, 22, and 32.

10. Ibid., p. 48.

11. Ibid., p. 24.

12. Ibid., p. 34.
13. Ibid., p. 79.
14. Ibid., p. 33.
15. Jawaharlal Nehru, *India and the World* (London: George Allen and Unwin, 1936), p. 220.
16. Cited in M.N. Das, *The Political Philosophy of Jawaharlal Nehru* (London: George Allen and Unwin, 1961), p. 46.
17. Ibid., pp. 192–3.
18. As noted earlier, Nehru wanted to develop nuclear energy for 'peaceful uses' and for India's 'protection'. See L.J. Kavic, *India's Quest for Security* (Berkeley and Los Angeles: University of California Press, 1967), p. 28.
19. Leonard Beaton, *The Reform of Power* (New York: Viking Press, 1972), p. 167.
20. Ibid.
21. Jawaharlal Nehru, *Foreign Policy of India: Texts of Documents, 1947–64* (New Delhi: Lok Sabha Secretariat, 1966), p. 243. The word 'destruction' is not defined. To destroy, according to a dictionary definition, means to annihilate. In the context of deterrence—namely, the utility in the nonuse of nuclear weapons—such weapons need never be used for destructive purposes.
22. Nehru, *Select Speeches*, p. 235.
23. Confidential interview, London, May 1971; confidential interviews, New Delhi, May–June 1971 and December 1971.
24. *Foreign Policy of India: Texts of Documents, 1947–64* (New Delhi: Lok Sabha Secretariat, 1966), pp. 241–3.
25. Confidential interview, New Delhi, December 1971.
26. Beaton, *The Reform of Power*, p. 50.
27. Confidential interviews, Ottawa and New Delhi, 1969–73.
28. Beaton, *The Reform of Power*, p. 50.
29. Thus, *External Affairs*, Department of External Affairs, Ottawa, March 1964, pp. 116–7, notes as follows: 'India will no longer be solely dependent on its coal and oil reserves as sources of energy. This is all the more important in view of the fact that these reserves are limited and not readily accessible'. These agreements with India 'represent a significant step towards the recognition abroad of Canadian progress in the achievement of the economic production of nuclear power. The station to be built at Rajasthan will be the first Canadian power reactor to be built outside Canada'. From these remarks, it should not be inferred that the economic motive is not important, but only that the economic motive may not be as

central as it is made out to be and that other motives may exist. One can also argue that the economic motive may have greater appeal for the donor than for the recipient.

30. Michael Brecher, *India and World Politics: Krishna Menon's View of the World* (New York: Praeger Publishers, 1968), pp. 116, 203, and 232.

31. Cited in K.P. Misra, ed., *Studies in Indian Foreign Policy* (New Delhi: Vikas Publications, 1969), p. 123.

32. Arthur Lall, 'Negotiating Disarmament', Cornell Research Papers in International Studies, 1964; and M. Samir Ahmed, 'The Neutrals and the Test Ban Negotiations', Carnegie Endowment for International Peace, Occasional Papers no. 4, February 1967, both describe this phase.

33. Scholarly work on the nuances of Indian attitudes and behaviour in the disarmament field is under-researched, although published documentation is available. For useful insights, see the following: J.G. Stoessinger, *The United Nations and the Superpowers* (New York: Random House, 1970), ch. 7; Paul C. Szasz, *The Law and Practices of the International Atomic Energy Agency*, Legal Series No. 7 (Vienna: IAEA, 1970); B.G. Bechoeffer, *Post-War Negotiations for Arms Control* (Washington, DC: Brookings Institution, 1961); M.S. Rajan, *India in World Affairs, 1954–56* (New York: Asia Publishing House, 1964), pp. 101–7.

34. Allan D. McKnight, IAEA, 'Safeguards: A Summary Account', mimeographed, prepared for the J.D. Bernal's Peace Library Conference on the Gas Centrifuge, undated, p. 1. Various aspects of the safeguards issue are discussed in an excellent volume, C.F. Barnaby, ed., *Preventing the Spread of Nuclear Weapons* (London: Souvenir Press, 1969).

35. See A. Gotlieb, *Disarmament and International Law* (Toronto: Canadian Institute of International Affairs, 1965), pp. 177, 188, and 193.

36. The full text is in *New York Times*, 6 April 1954.

37. J. Eayrs, *In Defence of Canada: Peacemaking and Deterrence* (Toronto: University of Toronto Press, 1972), p. 271.

38. Ibid., ch. 5; and Dean Acheson, *Present at the Creation: My Years at the State Department* (New York: Norton, 1969), ch. 35.

39. Bechoeffer, *Post-War Negotiations for Arms Control*, chs 3 and 4, discusses the public arms-control diplomacy of the United States during this period. Acheson's memoirs outline the kinds of attitudes that prevailed during the Truman era. David E. Lilienthal, *Change, Hope, and the Bomb* (Princeton, NJ: Princeton University Press, 1963) states that the basic assumptions about nuclear weapons since 1945 were challenged by him, but he does not seriously evaluate these assumptions. See particularly chs 2–4 of his book.

40. Eayrs, *In Defence of Canada*, pp. 277–9.

41. Ibid., p. 281.

42. For general history and overview, see M.S. Rajan, 'The Indo-Canadian Entente', *International Journal*, vol. 17, no. 4, Toronto, Autumn 1962. Entente is probably an exaggerated description of the relationship at that time.

43. Lester B. Pearson, 'The Development of Canadian Foreign Policy', *Foreign Affairs*, vol. 30, no. 1, October 1951.

44. Vincent Massey, *Canadians and the Commonwealth* (London: Oxford University Press, 1961), pp. 11–12.

45. Confidential interview, Ottawa, April 1971.

46. Some of the relevant documents are as follows: Agreement of the Canada–India Colombo Plan Atomic Reactor Project dated 28 April 1956, signed by Prime Minister Jawaharlal Nehru and Canadian High Commissioner Escott Reid; Agreement between the Government of Canada and the Government of India relating to the Rajasthan Atomic Power Station and the Douglas Point Nuclear Generating Station dated 16 December 1963, signed by H.J. Bhabha and Chester A. Ronning; Agreement between Atomic Energy of Canada Ltd and the President of India, 16 December 1963; Supplementary Agreement Amending the 16 December 1963 Agreement, dated 16 December 1966; Letter from Vikram A. Sarabhai to Canadian High Commissioner Mr Roland Michener, dated 16 December 1966; Letter from Vikram A. Sarabhai to Canadian High Commissioner Mr James George, dated 26 July 1968.

47. Confidential interview, Ottawa, April 1971.

48. The comments in this paragraph are based on confidential interviews, Ottawa, 1970–1.

49. UN General Assembly, *Official Records*, 3rd Plenary Session, 156th meeting, 4 November 1948, pp. 422–3.

50. H.J. Bhabha, 'The Need for Atomic Energy in the Underdeveloped Countries', Second United Nations International Conference on the Peaceful Uses of Atomic Energy, *Proceedings*, vol. 1 (Geneva: United Nations, 1958), p. 404.

51. Confidential interviews, London, Vienna, and New Delhi, May–June 1971.

52. Personal communication to author, 15 January 1973.

53. W.C. Clemens, *The Arms Race and Sino-Soviet Relations* (Stanford, CA: Hoover Institution Publications, Stanford University, 1968), p. 35.

54. Jawaharlal Nehru, 'Control of Nuclear Energy', *Select Speeches*, p. 193, our emphasis.

55. Ibid., p. 230.

56. Ibid., p. 235.

57. For a discussion, see Stoessinger, *The United Nations and the Super-powers*, ch. 8.

58. I am greatly indebted to Lt. General E.L.M. Burns for this comment.

59. Confidential interviews, Ottawa and New York, 1969–72. Officially, neither the Canadians nor the Indians admitted to the existence of a difference of opinion until the issue became public after 18 May 1974. Privately, of course, this was recognized as a major problem in Indo-Canadian relations. By the time India's prime minister, Indira Gandhi, visited Canada in May–June 1973, the lines between the Department of External Affairs and the atomic energy community in Ottawa, and between India and Canada had been rigidly drawn.

60. Ottawa, House of Commons, *Debates*, 2 November 1964, p. 9655, our emphasis.

61. Ottawa, House of Commons, *Debates*, 4 December 1968, p. 3477.

62. Szasz, *The Law and Practices of the International Atomic Energy Agency*, p. 549.

63. Ottawa, House of Commons, *Debates*, 20 January 1971, p. 2587.

64. This is the only Indo-US agreement on atomic energy that outlines the principles of the relationship. For its text, see *Foreign Policy of India: Texts of Documents*, 1947–64, pp. 229–40.

65. Homi Babha, 'Safeguards and the Dissemination of Military Power', *Disarmament and Arms Control*, vol. 2, Autumn 1964, p. 436.

5

The Shastri–Gandhi Years, 1964–74:
The External Dynamics

Introduction

This period saw the emergence of several major dynamics in India's nuclear *politics* and nuclear *policy*. The dynamism was revealed by the growing intensity of the nuclear debate within the Indian government, by the growing intensity and the broadening of the nuclear debate at different levels of state and society, and by the enlarged scope and changing orientation of Indian nuclear decisions. That is: (i) there was increased activity as well as increased volatility in the process of domestic debate and decision; (ii) there was a broadening, as well as a deepening, of the content of Indian policies concerning its external nuclear diplomacy and the nuclear base of its military and diplomatic strategies; and (iii) the structure of the Indian decision/debate process was established by the development of intra-Indian political elite contention in nuclear policy and by the emergence of a coalition of anti-nuclear Indian and anti-nuclear international/external forces that participated in the Indian nuclear debate in an extra-constitutional manner. This created a tension between 'nationalist' and 'global', or 'international', constituencies and their interests. The 1950s and the early 1960s saw the ascendancy of the pro-nuclear Indo–Canadian coalition that created the basis of India's Bomb programme. When the NPT became important in the US agenda in the 1960s, a parallel anti-nuclear coalition that brought together elements of Indian state and foreign government(s) and anti-Indian Bomb constituencies gained ground in India. Both the pro-nuclear and the anti-nuclear tracks coexisted during the Shastri–Gandhi years (1964–74).

Four major developments shaped this period:

(i) The PRC's nuclear development from the early 1960s (and later that of Pakistan) raised Indian policy (statist) and social (non-governmental, societal) consciousness about the importance of the nuclear question for India's diplomatic and military security and prestige. Here, an external development had a negative impact on the regional Sino–Indian and Indo–Pakistani equations.

(ii) The development of the nuclear Non-Proliferation Treaty (NPT) started in the early 1960s, and became an event by the mid-1960s when the USA and the USSR developed a common interest against horizontal nuclear proliferation. This major international development created an international legal and strategic division between the nuclear haves and the have-nots. It created a two-tiered nuclear world order that placed India at a legal, psychological, diplomatic, and a military disadvantage in relation to the five nuclear weapon states (including China) and the five permanent members of the UN Security Council (that again included China). This development marginalized Indian interests and prestige in the international nuclear sphere. It also marginalized India's plea for nuclear disarmament (that is, elimination of nuclear weapons) as the basis of international security because the NPT sanctified the existence of the five nuclear weapon states.

(iii) As a result of these international developments, a fierce debate emerged within India in the mid-1960s about the nuclear disarmament versus conventional defence versus nuclear deterrence dilemmas. Several schools of Indian nuclear thought emerged (discussed in Chapter 6). This was the first time that the secretive Indian governmental debate about the nuclear question acquired a societal (public, non-governmental) and political saliency, that is, it became a major issue of public importance. Hence all the circles in Figure 3.4 in Chapter 3 were engaged. For the first time in India's nuclear history, Indian nuclear *politics* and the Indian nuclear *policy*-making process reflected the interaction of forces within India and forces outside its borders. This debate was not settled during the Shastri–Gandhi years, but its emergence in the 1960s laid the basis of policy shifts in India's stance in the Comprehensive Test Ban Treaty (CTBT) negotiations in 1996, and in Indian nuclear testing in 1974 and 1998. This debate became a durable element in Indian politics and foreign policy, especially during the Indira Gandhi, Rajiv Gandhi, and Narasimha Rao eras.

(iv) Finally, out of this pattern came the first Pokhran test (1974), but its aftermath showed as well a pattern of Indian restraint against further nuclear testing. But there is another way to assess this 'restraint'. It was actually a sign of weakness, timidity, and vulnerability to external pressures, especially from the USA and the USSR, and it showed the influence of secretive foreign-linked Indian bureaucratic faction(s) in curbing India's nuclear development in the military sphere. This book dismisses the claim of 'restraint' as a cosmetic illusion, and argues that the Gandhis–Narasimha Rao years in particular saw the establishment of a powerful foreign-linked internal bureaucratic faction or coalition that degraded Indian nuclear nationalism and that made nonsense of India's diplomatic opposition to a discriminatory world nuclear order and Indian nuclear interests *vis-à-vis* China. The dynamics of such a foreign-linked faction or coalition is also discussed in Chapter 6.

The changes in the 1960s were significant. In the pre-crisis mode (1947–62), India was active in the development of the three-stage nuclear programme and it was active in advocating global nuclear disarmament as well. However, three events in the 1960s changed the context and the orientation of India's atomic and disarmament policies. The 1962 India–China war raised the issue of Indian defence preparedness and the need to give Indian diplomacy a military foundation. The 1964 Chinese test raised the issue of the utility of nuclear arms for Indian defence. Finally, the international and the Indian debate about the non-proliferation treaty (1961–8) raised the issue of the challenge to India's scientific and political independence under the new regime. These events impacted heavily on Indian decision processes and created bureaucratic and public debates. Philosophically, India was opposed to nuclear proliferation during the Shastri–Gandhi years, but the new circumstances and their impact on Indian policy thinking and behaviour showed that India's reaction to China and to the NPT during 1964–8 were related. They also showed that the philosophical and official policy stance against Indian nuclear proliferation was under pressure from within India and, as well, there was a process of engagement between the foreign-linked Indian bureaucratic faction (who favoured Indian nuclear disarmament and Indian non-nuclearization) and the coalition of elements of state and society in India who favoured the development and retention of the Indian nuclear weapons option and those who favoured its exercise.

The Indian concerns were revealed in the discussions between the US and the Indian governments. Having supported the goal of non-proliferation in the early 1960s, India veered away from the NPT during 1966–8, partly because the treaty was discriminatory, and partly because it did not address India's China problem. In Indian government circles, the proposition emerged that in consideration of a nuclear threat and nuclear war, when one country (China) had nuclear arms and the other (India) did not, the nuclear option could not be left in the hands of one country only. In the long run, China had tremendous influence in Asia and there was potential for trade with India as well. In the short to medium run, China possessed the initiative to cause disturbance on the extended Himalayan border short of war, whereas India lacked the strategic initiative because the Indian diplomatic and military mechanism was reactive in nature. Such an attitude was inbred in the Indian political and strategic culture.[1]

In these circumstances, the defence aspect entered India's NPT policy in the 1960s and it led to three decisions: *to develop and to retain the nuclear weapons option; to contain the demand for nuclear arms,* and *to contain the pressure to sign the NPT*. Thus, India's nuclear policy became three-sided or three dimensional in this period. The demand for nuclear arms was contained on the basis of the following premise. Given the political will, India could go nuclear but there was no realistic government assessment to prove that nuclear arms could help alleviate India's immediate defence problems. Hence, it was first necessary to ensure that India's armament policy was tied to immediate defence problems and the nuclear weapons option was tied to the long-term contingency. No doubt China was a real nuclear power on India's border, but the China threat in the 1960s was primarily conventional in the opinion of Indian defence planners, and India possessed sufficient capability to deal with that kind of threat. These considerations and approach led to the emergence of the paradigm which is outlined in Table 5.1.

In this paradigm, India veered away from its faith in the possibility of its own nuclear disarmament. *The prospect of Indian nuclear abstinence was degraded in Indian policy thinking in the late 1960s compared to the attitude of the late 1940s; and the utility of a secret nuclear weapons option in contingency planning was upgraded*. But at the same time, India continued to seek the nuclear disarmament of others, especially China, because this was in India's self-interest. It was in a weak country's interest to create a military balance or to reduce the imbalance in the distribution of power by limiting the armaments of a military power like China. Here India's interest in nuclear disarmament

TABLE 5.1
Structure of India's Nuclear Posture and Domestic Nuclear Constituencies, 1964–74

Theme	Nuclear Disarmament for World	Nuclear Abstention for India	Global Arms Control NPT/CTBT/PTBT	Development of Indian Nuclear Weapons Capability
Decision-maker (s)	• Politically leaderless; MEA	• Ministry of Finance • Section of MEA • Indira Gandhi (PM from January 1966)	• Section of MEA • MOD† • PM Indira Gandhi*	• PM (Shastri, 1964–5, Indira Gandhi, 1974)* • AEC • Space • Section of MEA
Level of debate	• Interstate	• Indian society • Indian bureaucracy	• Interstate	• Inner circles of government • Public opinion and intellectual opinion

Triggering events:
• PRC nuclear testing
• NPT

Notes:
† The explosive device in the 1974 test was fabricated in a defence laboratory but the Ministry of Defence (MOD) and the armed forces did not take an official position in the Indian nuclear debate. They seemed to be passive observers. She cancelled Shastri's decision, in January 1966, to authorize the preparation of a nuclear test.
* Mrs Gandhi was ambivalent about India's nuclear policy. She initially favoured signing the NPT but changed her mind under Cabinet and political pressure (1968–9).

was driven by a security consideration despite the appearance of a principled stand.

The pattern of India's nuclear activities in the 1964–74 period was intense. Table 5.2 is an overview of the technical activities in the nuclear and space spheres, the diplomatic activities and the decision

TABLE 5.2

Overview of Indian Nuclear Activities, Shastri–Gandhi Years, 1964–74

Technical Activity	*Diplomatic Activity*	*Decision-making About Indian Nuclear Arms*
Plutonium was separated at Trombay, 1965. Electronics Corp. was established, 1967. Uranium 233 was separated from thorium, 1970. Purnima-I, plutonium fuelled facility started up, 1972. PNE was tested, 1974.	• NPT is debated, 1961–9. • Security guarantees against PRC are examined, 1964. • India continues to push for nuclear disarmament, 1947–present.	• India seeks the legal and technical ability to develop its nuclear weapons option, 1964–74.* • India decides against the exercise of its nuclear option until its first test (May 1974) and maintained its opposition to nuclear testing after it first test.

*The process started in the mid-1950s when Canada–India nuclear supply arrangements were finalized.

making concerning India's nuclear weapons status. The technical activity reveals a commitment to the development of a nuclear weapons option and the start-up of a space programme that had dual-use, civil–military potential. So the technical activity showed an incremental and covert acquisition of the capacity of a bomb programme and a Missile programme. The diplomatic activity was consistent with the Nehru–Bhabha years. The pattern and process of decision-making, however, underwent a significant enlargement and empowerment of a number of constituencies within India: the pro-Bomb and the anti-Bomb; those who sought nuclear disarmament as a matter of policy and principle and those who sought it as a matter of tactics and Indian interests; those who primarily wanted global (including Chinese nuclear disarmament) and those who primarily sought India's nuclear disarmament; those who sought national security through enhanced conventional defence measures and those who sought it through a shift towards nuclear deterrence as a radically different basis (compared to conventional defence) of Indian security. This chapter highlights the external dynamics in the Indian and nuclear/space decision process. The next chapter deals with the internal dynamics. The story is that the enlargement of the process, the empowerment of diverse and competitive constituencies, and the emergence of a pattern of alliance and polarity in the Indian decision process occurred in the Shastri–Gandhi years; and this pattern continued thereafter. That is, a system change occurred in this period. It contrasts with the pattern of alliance and polarity of the prehistory and the Nehru–Bhabha eras, and it became the basis of a power struggle among the different constituencies which was settled by the 1998 tests. Figure 5.1 outlines the arguments and the players in the nuclear debate in this period.

Changing Indian Nuclear Dynamics in the 1960s: The International and Regional Aspects

There are two ways to analyse India's nuclear debates in the 1964–74 era. The first perspective sees the nuclear issue essentially as a power play among the various Indian elites, within and outside the government; here the internal dynamics are emphasized. The second perspective sees the nuclear issue as a power play, a strategy, by India to enter into the calculations of the major power which they opposed. Even if India's contribution to the US–USSR–PRC game was marginal, according to this perspective there was value in 'staying in the game'. In this focus, the external dynamics of strategic interactions between India and the powers are emphasized. The China problem appears in both perspectives, but it is not central in the total picture of either perspective—that is, the 'nuclear-option' strategy applies partly to China's threat, partly to India's aspiration to change the character of the international system, and partly to differing loyalties of bureaucratic actors to pro-US, pro-Soviet, and pro-China lobbies in India. This chapter emphasizes the importance of studying both the internal and external dynamics because of their interdependence since the 1960s.

Two preliminary observations should be made before one examines the contours of India's external and internal nuclear dynamics. First, India's nuclear debate did not start with China's first test in 1964. In fact, there has been an ongoing nuclear debate within India's foreign-

policy and atomic-energy establishments since the mid-1950s at least.
The debate was intra-governmental. It centred on the official relationship and the personal friendship between Indian Prime Minister Nehru
and the distinguished scientist, and subsequently first chief of the Indian
Atomic Energy Commission, Dr Homi Bhabha. Upto 1964, these two
personalities symbolized the two facets of India's disarmament and
security policies. Nehru reflected openly his mistrust of superpower-
directed international security regimes while advocating balanced and
controlled nuclear disarmament. Here, Krishna Menon seemed to influence Nehru's disarmament thinking to an extent.

Bhabha, however, extended his mistrust of the superpowers into a
mistrust also of disarmament as a strategy.[2] His pioneering work to create a modest and sophisticated atomic energy programme was based on
this premise.[3] He recognized the political value of nuclear weapons.
Even in the 1950s, India's nuclear programme was so structured that it
could be converted into a weapons programme provided the government of India was willing to take the decision and to provide the necessary resources.[4] Consequently, even during the 1950s, India was not
irrevocably committed against the future use of atomic energy for
military purposes. This premise was carried into India's post-1964
diplomacy in the Geneva disarmament committee (that is, the ENDC).

India's diplomatic strategy in the ENDC gained visibility from
Western speculation about India's nuclear intentions. The pro-bomb
lobby urged the Indian government to sanction a nuclear-weapons
programme, but India's nuclear programme gained wider public recognition as a result of the technical information about India's nuclear
programme that was known to select scientific circles and that was
publicized by Leonard Beaton and John Maddox.[5] Their assessment was
that India at that time was against the bomb, although India possessed
the means to go nuclear and the Nehru–Bhabha leadership had an incentive to retain the nuclear weapons option.

It was in the context of India's ongoing reappraisal of its China
policy that China's first atomic explosion occurred.[6] Prior to this, the
Indians had taken some military and political measures to strengthen itself to meet China's threat in the Himalayas. With the explosion, the
Indian security debate acquired a fresh issue, namely, to secure a
nuclear and a diplomatic response to China.

Dr Raj Krishna, an Indian economist with an international reputation,
was the first articulate exponent of the pro-bomb lobby.[7] He sought an Indian nuclear response against China's missile threat. He put forth several

premises and arguments, including the following: (1) India faced an expansionist Chinese regime;[8] (2) China had won international respect because of its determination to organize power in defiance of the great powers;[9] (3) India needed a viable India–China balance and an Asian balance of power:[10] this was defined as India's central aim; (4) an independent strategic nuclear deterrent was obviously beyond India's capacity;[11] (5) India needed a division of labour in deterrence, with the superpowers jointly providing strategic deterrence and India providing tactical deterrence: It was contended that there was harmony of interests in this regard between India and the superpowers;[12] (6) Indians needed to differentiate between the question of strategic abstention and tactical abstention, between short-term dependence on the West and long-term dependence;[13] (7) economic cost was not a real constraint in India's nuclear policy, and one needed to view national security as a combination of defence and development and not just either defence or development;[14] (8) disarmament and proliferation were not necessarily mutually exclusive strategies, but rather India needed to pursue the goal of disarmament as a long-term prospect, utilizing nuclear-arms acquisition as an intermediate strategy;[15] (9) it was not in India's interest to sign a Partial Test Ban Treaty (PTBT) unless China had done the same;[16] (10) having made the mistake of signing the test ban, in view of China's non-adherence, India had a case for withdrawal;[17] and, finally (11) the 'only' short-range choice for India was to secure 'some' nuclear capability and 'some' guarantees from friendly nations.[18]

Other Indian elite arguments opposed Raj Krishna's advice. The opposing arguments debated the economic cost of a weapons programme, and its foreign policy and military effects. Thus, R.K. Nehru, formerly secretary general of the Indian Ministry of External Affairs, argued as follows:

A country which when exposed to a threat refuses in the interests of the world community to develop nuclear weapons has the right to demand that some progress should be made in the direction of arms control and disarmament.[19]

Another former secretary general of the Ministry of External Affairs, M.J. Desai, argued:

India will be playing straight into the hands of China if because of fear of emotional reaction or prestige considerations, it enters into a nuclear race with China. The enormous diversion of resources . . . will retard India's economic and social development programmes indefinitely and . . . not only weaken India internally but eliminate it as a political factor in Asia and Africa.[20]

Desai then went on to state his professional opinion that

... if India cannot maintain its superiority regarding carriers and nuclear weapons vis-à-vis China, anything less will only tempt China to use nuclear weapons against India in a so-called defensive or pre-emptive strike.[21]

Finally, on one extreme side of the political spectrum was the lonely voice of former defence minister and Nehru's confidant on disarmament, Krishna Menon. He urged Indians to pursue with vigour the strategies of disarmament and peaceful coexistence. To quote him:

In the field of foreign policy, India should not remain inhibited by the shock of Chinese invasion. Her concern about nuclear peril, about disarmament and coexistence must be reactivated. It is not in our interest to permit doubts to be engendered to our declared policy and integrity in respect of the nuclear weapons.[22]

Menon's preference for nuclear disarmament had not changed in the 1960s (from the 1950s), but the thrust of his remarks was unclear. In his wide-ranging interview with Michael Brecher, he had insisted on the undesirability of 'talking' about the destructive uses of nuclear weapons in India, because no 'new factor' had arisen. He dismissed Brecher's suggestion that China's offensive nuclear capability was such a new factor. He felt that China's bomb-making plans were known to Indian authorities and that the danger of Chinese offensive capability against India was not immediate.[23] It was unclear whether Menon's admonition applied only against public talk until Chinese capabilities posed an immediate threat to India or whether his admonition was broader in scope and excluded a reappraisal of the evolving global alignments in the 1960s and the effect of such changes on Indian strategies and interests. Seemingly, it was the latter, as he consistently opposed an Indian nuclear weapons programme and favoured India's adherence to the NPT.

By 1965–6, it became clear that India's public security policy debate had developed outlines of two different perspectives on the question of nuclear weapons. The first school of thought provided a recapitulation of India's traditional world-order concern. In this view, nuclear disarmament and general and complete disarmament on a universal and comprehensive basis were required to make the world safe against a nuclear world war. In the 1950s, this had been the vehicle for India's participation in the international disarmament debate.

The second school advocated a revision of the old approach. This school sought a deterrent role for India. It sought to revise non-alignment by asking for formal security ties with the superpowers and rapid Indian effort to 'go nuclear' to establish an India–China nuclear balance, in addition to an India–China conventional military balance. This school, therefore, sought a radical reappraisal of India's foreign and security policies, and the premise was that China's threat was a central problem in Indian foreign relations.

A deeper examination of India's NPT diplomacy suggests a third approach. This synthesized a part of the traditional 'nuclear disarmament' school with a part of the radically revisionist 'Indian bomb' school. The latter focus strengthened India's opposition to international safeguards and moderated, by implication, India's commitment to nuclear disarmament. Furthermore, by emphasizing India's security problems, the new approach probed the nature and scope of the superpowers' commitments to Indian security.

This approach originated after 1962 and evolved during the period 1964–8. Essentially, it expanded the framework of India's political strategy, stressing a nuclear option but non-weapons stance. In the 1950s, India talked about nuclear disarmament, while it obviously benefited from Canada's policy of disseminating vitally needed and sophisticated CANDU technology to India. After 1964, India started to talk about horizontal and vertical non-proliferation security issues, just when the superpowers appeared to be ready jointly to secure international restrictions on dissemination and just when they appeared unable to agree on a need to contain China via India by offering India a joint superpower guarantee against China. After Indian Ambassador L.K. Jha started to explore the possibilities of joint Soviet–US security assurances, it was found that the idea of a security guarantee against China was untenable because Soviet and US policy premises were different on the issue. India found it difficult to persuade the United States to join with the USSR in providing a joint security assurance outside the Security Council framework, where China's veto would apply. Indo–Soviet discussions on this issue reached a point where drafts of an agreement were being discussed, but the Soviets were unwilling to approach the White House on India's behalf and left India free to persuade the United States to join the Soviet effort to strengthen Indian security. The Indian concern was primarily with the political uses of nuclear weapons, with the utility of its possession, and its skilled non-use (to borrow a phrase from Bernard Brodie) in the context of China's permanent seat at the Security Council. The question of the military uses of Chinese nuclear weapons was not an 'immediate' problem for India during 1965–8 because China at the time did not possess the nuclear means to threaten India, nor did it have such an incentive, given its conventional superiority.

The sources of change in India's security policy were internal and external. It was internal inasmuch as it dealt with the challenge of India's pro-bomb lobby. Externally, it reacted to the pattern of Soviet–US détente diplomacy in arms control. The Indians detected a pattern of superpower concert in international relations. A brief review of the developments during 1963–4 makes this clear.

After the Baruch plan, the first non-proliferation proposal was a part of the partial disarmament plan submitted by the United States, United Kingdom, France, and Canada in 1957 to the five-nation subcommittee of the UN Disarmament Commission. This plan included the cut-off, test ban, and bans on the acceptance and transfer of nuclear weapons by NNWSs, 'except under arrangements to assure their use for defensive purposes only'.[24] This was a non-dissemination proposal. Similarly, in 1961, the Irish resolution on non-dissemination was unanimously accepted by the UN General Assembly. This called for an agreement

under which the nuclear states would undertake to refrain from relinquishing control of nuclear weapons and from transmitting the information necessary for their manufacture to States not possessing such weapons, and provisions under which States not possessing nuclear weapons would undertake not to manufacture or otherwise acquire control of such weapons.[25]

According to a US government study, 'by 1963 [the United States and the USSR] had begun private discussions on non-proliferation as a collateral measure'.[26] Arnold Kramish, an extremely knowledgeable observer of the nuclear scene, notes the beginning of the practice of Soviet–US agreement as the basis of shaping the arms-control consensus. According to him,

The Irish Resolution adopted by the General Assembly of the United Nations on 20 December 1961 produced the first international initiative towards a treaty which would freeze the nuclear status quo. Most of the significant agreement on the working and terms of such a treaty has been reached on a secret tête-à-tête basis between the United States and the USSR—a circumstance not wholeheartedly appreciated by the other nations who would be most profoundly affected by such a treaty. Some ephemeral insights into the early nature of these contacts can be found in various documents, such as the 1963 Sino-Soviet exchanges.[27]

During 1963–4, two themes appeared in Soviet–US arms-control relations. The first theme was overt and dealt with the problem of inspection. The second theme was covert. It dealt with the superpower view that an arms-control agreement required, as a *sine qua non*, agreement between the superpowers, and this was held to be necessary and sufficient to achieve international security.

The year 1963 seems to be an important turning point in Soviet–US arms-control diplomacy. Following the Kennedy–Khrushchev exchanges during 1963,[28] there were further exchanges during 14–31 January 1963. In an address by Khrushchev at the Sixth Congress of the Socialist Unity Party of Germany on 16 January 1963, the Soviet leader declared the following:

As far as the socialist world system is concerned, we have always been and still are in favour of strengthening peaceful coexistence of peaceful economic competition between the two systems, of settling disputed issues by negotiations.[29]

On 31 January 1963, US Arms Control and Disarmament Agency (ACDA) Director William Foster noted that there had been 'private exploratory talks' between the superpowers. He noted that the 'Soviet Union has proposed that the negotiations now be returned to the Eighteen-Nation Disarmament Committee in Geneva'.[30] On 1 February 1963, Secretary of State Dean Rusk thought that there were 'other factors in the situation'—that is, other than the question of inspection or international verification of a test ban.

In a news conference on 21 February 1963, Kennedy disclosed the rationale behind the test ban negotiations. To quote him:

Well, in my judgement, the major argument for the test ban treaty is the limiting effect it might have on proliferation . . . Now, on the question of France, France has been recognised as a nuclear power by the Soviet Union. It would be up to the Soviet Union to make a judgement as to what action they would take on the treaty, if France continued to test. This is a matter which we will have to discuss with the Soviet Union. In addition, we are concerned about other countries testing . . . There is no guarantee, if we sign a nuclear test ban, that it will end proliferation. It is, however, our feeling that the Soviet Union would not accept a test ban unless they shared our view that proliferation was undesirable, and it might be a weight in the scale against proliferation, and I so regard it.[31]

The link between the test ban and nuclear proliferation was elaborated by other senior US officials. Secretary Rusk argued as follows:

Among the dangers to the United States from continued testing by both sides I would consider the danger of the further spread of nuclear weapons to other countries of perhaps primary importance. Unlimited testing by both the United States and the Soviet Union would substantially increase the likelihood that more and more nations would seek the dubious, but what some might consider prestigious, distinction of membership in the nuclear club . . .

A test ban would not of itself solve the problems of proliferation of nuclear weapons. It should be recognised that at least one present nuclear power and one power apparently bent on developing nuclear weapons might not be persuaded to subscribe to the test ban treaty from the outset. However, many potential nuclear powers might at this stage be induced to accede to the treaty.

Moreover, a nuclear test ban could lead to further steps which would deal more directly with the proliferation problem. I am referring here to the possibility of an agreement on the one hand by the nuclear powers not to transfer control of weapons or to give assistance in weapons development to countries not already possessing them and, on the other, by the non-nuclear powers not to produce or acquire nuclear weapons of their own.[32]

The bilateral and the superpower basis of the test ban, and the third-party orientation in the superpowers' effort to secure a test ban, became explicit in Kennedy's news conference on 8 May 1963. He pointed out, 'If we don't get it now, I would think perhaps the genie is out of the bottle and we'll never get it back in again'.[33] In a radio–television address on 26 July 1963, Kennedy expanded his reasoning against further proliferation. To quote him:

During the next several years, in addition to the four current nuclear powers, a small but significant number of nations will have the intellectual, physical and financial resources to produce both nuclear weapons and the means of delivering them . . .

I ask you to stop and think for a moment what it would mean to have nuclear weapons in so many hands, in the hands of countries large and small, stable and unstable, responsible and irresponsible, scattered throughout the world. There would be no rest for anyone then, no stability, no real security, and no chance of effective disarmament. There would only be the increased chance of accidental war and an increased necessity for the great powers to involve themselves in what otherwise would be local conflict.

We have a great obligation—all four nuclear powers have a great obligation—to use whatever time remains to prevent the spread of nuclear weapons.[34]

Earlier, in his wide-ranging speech on the US–Soviet relations before an American university audience in Washington, DC on 10 June 1963, President Kennedy had underlined the bilateral basis of arms control. He pointedly identified the 'common interest' of the two superpowers in questions relating to war and peace. He stated categorically that the 'two strongest powers' bore the heaviest burdens.[35] Khrushchev expressed 'satisfaction' with the 'call for better relations' between the two countries and emphasized his willingness 'to find a solution to outstanding problems, to establish good relations between our great powers'.[36]

French and Chinese views of superpower activity outlined third-party suspicions about the détente as the basis for international security. Third party sentiment against the détente emerged even before the superpowers began to support the détente publicly. President Charles de Gaulle responded on 14 June 1963 by saying that 'alliances have no absolute virtues' irrespective of the sentiments on which they were based and France intended to 'have its national defence'. On 29 July 1963, he elaborated on the international implications of the test ban. To quote him:

The empire of China, its [Soviet Russia's] neighbour for 6,000 miles, inhabited by 700 million men, an empire that is indestructible, ambitious and deprived of everything—all that can, in effect, introduce some new elements into the concerns of the Kremlin and lead it to insert a note of sincerity in the couplets that it devotes to peaceful coexistence. And, thus, the United States which, since Yalta and Potsdam, has nothing, after all, to ask from the Soviets, the United States sees tempting prospects opening up before it. Hence, for instance, all the separate negotiations between the Anglo-Saxons and the Soviets, which, starting with the limited agreement on nuclear testing, seem likely to be extended to other questions . . .[37]

The Chinese reaction was harsher than the French one. It appeared in several categories: The USSR had sold out Chinese interests.[38] The USSR was colluding with US imperialism with the aim of menacing China.[39] The USSR, like the United States, did not really believe in nuclear disarmament since 1956. And, finally, the USSR was aiding the 'Indian reactionaries' rather than China. The following quotations describe China's reasoning.

It is not only at present that the Soviet leaders have begun to collude with US imperialism and attempt to manacle China. As far back as 20 June 1959, when there was not yet the slightest sign of a treaty on stopping nuclear tests, the Soviet Government unilaterally tore up the agreement on new technology for national defence concluded between China and the Soviet Union on 15 October 1957, and refused to provide China with a sample of an atom bomb and technical data concerning its manufacture. This was done as a presentation gift at the time the Soviet leader went to the United States for talks with Eisenhower in September.[40]

From 1946 to 1956, the Soviet Government insisted on the complete prohibition of nuclear weapons. They were correct then and we firmly supported them. In their summary report to the 20th Congress of the Communist Party of the Soviet Union in 1956, the Soviet leaders divorced the cessation of nuclear tests from the question of disarmament.[41]

The year 1964 witnessed an elaboration of the trend of bilateralism in superpower arms control diplomacy. In a letter to Premier Khrushchev, the US President outlined the need to develop new proposals to prevent the spread of nuclear weapons.[42] In a message to the ENDC, on 21 January 1964, President Lyndon B. Johnson said the following:

to stop the spread of nuclear weapons to nations not now controlling them, let us agree:

(a) That nuclear weapons not be transferred into the national control of states which do not now control them, and that all transfers of nuclear materials for peaceful purposes take place under effective international safeguards.[43]

The Soviet memorandum of 28 January 1964 to the ENDC accepted the principle of preventing the spread of nuclear weapons and reasoned as follows:

A widening of the circle of States possessing nuclear weapons would increase many times over the danger of the outbreak of a thermonuclear war. At the same time, a widening of the circle of nuclear states would also make it much more difficult to solve the problem of disarmament.[44]

On 3 April 1964, in a news conference, Rusk pointedly outlined the anti-China rationale in Soviet–US non-dissemination strategy. To quote him:

Now, on our side we have a very substantial interest in the non-dissemination idea as it applies to Peiping, but there is no evidence whatever that Peiping would engage in the kind of agreement that we have been talking with other governments about, and so at least some of our sense of urgency diminishes if it is clear that Peiping will not take part.

But I would like to add this further note. The fact that it might be difficult to bring this question to a formal agreement is not the whole story. It is my impression that Moscow, Paris, London, Washington have a certain coincidence of Policy on this matter.[45]

On 2 July 1964, before the Eighteen-Nation Disarmament Committee, Arms Control and Disarmament Agency (ACDA) of the US government Director Foster clarified the thrust of the US strategy on safeguards on peaceful uses of atomic energy. To quote him:

We continue to support the idea that all transfers of fissionable materials for peaceful purposes should take place under effective international safeguards. This proposal is intended to fill a gap left by the IAEA Statute to which I referred earlier. Whenever that Agency participates in some way in assistance to nations in their peaceful nuclear programmes, the Agency system of international safeguards applies. However, this is not necessarily the case for transfers between States outside the IAEA framework. Our proposal is that international safeguards should apply to such transfers as well.[46]

Khrushchev's fall from power was accompanied by the announcement of China's first nuclear test on 16 October 1964. The statements by President Johnson and Rusk regretted China's entry into the nuclear club. Yet, the persisting usefulness of a policy of anti-proliferation was noted by Secretary Rusk:

But on the other hand, even though Peiping has exploded such a weapon or device, it still is important that these weapons not be distributed generally around the world. The capacity to make them is now in the hands of at least 15 or 20 countries. The cost of making them is continually coming down as technology advances, and, as has been pointed out many times, the problems of handling nuclear weapons will go up geometrically as more countries get them.

So there would still be some point in trying to work out arrangements for limiting the proliferation of these weapons.[47]

On October 18, in a radio–television address, Johnson noted that China's test and the fall of Khrushchev did 'not change our basic policy. They just reinforce it', and 'Nations that do not seek national nuclear weapons can be sure that, if they need our strong support against some threat of nuclear blackmail, then they will have it.[48]

This was the international setting in which India's diplomatic strategy evolved after it signed the partial test ban treaty. India reacted to three themes in US–USSR arms-control strategies. First, India rejected the US aim to institute international safeguards on peaceful atomic activities.

Secondly, the goal of nuclear disarmament continued to appeal to India because its implementation would favour the weaker countries. During 1963–4, therefore, India supported several General Assembly resolutions on this topic. For example, it supported the resolution 1908 (XVIII), 27 November 1963, which sought general and complete disarmament under effective international control. It supported resolution 1909 (XVIII) of the same date, which sought to prohibit the use of nuclear and thermonuclear weapons. On the same date, it supported resolution 1910 (XVIII), which called for an urgent need to suspend nuclear tests. It favoured resolution 1911 (XVIII) of the same date on the denuclearization of Latin America. Finally, it favoured resolution 1931 (XVIII) of 11 December 1963, which dealt with the conversion to peaceful needs of the resources released by disarmament. These themes conformed to India's traditional disarmament diplomacy. They reflected a fundamentalist position that sought to transform the world order through total disarmament. Thus, on 24 March 1964, Ambassador V.C. Trivedi noted in the ENDC as follows: 'Disarmament is not an end in itself but a means to an end', and 'The objective of a peaceful, progressive and just world is impossible of realization unless the world is first disarmed'.[49]

The third aspect of India's diplomacy underlay the controversy between India and the superpowers. The superpowers tried to utilize arms control to create and stabilize the US–USSR détente; India had no such commitment. This aspect laid the foundation for the third school of Indian nuclear thought, as noted above.

In the 1950s, India's disarmament policy was 'talk' rather than 'negotiations' involving India's central security interests. In contrast, the basic premise in the third school was that there could be no real negotiations between India and the nuclear superpowers because the fundamental policy of the superpowers was basically diverse from India's. This premise became central to India's NPT diplomacy around 1965—that is, after Indians recognized the implications of the Soviet–US conversations on arms control during 1963–4.[50]

Overall, the third approach to Indian security—as expressed in the ENDC after 1964—seemed to borrow its strategy from different sources—internal and external. One internal source was that it referred to the traditional Indian concern for nuclear disarmament. Another internal source was that it referred to the public sentiments within India to secure a nuclear response to China after the 1962 crisis. The third source was external; it reflected a borrowing of Soviet arguments against the Baruch plan. India's fight against international control over atomic energy seemed to be structured on earlier Soviet arguments. Finally, after 1963, India borrowed its arguments from another external, albeit an unlikely, source; it adopted China's arguments of 1963 against the danger of superpower détente and superpower imperialism.

During 1963–4, a contrast between the first and the third schools of thought to security and disarmament seemed to emerge in India's stance. During 1963, the UN resolutions, which India supported, expressed the approach of the first school of thought. (Ambassador

Trivedi's statement of 24 March 1964 also expressed the view of this school.) By 27 August 1964, in the ENDC, the complexities and the changes in India's disarmament diplomacy started to take shape. According to Ambassador R.K. Nehru, India had 'no intention of producing or acquiring nuclear weapons', but 'if a convention is to be effective, it will require the active support of all States, and more particularly of States which possess such weapons'.[51] In India's August 27 statement, it became clear that India wanted horizontal and vertical non-proliferation, that is, non-proliferation that was universal and comprehensive, signed by all states including China. Furthermore, in the memorandum submitted by eight nations to the ENDC on 14 September 1964, the Indian delegation stated categorically, as follows:

We also agree that the use of nuclear energy for production of weapons should be prohibited under international control and supervision. However, we cannot agree to any measures which might have the effect of restricting the peaceful utilisation of nuclear energy, or establishing some form of control which would be detrimental to the interests of the less developed countries, or would discriminate against them. The control should be restricted to plants which produce fissile material so as to prevent any country, whether developed or less developed, from making nuclear weapons in any significant manner. The present system of IAEA Safeguards should not be extended to equipment and devices serving a peaceful purpose as this would widen the gap between the developed and developing countries.

We would welcome the transfer of fissionable material stocks, in increasing quantities, to peaceful uses.[52]

Overall, in 1964, India's disarmament diplomacy was to encourage discussions of the proliferation issue in its entirety rather than only non-dissemination in international forums, to criticize the Chinese for their nuclear testing in violation of world opinion, to remind the Chinese about the principles of peaceful coexistence, to encourage the Chinese to sign the partial test ban treaty, and to score propaganda points *vis-à-vis* China.[53] Secondly, it reiterated a concern to promote the peaceful uses of atomic energy for the developing countries.

India's post-1964 nuclear responses to the challenges of the superpowers and China fall into two categories. During 1964–5, one sees a continuation of the traditional disarmament jargon about 'world peace through disarmament', although at this time, India's policy had started to shift.[54] After 1965, one sees the emergence of a low-key profile of India's security strategy. The speeches of three Indian ambassadors deserve notice since these symbolize the sense of change and transition between the 'old' and the 'new' components of India's atomic diplomacy. Ambassador Nehru voiced the old Indian concerns about the need for disarmament, while Ambassador B.N. Chakravarty reflected the transitional phase, which finally culminated in subtle and substantial modifications of India's posture by Ambassador Trivedi after 1965.

India Shapes a Strategy, 1965–7

Indian speeches in the disarmament debate during 1965 revealed a reorientation in strategy. Ambassador V.C. Trivedi, an expert in disarmament and atomic energy questions, provided a fresh spark to Indian interventions. He reiterated several familiar world concerns. But the selective focus, the timing, and the context in which his arguments were made, suggested that this was no mere repetition of an old story.

A contrast between Trivedi's strategy in the ENDC and that of Chakravarty in the UN reveals an evolution of India's strategy. Trivedi was in the headquarters of the Ministry of External Affairs when Chakravarty's statement was made. Trivedi had an important input in preparing the Indian position.

In Chakravarty's statement of 4 May 1965, the conditions of a viable non-proliferation agreement were stipulated as follows:

1. An undertaking by the nuclear powers not to transfer nuclear weapons or nuclear weapons technology to others.

2. An undertaking through the UN to safeguard the security of countries which may be threatened by powers having nuclear weapons capability or about to have such capability.

3. An undertaking not to use nuclear weapons against countries which do not possess them.

4. Tangible progress toward disarmament, including a comprehensive test ban treaty, a complete freeze on the production of nuclear weapons and means of delivery as well as a substantial reduction in the existing stocks.

5. Finally, an undertaking by non-nuclear powers not to acquire or manufacture nuclear weapons.[55]

Chakravarty emphasized that the proposal had to be integrated and

It is no use telling countries, some of which may be even more advanced in nuclear technology than China, that they should enter into a treaty which would stipulate only that they must not acquire or produce these weapons.[56]

Finally, there was a signal that superpowers' guarantees had to be credible. To quote him:

Again, it is no use telling them that their security will be safeguarded by one or another of the existing nuclear powers. Such an assurance has to be really dependable.[57]

The substance of Trivedi's strategy was to create an internationally viable political foundation for India's nuclear option and to coordinate India's nuclear policy and foreign policy, given the decision-making uncertainties in India in the late 1950s and the 1960s.[58]

His hard-hitting statement of 12 August 1965 revealed the new orientation. First, it emphasized a need to make a 'clear and unambiguous distinction between the national decisions of countries on the one hand and the obligations to be assumed by them as signatories to an international instrument on the other'.[59] Secondly, it emphasized that the crux of the proliferation problem concerned the attitudes and behaviour of the existing nuclear powers, not those of potential proliferators.[60] Thirdly, it noted that 'the question of an undertaking through the United Nations to safeguard the security of non-nuclear nations' was inadequate and 'not a correct or complete reading of our proposal'. The question of security guarantees was described as 'peripheral', not central to the issue of nuclear disarmament.[61] It was suggested that a credible plan for non-proliferation should first produce nuclear disarmament by the existing nuclear powers and, second, create obligations by the non-nuclear powers against the acquisition or manufacture of nuclear weapons.[62] Finally, the point was made that

Institution of international controls on peaceful reactors and power stations is like an attempt to maintain law and order in a society by placing all its law-abiding citizens in custody while leaving its law-breaking elements free to roam the streets.[63]

The second major Indian contribution to the non-proliferation debate came in Trivedi's statement to the First Committee of the General Assembly on 26 October 1965. This statement advertised India's modest but sophisticated atomic energy programme.[64] This statement was a frontal challenge to the Western approach to the nuclear treaty.

Three approaches to the issue were outlined: The first, called the 'non-aligned, non-nuclear approach', said Trivedi, was the approach of the non-aligned states. It called for eventual elimination of nuclear arms from world politics and for nuclear abstention by the non-nuclear states. The second approach required a moratorium on future proliferation for a short period of time during which the nuclear powers would cease further production and start a programme of reduction of existing stockpiles. The third approach was the one that the superpowers adhered to. This sought security through military alliance and sought barriers to future proliferation. Trivedi felt that an international treaty, to be effective, required the support of the entire international community,[65] that 'future proliferation is a consequence of existing proliferation and that one cannot deal effectively with the consequence without dealing with the cause'.[66]

During 1966–7, a sharper focus was given to the preceding views. The statement of 15 February 1965 made several other points: No prestige ought to accrue to states that possessed nuclear weapons.[67] India's approach to the issue of the security of non-nuclear states was clearly defined to mean that 'security is not synonymous with protection, no matter how powerful the protector or how sincere'.[68] Finally, the political context and the political effect of a nuclear non-proliferation treaty were spelled out. To quote Trivedi:

The problem of negotiating a treaty on non-proliferation has implications far beyond the realm of proliferation of nuclear weapons or even of general and complete disarmament. The attitudes that we take and the approaches we adopt on this will reflect our attitudes and approaches on international relations in general. It is therefore imperative that we take a global approach on this issue, take into account the needs and requirements of all members of the international community and follow an approach which reflects our firm adherence to the sovereign equality of all nations and to the principles of equality and mutual benefit. Otherwise, we shall be repeating the failures of the League of Nations.[69]

If this statement expressed a philosophical tone, the May 10 statement focused on specific aspects of the proposed nuclear treaty. Here some specifics in India's negotiating strategy became apparent. India argued that, to stop proliferation, one needed to erect barriers against the transfer of nuclear technology not only by a nuclear power to a non-nuclear power but also by one nuclear power to another nuclear power. This was meaningful in the context of a view of China as 'an incipient nuclear weapon Power, a Power which does not as yet have either a stockpile of nuclear weapons or a developed system of delivery'.[70] Thus, India's concern probably focused on the possibility of future transfers of nuclear or missile technology to China by states (such as the United States) interested in managing the global balance and the Sino–Soviet military balance. This position also directed attention to the extensive nuclear material and technology transfers between the North Atlantic Treaty Organization (NATO) countries.

The statement of 7 November 1966 also deserves mention. It offered several insights about India's approach to political–military problems in world politics. Trivedi argued that nuclear weapons did not provide security or 'stable security', that security was not a question of seeking protection from nuclear weapons powers, that security questions could not be discussed in large and open forums such as the Geneva Non-Nuclear Weapons Countries Conference, that national security ought to be examined in the context of international security, and, finally, that the issue of peaceful uses of nuclear energy was separate from the issue of proliferation.[71]

During 1967, Trivedi's position evolved further. His arguments, voiced as a civil servant, gained support at the political level in India. Thus, Foreign Minister M.C. Chagla's statement of 27 March 1967 summarized Trivedi's central concerns but injected an element of uncertainty. He noted India's 'special problem of security against nuclear attack and blackmail' and emphasized that this had to be 'taken into full account before our final attitude to a non-proliferation treaty is determined'.[72] This indicated that even though the overall political stance in India favoured the line that Trivedi had outlined in Geneva, this was not India's final position—that is, reliable superpower security guarantees could be traded for India's acceptance of the NPT. One can thus understand why some of Trivedi's statements were hedged to provide for the growth of policy in the direction of a weapons programme or a continuation of the policy of proliferation of peaceful nuclear technology.

Chagla's statement of 27 April 1967, in contrast with his previous statement, was more definite and comprehensive. It linked India's signature on the NPT to the availability of a security guarantee, but it noted that other aspects were involved. An emphasis emerged about the consistency between NPT provisions and the General Assembly resolution 2028 of 1965. More importantly, it stated that India's signature on the NPT was not linked to that of China's, for two reasons: China's signature was a 'utopian dream', and secondly, even if China signed, it would do so as a nuclear power in terms of the treaty.[73] The point was clear that a signature by a nuclear-weapons state was not meaningful since the NPT permitted vertical proliferation.

With a stronger political mandate, Trivedi focused on the contradictory and discriminatory features of the superpowers' non-proliferation treaty drafts. In his statement of 23 May 1967, he stressed the danger of atomic apartheid. He recognized that there were several common features between peaceful and military explosive devices but felt that this was not the central issue: Technology itself was not evil, but the concern was the use that was made of it. Then he went on to make two telling points. First,

No real or effective effort is being made to deny prestige to possession of nuclear weapons. On the contrary, reports indicate that the nuclear-weapon Powers are being given an overwhelmingly privileged position in the propositions which are being elaborated these days. As time goes on, the nuclear-weapon Powers are apparently contemplating ever increasing provisions of discrimination . . . The nuclear weapon Powers want comprehensive controls over the peaceful activities of civil nuclear Powers. They even want to prohibit the civil nuclear Powers from undertaking peaceful explosions purely for their economic development even if such peaceful pursuits take place under international supervision.

All these projects will, however, have just the opposite effect. A discriminatory treaty which gives a privileged licence to the existing nuclear-weapons Powers to proliferate at will and which heaps ever-increasing prohibitions on non-nuclear Powers will in itself be the strongest incentive to a new country to embark on a nuclear weapons programme.

Second, the contradiction in the superpowers' case about increasing security through non-proliferation was noted:

These powerful nuclear-weapon nations say that the non-nuclear nations would safeguard their security by forswearing nuclear weapons forever in the midst of mushrooming proliferation by the nuclear weapon Powers themselves.

This is, however, not the precept which they have themselves followed, and in fact they rejected it for themselves when it was time for them to decide.[74]

Finally, in his statement of 28 September 1967, Trivedi linked India's position to the history of the disarmament negotiations. He reminded the superpowers that the Baruch plan had failed because it sought to restrict research and development in national atomic energy programmes, and, in addition, he noted that the 1961 Joint Principles enunciated by the two superpowers had emphasized the importance of the principles of balance and security for all.

Such a perspective had been utilized by the Soviet Union *vis-à-vis* the United States in the Baruch plan debates. Trivedi's detailed knowledge of the history and nuances of the disarmament negotiations embarrassed the superpowers. Furthermore, his proposed amendments were simple but startling because these would have undermined the basis of the superpowers' anti-proliferation strategy. In his detailed critique of the proposed treaty, he urged the superpowers to separate the dissemination and the anti-proliferation objectives and to control both kinds of activities by all states. The idea of controlling peaceful explosive activities was rejected. The Indian delegation proposed deletion of all references to the terms 'or nuclear devices' in Article I of the draft treaty. Finally, it was urged that Article III be amended to exclude the term 'non-nuclear weapon States' so that the treaty could be non-discriminatory and universal in its scope.[75]

Following Trivedi's departure from Geneva in late 1967, India's disarmament and atomic energy diplomacy slipped into a low gear.[76] Yet he had permanently altered India's disarmament stance of the 1950s. Two points emerged clearly in his articulation of India's political and security position. First, the question of security guarantee from the superpowers to India was quite apart from the question of NPT. The credibility of the security assurances depended on the specific international context in which a security guarantee was applied to a military crisis. In view of the poor historical record of security guarantees, little credence could be given to a formal resolution in the United Nations, particularly when the veto was available to the major powers, including those against which India needed security assurances.

Second, superpower efforts to control the peaceful atom appeared to be a part of a philosophy to neglect third-party interests. Thus, India's NPT behaviour implied that the peaceful atom helped its modernization needs, and it challenged the political implications of superpower détente in arms control.

This challenge was explicit in Trivedi's proposed amendments to the nuclear treaty, as noted above. The amendments sought to remove international control on 'peaceful' nuclear explosive devices of the NNWSs. These proposed amendments, given superpower policies to the contrary, suggested that India's preference for proliferation of peaceful nuclear technology created a grey zone of horizontal proliferation in terms of superpower values—that is, in terms of Article II of the NPT, even if the potential horizontal proliferator (India) did not claim a desire to manufacture or test nuclear weapons. It meant that the letter and spirit of the NPT would be violated not only if India actually manufactured nuclear weapons but even if it exploded a peaceful underground nuclear device.

This innovation, however, could not hide a paradox, or a contradiction, in India's nuclear positions. (An Indian official could always argue that the 'contradiction' was necessary to the growth of India's nuclear policy and foreign policies.) The contradiction centred on two fundamental propositions. On the one hand, India believed in national, peaceful atomic technology proliferation, including that of nuclear devices for peaceful purposes. But, on the other hand, India took the categorical view that it continued to decide against nuclear weapons. Admittedly, the admonition against nuclear weapons could change since the constraints were political and moral, not legal. These positions had the effect of bringing India to the threshold of a weapons programme, leaving India pitched delicately on the brink—diplomatically and in terms of weapons technology.

This discussion revealed a substantial development of India's stance on the US–USSR effort to develop a non-proliferation regime. The discussion shows that many subtle and fundamental nuances had appeared in India's attitude and policy on non-proliferation by the time the Nehru era was ending and the Shastri–Gandhi era started. However, the Shastri–Gandhi years were important because, despite the background diplomatic work done by Indian diplomats on the NPT, the decision to accept or reject the NPT and the decision to undertake Pokhran I (May 1974) occurred during the Shastri–Gandhi years. This period is noteworthy for considerable oscillation in both areas: the question of the NPT and the question of Indian nuclear testing. The following chapter discusses the pattern of the Indian leadership behaviour on the two issues and then assesses the structure and pattern of internal dynamics during 1964–74.

ENDNOTES

1. George Tanham, 'Indian Strategic Culture', *The Washington Quarterly,* vol. 15, no. 1, Winter 1992.
2. Confidential interviews, London, May 1971.
3. Ibid.
4. Ibid.
5. Leonard Beaton and John Maddox, *The Spread of Nuclear Weapons* (New York: Frederick A. Praeger, 1962).
6. Sisir Gupta, 'The Indian Dilemma', in Alastair Buchan, ed., *A World of Nuclear Powers?* (New York: American Assembly, 1966), p. 56.
7. Raj Krishna, 'India and the Bomb', *India Quarterly,* Indian Council of World Affairs, New Delhi, April–June 1965.

8. Ibid., p. 119.
9. Ibid.
10. Ibid., p. 120.
11. Ibid., p. 127.
12. Ibid., p. 128.
13. Ibid.
14. Ibid., p . 131.
15. Ibid., p. 134.
16. Ibid., p. 135.
17. Ibid., p. 136.
18. Ibid.
19. R.K. Nehru, 'The Challenge of the Chinese Bomb', *India Quarterly*, January–March 1965.
20. M.J. Desai, 'India and Nuclear Weapons', *Disarmament and Arms Control*, Autumn 1965.
21. Ibid.
22. In *Seminar*, New Delhi, November 1965.
23. In Michael Brecher, *India and World Politics: Krishna Menon's View of the World* (New York: Praeger Publishers, 1968).
24. *International Negotiations on the Treaty on the Nonproliferation of Nuclear Weapons*, US Arms Control and Disarmament Agency, Washington, DC, January 1969, p. ix. (Hereafter cited as *International Negotiations*.)
25. *The United Nations and Disarmament, 1945–70* (New York: United Nations, 1970), p. 263.
26. *International Negotiations*, p. ix.
27. Arnold Kramish, 'The Watched and the Unwatched: Inspection in the Non-Proliferation Treaty', *Adelphi Papers*, no. 36 (London: International Institute for Strategic Studies [IISS], June 1967), p. 2.
28. US Arms Control and Disarmament Agency, *Documents on Disarmament, 1962* (Washington, DC: Government Printing Office Series; hereafter cited as *Documents*), vol. 2, pp. 1239–42, 1277–9.
29. Ibid., p. 11.
30. Ibid., p. 28.
31. Ibid., pp. 59–60.
32. Ibid., p. 109.
33. Ibid., p. 183.
34. Ibid., pp. 254–6.
35. Ibid., pp. 217–8.
36. Ibid., p. 228.

37. Ibid., p. 264.
38. Ibid., p. 270.
39. Ibid., p. 358.
40. Ibid., pp. 363–4.
41. Ibid., p. 365.
42. *Documents*, 1964, p. 5.
43. Ibid., p. 8.
44. Ibid., p. 15.
45. Ibid., pp. 140–1.
46. Ibid., p. 253.
47. Ibid., p. 461.
48. Ibid., p. 468.
49. Ibid., p. 107.
50. Confidential interviews, New Delhi, July–August 1973.
51. *Documents*, 1964, pp. 376–7.
52. Ibid., p. 410.
53. See letter from Prime Minister Lal Bahadur Shastri to Premier Chou En-lai, 27 November 1964 and General Assembly address of India's Foreign Minister, 14 December 1964, in ibid., pp. 487–91 and 527–30, respectively.
54. Confidential interviews, New Delhi, July–August 1973.
55. *Documents*, 1965, p. 148.
56. Ibid.
57. Ibid.
58. Confidential interviews, New Delhi, July–August 1973.
59. *Documents*, 1965, p. 334.
60. Ibid., p. 335.
61. Ibid., p. 336.
62. Ibid., p. 338.
63. Ibid., p. 339.
64. Ibid., p. 492.
65. Ibid., p. 498.
66. Ibid., p. 493.
67. *Documents*, 1966, p. 17.
68. Ibid.
69. Ibid., p. 22.
70. Ibid., p. 283.
71. Ibid., pp. 702–3.
72. *Documents*, 1967, pp. 177–8.
73. Ibid., pp. 204–6.

74. Both quotes are in ibid., pp. 236–7.
75. Ibid., pp. 433–9.
76. For the relevant statements, see Ambassador M.A. Hussain's statement to the ENDC on 27 February 1968 and his statement to the First Committee at the UN General Assembly on 14 May 1968; Ambassador G. Parthasarathi's statement to the Security Council on 19 June 1968 discussed some of the general issues concerning the balance of power and the arms race; the concerns about the balance of power and 'spheres of influence' aspects of international politics were outlined in Foreign Minister Dinesh Singh's statement at the General Assembly on 2 October 1969 and in his statement to the Indian Parliament on 8 April 1970.

6

The Shastri–Gandhi Years, 1964–74: The Internal Dynamics

Introduction

The internal dynamics in the period 1964–74 were highly significant because of the heightened interplay and tension between external and internal compulsions in Indian nuclear decision-making. In this period, the technical activity in the nuclear sphere continued to show incremental growth and qualitative development (Figure 5.1). The diplomatic posture also showed a development of nuance and firmness; in fact, the diplomatic posture of the Nehru–Bhabha years was built up during this period. But in the area of nuclear decision-making, this period was significant in three ways.

(i) Five major nuclear decisions were made in this period.

(a) the Shastri decision in late 1965 to authorize the Indian Atomic Energy Commission (AEC) to prepare for a nuclear test was cancelled by Indira Gandhi in early 1966.

(b) After an internal debate, the Gandhi government decided against signing the nuclear non-proliferation treaty (NPT).

(c) India's first nuclear test (Pokhran I) was conducted in May 1974.

(d) Following this test, the Indian government declared that it would not conduct more tests, that it did not seek nuclear weapon status, but that it would retain its nuclear option.

(e) Following China's first nuclear test in October 1964 and in the context of its deliberation of the NPT, India sought Great Powers' security guarantees but concluded that they lacked credibility.

(ii) The zigzag pattern of Indian nuclear decision-making revealed a heightened power struggle within India. This involved a number of players: Indira Gandhi; key Cabinet members; key members of the Indian bureaucracy; Indian nationalistic forces which were represented in the Indian bureaucracy and had a voice in the Indian media, academia, and parliamentary circles. The power struggle involved three powerful tendencies in the Indian body politic: pro-Western, which sought Indian *non*-nuclearization, that is, 'don't go nuclear' (as distinct from *de*nuclearization which requires a rollback of the existing process); pro-Soviet, which sought continued Indian commitment to global nuclear disarmament and as well required Indian non-nuclearization because the Soviet Union became a co-partner of the USA in the NPT; and finally, Indian nationalistic forces at the levels of state and society which sought to retain the nuclear option as a minimum, and to exercise it and develop a nuclear weapons stance. The Indian players fell into the three categories.

(iii) During this period, we see the reinforcement of the pro-Western tendency in Indian nuclear decision-making as a result of the emergence of foreign-linked Indian factional politics at the state (Indira Gandhi and bureaucracy) and societal levels (Indian media and academic). Foreign-linked factionalism in Indian nuclear decision-making intensified and polarized the decision process; it produced a zigzag pattern of decision-making with signs of oscillation (ambivalence), ambiguity, and secrecy, or lack of transparency in the Indian nuclear sphere. But surprisingly, given the powerful patronage of the US and the Western powers of Indian foreign-linked factions, the nationalistic forces did not lose the game.

How did the three domestic (and international) tendencies shape Indian nuclear decision-making in the Shastri–Gandhi years? How did Indira Gandhi/Shastri shape the tendencies—did leadership make a difference to the nuclear decision process? What was the relationship between the foreign-linked Indian bureaucratic and leadership *politics* and nuclear policy making *process* in this period? To a discussion of these questions we now turn.

The Constants and the Variables in Shastri–Indira Gandhi's Nuclear Decision-Making

There were three main constants in Indian diplomatic and military affairs that affected decision-making in this period. First, a power struggle and balance of power—a form of competitive coexistence—existed among the three tendencies in Indian statist and social behaviour and thought, which were noted earlier. Secondly, external military and diplomatic pressures were exerted on India by China, Pakistan, the USA, and the USSR with a view to contain Indian military and nuclear activities which challenged their interests and policies, for example in the 1965 and 1971 wars, and with respect to the NPT regime. Thirdly, India's scientific establishment continuously developed Indian nuclear weapons capability, and India's diplomatic establishment developed a diplomatic position that challenged Western and Soviet norms concerning international nuclear controls and non-proliferation.

These constants were in play during the Nehru years but they gained in importance in the Shastri–Gandhi years because of new international developments (South Asian wars, NPT, Chinese nuclear testing) in the 1960s and because of differences in the leadership styles and motives of Nehru's successors. The latter became the variable in Indian military and nuclear behaviour in the Shastri–Gandhi years. The third constant has been discussed in previous chapters. This chapter will therefore, highlight the first constant and the single new variable. The second constant is well understood by students of Indian diplomatic and military affairs and as such will not be discussed here.

The first constant refers to the existence of a fierce power struggle between three tendencies which dominated the Shastri–Gandhi years. The first one was, and still is, represented by the pro-Western group which sought to align India to the Western camp, politically and economically. The sign of this tendency was the encouragement which Western thinkers and practitioners have continually offered in favour of the development of a brand of Indian Utopianism, that is, a belief in non-violence, peace talk, East–West bridge-building, disarmament, diplomacy, peaceful economic development, and avoidance of an Indian military build-up and nuclear, naval, and space development. Nehru, the overt critic of the United States, was also the symbol and representative of this tendency. Even after the Nehru line was discredited in 1962, this kind of thinking, which had deep roots among officials who had been recruited into the diplomatic service in the 1940s, 1950s, and the early 1960s, continued to work its way through the policy process, but with one major difference. In the 1940s and the early 1950s, this approach was the dominant tendency in Indian statecraft. In the 1950s—Indian diplomatic practitioners—Nehru and his circle of advisers—started to tilt towards Moscow regarding Kashmir, disarmament, and Korean affairs, and Moscow tilted towards Delhi and the Nehrus; this was in the mutual interest of both the countries and their policy elites. After the 1960s, the pro-West tendency had become a subordinate tendency in Indian security thinking but it nevertheless retained pockets of great influence in key decision-making circles on selected issues.

The second tendency was represented by the pro-Soviet group. Nehru, the Fabian socialist, assisted by Krishna Menon, legitimized this tendency by his approach to the USSR in the 1950s. However, its character changed with the ascendancy of Indira Gandhi in the late 1960s and with the increased significance of Indo–Soviet relations in India's foreign and defence mechanisms as well as in Indian politics. The benchmarks of this tendency lay in continued disarmament advocacy by India and the Soviet Union, the USSR's support to India on Kashmir, India's utility as a pro-Soviet force in the Third World and the UN, and India's military and industrial build-up under Soviet auspices. The latter suggested a Soviet motivation to help India, to shape the superpowers' competition in the subcontinent, but also to induce Indian dependence on the USSR. In the framework of Indian politics, there was an apparent polarization between the Rightists and the Leftists, and in the framework of Indian foreign and military relations the two tendencies appeared to be different, if not opposite, ideological and policy poles. However, in the 1960s, US–USSR relations began to converge; at the global level, the US and the USSR sought détente and arms control; in the Indian subcontinent, both sought to protect Pakistan in different ways, and both sought to prevent total Indian military victory over Pakistan. With the emergence of a cooperative coexistence between the two, the domestic Rightist versus Leftist polarization within India lost its meaning. While the ascendancy of the pro-Soviet group in Indian foreign affairs during the 1970s and the early 1980s was apparent, the practical effect of the 'Rightist' and the 'Leftist' international camps was to seek the integration of Indian politics and Indian security policy with the interests of the two camp leaders. This was the setting in which the third tendency exerted itself.

The third tendency reveals the growing influence of Indian nationalistic elites and public opinion since the 1940s. We should understand this tendency because it is a strong and a permanent undercurrent which has exerted itself at crucial times, even when the second, pro-Soviet tendency, appeared to be dominant. The third tendency had begun even to alter Indira Gandhi's thinking after 1979 (even though her leadership style remained unchanged). In Indian foreign and military affairs, this tendency had increased influence in the policy process, but it is still not in command. Shastri was a true exponent of this tendency. He authorized the Indian Army to take Lahore and Sialkot if it could in the 1965 military campaign. He ordered the Army to cross the international Indo–Pakistan border to relieve the Pakistani military pressure in Kashmir; and he authorized H.J. Bhabha to prepare the groundwork for an Indian nuclear test. Shastri was challenging the Nehru legacy which was a policy of no war with Pakistan, an unstable ceasefire in Kashmir, and a dependence on a diplomatic solution with Pakistan. Shastri also challenged the US–USSR preference for a no-war Indo–Pakistan environment because regional warlike initiatives would force the superpowers to take sides, to take risks and to risk their self-appointment as guardians of world and regional order(s). Shastri's behaviour was a sign of the presence and assertiveness of the third tendency even when the first and second ones appeared to predominate in Western and Soviet scholarship. Indian nuclear diplomacy as well as in the technical activity and organization of Indian nuclear science was another sign of the assertiveness of the nationalistic tendency, as was India's war behaviour in the 1971 Bangladesh campaign.

The variable concerned Indira Gandhi's mental make-up and its impact on the pattern and process of Indian strategic decision-making. Our perspective is that there was an evolution, that is, betterment in the form of the modernization of the Indian defence mechanism after the 1962 crisis, but this process was autonomous; routine defence modernization occurred independently of the Prime Minister's motivations, interests, and imperatives. That is, routine, inertial, adjustments in Indian defence planning occurred after 1962; here the key actors were the Ministry of Defence and the armed services. And here professional assessments of short-term and long-term external threats and Indian requirements shaped the process to develop, coordinate, and concentrate the strength of the Indian military machine. But this machine has never (and rightly so) become a state within a state. It has remained responsive to supervision by the elected political leadership and the non-elected but legitimate civil bureaucracy.

In both her internal policies and her external postures, Indira Gandhi sought spectacular drama. Here we need to see Indira Gandhi, indeed the Nehru family, as actors, and Indian politics, as well as the Indian foreign policy mechanism, as a theatre where the aim is to create an illusion of reality and to achieve a rapport with the audience to achieve an effect of the moment. Here the psychological compulsion is to create a string of favourable effects, a string of temporary successes where the inner realities are carefully obscured from public and critical scrutiny; and the posture and the temporary success is not the tip of the iceberg which would reveal the existence of a policy. Thus, after *Garibi Hatao* ('Remove Poverty') helped win the elections, Indira Gandhi did not come up with any policies to produce radical or evolutionary economic and social change for the Indian poor. Her January 1966 decision to cancel the nuclear test project may be attributed to inexperience, to the pressure of other priorities (that is, staying in power) and to the nature of bureaucratic advice. Her decision in February 1968 not to sign the NPT reflected fear of Cabinet disapproval, the nature of bureaucratic advice, and the recognition that the Treaty was not popular in India. The internal setting was such that Indira Gandhi was in the process of gaining her ascendancy in Indian politics in the late 1960s and she neither understood nor cared for nuclear affairs. Yet here she was making the case against the NPT on grounds of principle and national interest. 'Principles' were a vital part of her and India's nuclear *posture* on the Treaty but they had nothing to do with the *motivation* behind this decision. *The 1974 Pokhran test was the product of scientific advice, a diplomatic demonstration to the major powers in India's environment, a popular gesture and a method to disarm India's bomb lobby but, here again, because of bureaucratic advice, external pressures and her unfamiliarity with the subject, Indira Gandhi failed to pursue the test to its logical conclusion. Her defiant nuclear posture did not become a long-term policy.* In all these instances, Indira Gandhi's mental compulsion was not to formulate policies but to engage in *ad hoc* policy action where her primary motivation was to promote her ascendancy in Indian politics and to take advantage of the immediate situation. In other words, because of her psychological compulsions, she made decisions about security matters, she participated in events but she did not make policies which settled problems or showed a strategic plan or a pathway. The result of her mental make-up was that the power struggle among the three competitive tendencies continued during the Gandhi years and India remained vulnerable to diverse external and internal influences.

This is why, with one exception, nothing positive happened in the field of foreign affairs and national security during the 1966–9 period in India. Indira Gandhi did little or nothing about defence promotion and foreign policy projection during this period. Defence modernization reflected the evolution (improvement) of defence consciousness and preparation on the part of the Indian bureaucracies in the aftermath of the wars in 1962 and 1965. She made two major national security decisions in this period. The first, made in early 1966 shortly after Shastri died, was to cancel Shastri's decision in late 1965 (after the Indo–Pakistan war) to authorize India's atomic energy establishment under Homi Bhabha to actively pursue the development of an Indian nuclear weapon option. Shastri and Bhabha died in January 1966 and Indira Gandhi cancelled the project and reversed the scientific and political momentum of test-planning. The decision was momentous because had India tested in 1966 even a crude device, it could have escaped the pressure of the NPT regime. It could have become a nuclear weapon state in terms of the treaty's language. It could have saved India from much subsequent diplomatic pressure by both the West and the Soviet Union to join the Treaty and to reject the Indian nuclear option. (This was another major issue where Soviet and American interests converged against India beginning in the second half of the 1960s.)

Her other decision, made in February 1968, was not to sign the nuclear non-proliferation treaty. She gained the political credit in India for upholding India's independence and for taking a principled stand against a discriminatory treaty. In fact, Indira Gandhi would have signed the treaty but for a high-powered bureaucratic coalition led by a fellow Kashmiri (her foreign secretary T.N. Kaul) who read the mood in the Indian cabinet and the public correctly. Considerations of her own, and her party's prestige, and the pressure of bureaucratic politics from below, and not a carefully considered assessment of the national interest governed Indira Gandhi's decision against the nuclear treaty. The NPT decision revealed Indira Gandhi's vulnerability to 'good' bureaucratic advice and pressure, just as her decision in the early days of her prime ministership to cancel the nuclear testing project revealed her vulnerability to 'bad' advice by her scientist–politicians and civil servants. The hypothesis is that during 1966–9, Indira Gandhi's priority was to establish her ascendancy in Indian politics; that is, the domestic imperative was paramount. Consequently, her decision-making about diplomatic–strategic (in this case nuclear) questions reflected the primacy of domestic-political and bureaucratic inputs, advice, and pressure. Foreign policy theory asserts that a country's external policies are formed in response to external threats, that is, foreign and military affairs are pursued in relation to external considerations. This was not true in the case of Indira Gandhi's attitudes and decisions in the two instances during 1966–9. Although her domestic political compulsions and her inexperience in nuclear and diplomatic affairs may explain this style and pattern of national decision-making, the impact of her (or any leader's) mental make-up is significant when leadership personality, not high-quality institutional or staff work is the basis of national or public policy making. A test of the soundness of our assertion is that Indira Gandhi's mental make-up still shaped the style and substance of strategic decision-making even after she had consolidated her domestic power base. She (and later her son) remained vulnerable to foreign-linked bureaucratic and political activity in the national security sphere as a result of her mental make-up and leadership style.

The hypothesis about the leadership variable is that a mental outlook that reflects personal insecurity of the leader will result in a closed, elitist, and secretive decision-making process which is vulnerable to 'good/bad' inputs by those who can gain access to this process.[1] When decision making is lifted to this level, it becomes highly personalized; and the discipline of an institutionalized process and organized bureaucratic and parliamentary and public debate is lost or weakened. Furthermore, leadership action acquires the character of theatre rather than policy development. The latter requires settlement of debate(s) among conflicting tendencies or approaches; it requires decision or ir-revocable choice(s) which resolve dilemmas. A hallmark of the Indira Gandhi years was that she did not settle a single nuclear issue. Instead, by refusing to sign the NPT and by refusing to go nuclear, she boxed India into a situation of continuous pressure by forces within and out-side India who wanted a non-nuclear India. She did not enhance India's national security or prestige by her nuclear actions and she left a dif-ficult legacy for her successors. She did not take the difficult decision to go nuclear (nor did her father) when the opportunity existed and when the opportunity-costs were manageable. But this hypothesis has a corollary. The leadership variable (involving the nuclear behaviour of Indira Gandhi, Rajiv Gandhi, and Narasimha Rao) boxed India into a no-NPT, no-nuclear weapons stance, but at the same time, Indian bureaucratic politics and the nationalistic societal tendency also boxed in these leaders from signing the NPT and from abandoning India's nuclear weapons option. That is, the first (power struggle between the three tendencies) and the third constants (option-building by Indian scientific and diplomatic mechanisms) checked the second constant (ex-ternal pressures) and the leadership variable.

The Role of Bureaucratic Politics

The post-Nehru years, nonetheless, were significant in opening up channels of discourse within the Indian government and in Indian polity and society. During the 1964–8 period, the Indian government faced three issues: whether India should sign the NPT; whether India should accept the weak US–Soviet security assurances through the UN Security Council; and, finally, whether India should establish a crash plutonium bomb programme and/or to have a peaceful nuclear explosion. The first aspect surfaced during November 1967 to February 1968, after agreement on Article III was reached between the superpowers.[2] The issue of security guarantees was present up to 1968; it appeared in Indian arguments in Geneva as well as outside the ENDC format. The third issue was present in the Indian nuclear debate since 1965.

Ambassador Trivedi had noted in the Eighteen-Nations Disarmament Conference (ENDC) that there were three approaches to international security. The first one sought security through a non-alignment and non-weapon stance. The second sought security through a moratorium on the further spread of nuclear weapons. The third sought security through military alliances.[3]

To assess the significance of Trivedi's description of these three approaches, one should note the difference between India's NPT stance and the three approaches. Two points merit attention. First, the process of a high-level international debate on international nuclear policy revealed an Indian nuclear option which publicly, prior to 1965, did not even exist. To make such an option visible was Trivedi's main aim.[4]

Secondly, Trivedi's speeches conveyed the impression that post-1964 India did not really seem to fit completely into either of the three approaches. With a potential capacity for military application, and in the absence of a legal renunciation of nuclear weapons, India's nuclear option meant that India no longer fitted into the 'pure' non-nuclear approach. In fact, Indian statements at the highest level shifted. In 1961, Nehru had publicly stated categorically that India would not produce nuclear weapons, 'whatever may happen'. But Prime Minister Indira Gandhi told the Indian Parliament in 1968, 'India is making every effort to develop nuclear know-how and capacity. The belief that China can attack any country with nuclear bombs is misconceived.' Similarly, she told the Parliament that there was no substitute for military preparedness, but at that time, she rejected the suggestion for a change in India's peaceful nuclear policy.

Neither did Trivedi's speeches suggest that India's behaviour during 1964–8 and after 1968 fit the second approach. This approach sought international security by preventing the further spread of nuclear weapons. It assumed that horizontal nuclear proliferation was imminent and that there would be nuclear dominoes. Both premises were questionable. Knowledgeable Indians argued that the danger was exaggerated by the superpowers, and, in any case, if it was true, there was little the nuclear superpowers could do about it. Instances of French and Chinese deviance from the superpowers' non-proliferation policies revealed the impotence of the superpowers in this regard. Moreover, India had managed to escape international inspection of all its peaceful nuclear activities as a result of its policies of the 1950s. As such, in India's case, the superpower anti-proliferation strategy was really like closing the door after the horse had bolted.

The third approach sought security through alliance politics and through the stability of the superpower deterrents. It required vertical proliferation, given the superpower premise that they needed strategic power to negotiate with each other and to protect their allies and clients. By contrast, the Indian foreign policy premise from the 1950s on was that absolute levels of strategic power did not matter and that alliances did not necessarily promote the security of their weaker members. Accordingly, this superpower approach was also rejected in India's NPT strategy.

The novelty of the Indian bureaucratic behaviour on the NPT during 1965–8 lay in the context of an ongoing reappraisal of the military factor in Indian foreign policy. It rested on the nature of the strategic threats in the Indian security environment and on the sufficiency of the Indian diplomatic and military means to fight or deflect the threats. In this sense, to make the Indian nuclear weapons option visible was not necessarily to take a step toward an Indian weapons programme. It was an insurance—by keeping abreast of modern nuclear technology—in that direction should China become a nuclear threat to India. But clearly, the option meant that the non-nuclear approach of the 1950s was irrevocably modified. This message was grasped by audiences within and outside India. In other words, the nuclear-option approach to Indian security complemented India's strategy to seek security through a modern military machine, to defend and deter conventional military threats from Pakistan and China.

Seeking security guarantees from foreign powers or developing an Indian bomb on a crash basis were the two most controversial issues in India's nuclear debate. Both questions dealt with the China problem. Ideally, given the implication of a nuclear China, the Indian military should have been involved intensively with these questions. But, unlike US and Soviet military elites, the role of the Indian defence services was different at the time. As George Quester pointed out: 'Happily for the tradition of democratic civilian rule in India, these opinions [military ones] are far from decisive, and are not very openly expressed.' He notes, however, that:

Yet, there is little evidence of any enthusiasm for nuclear weapons in the Indian Army, or even in the Indian Air Force, on the simple fear that a nuclear weapons program would mushroom into something very costly, drawing funds from conventional weapons which for the moment seem more urgent.[5]

This observation directs attention to the priority that the Indian defence people assigned during 1964–8 to conventional defence means against China. It also points to a deliberateness in Indian assessments of the threat potential. Otherwise, considering that the Indian army would clearly benefit from a decision to adopt tactical weapons and the Indian air force would clearly benefit from a strategic weapons programme, the lack of enthusiasm for nuclear weapons by the Indian army and air force is hard to explain.[6]

Actors and Influences in the Nuclear Debate, 1964–8

On the foregoing questions, there were three types of actors. (1) Ambassador Trivedi and the Indian delegation to the ENDC constituted the first type. (2) Those in the Ministry of External Affairs and in charge of foreign aid relations who wanted India to sign the NPT and accept the security assurances offered by President Johnson (October 1964) and Premier Aleksei Kosygin (February 1966) and eventually by the two in the United Nations represented the second type.[7] Finally, (3) the political leaders including Prime Minister Shastri and his successor, Indira Gandhi, represented the third type.

The justification for distinguishing between the first and the second types is a straightforward one—namely, they represented differences of opinion on the basic approach to the NPT and towards the superpowers. The emphasis here was on the effects of India's NPT stand on India's relationship with the superpowers. The justification for differentiating between the first and the third types is of a different kind. Whereas the first type argued the Indian case as a matter of principle and national interest, the third type, since it represented politicians, argued on the basis of political expediency—namely, the rejection of the NPT because Indian public opinion revealed public opposition to the NPT. Thus, Ambassador Trivedi and the Indian cabinet argued against the NPT, but for different reasons.

In view of the lack of archive material and a lack of conceptual tools, this section does not analyse the relationship between individual civil servants and individual politicians. Similarly, the relationship between the Indian defence services and the External Affairs Ministry, on questions related to the NPT, are not discussed in this section. There are two reasons for this. In strategic questions, except those dealing with territorial defence, the Defence Ministry could not initiate the process of consultation with the External Affairs Ministry or the prime minister's secretariat (which came into being in July 1964). The Defence Ministry, however, could be consulted by the political agencies, but even then its opinions would relate to the 'military' implications of a particular issue. In other words, there was no real two-way dialogue between the military and political staffs in India in matters involving long-term strategic planning as was the case in the British Raj. The 'rules of the game' underlying the principle of civilian control of the military are still such in India that the services lack the authority or the political clout to initiate analyses or make representations, except when their views are requested or if the views relate to specific budgetary requests. In questions relating to atomic energy and the NPT, the consultative process did not touch the defence services even marginally.

The First Cut in Indian Nuclear Decision-making (2 June 1964– 11 January 1965): Brecher's Analysis of the Shastri Era[8]

Brecher presents a controversial view of nuclear decision-making during the Shastri era. According to him, the domestic political setting appeared somewhat as follows. The new prime minister had stepped into the shoes of the late Jawaharlal Nehru and was unsure of his political strength. The problems of food and language 'dominated' the Indian government, and the cabinet and its emergency committee emerged as the decision-making organs in foreign affairs. He notes the growth of the position of the prime minister's secretariat—set up to aid the prime minister. According to him,

Long before the end of Shastri's first year, then, the Prime Minister's Secretariat had become not just an 'information pipeline' to the Prime Minister or even merely a channel for the reverse flow of decision; it was also a formidable influence in the making of decision.

From this, Brecher hypothesizes that the 'pyramids of decision in foreign and domestic policy have changed' after the Nehru succession. The institutional framework appeared somewhat as follows.

TABLE 6.1
Comparative Institutional Framework of India's Foreign Policy
(under Nehru and Shastri)

Foreign Policy under Nehru	*Foreign Policy under Shastri*
Nehru	Emergency Committee of Cabinet
Menon (until 1962)	Prime Minister and Prime Minister's Secretariat
Foreign Affairs Committee of Cabinet (until 1962)	External Affairs Minister
Emergency Committee of Cabinet (after 1962)	Committee of Secretaries
External Affairs Ministry	External Affairs Ministry

In the nuclear field, Brecher notes,

Yet the Prime Minister himself has also taken the initiative in foreign policy, as with the decision not to produce the Bomb—which, by his own admission, was never brought to Cabinet. So too with his proposal for a nuclear shield in his discussions with Prime Minister Wilson in October 1964—which was unknown to his colleagues or staff . . .

All this has tended to denigrate the influence of the External Affairs officials, for Nehru regarded himself and was accepted, as a professional; civil servants outside the Ministry have acquired influence—at their expense.

Finally, Brecher notes a shift in the overall orientation of Indian foreign relations. To quote him again:

Dé-Nehruisation is most evident in the sphere of foreign policy, notable in the withdrawal of India from intense involvement in the outer perimeter—India's neighbours . . . It will become more marked in the future. Non-alignment remains the formal basis of India's policy, but this has been transformed, in practice, into bi-alignment with the superpowers; equidistance from the United States and the Soviet Union has been replaced by equal proximity; such was the impact of the China debacle and India's lesser prestige in the world.

Indian Nuclear Decision-making in the Shastri Era: The Second Cut

Many generalizations—about the sources of Indian foreign policy and about India's external involvements—seem excessive in Brecher's analysis. This is particularly true with respect to his analysis of India's nuclear policy at that time. Shastri is shown to have decided 'not to produce the Bomb'. Yet the fact that the matter was not brought before the Indian cabinet suggests another explanation—namely, that the issue at that time was not important enough to merit a decision and the 'decision' not to produce a bomb in 1965 was simply a reaffirmation of the earlier decision not to produce nuclear weapons 'at present'. A 'decision' implies a shift, and there was no shift in 1965.

The analysis here, in this book of India's nuclear policy during the Shastri era, given the previous history of India's arms control and nuclear policies, differs significantly from Brecher's analysis. It challenges two streams in Brecher's perceptions. The first set of perceptions deals with the general orientation of Indian foreign relations after Nehru. The second set deals with the role of the Indian Ministry of External Affairs. Brecher's analysis is not intended to be a convenient whipping boy. It is meant to give us a starting point—a point of departure—for our view of Indian decision-making on the NPT. The point that will be made is that the position of the Indian Ministry of External Affairs did not decline—as Brecher thinks it did—and, if anything, during 1965–8, the position of the ministry was consolidated and strengthened. The role of Trivedi in the ENDC is a case in point.

As the preceding chapters have shown, Indian interventions in international conference diplomacy hardly revealed a 'withdrawal of India from intense involvement in the outer perimeter—the global system'. If anything, it demonstrated the exact opposite—namely, intense Indian involvement in the debate on nuclear proliferation.

In a single paragraph, Brecher reveals a contradiction. On one hand, he argues that India withdrew from intense involvement in global politics and instead concentrated on subcontinental politics. On the other hand, he argues that Indian non-alignment became transformed into a bi-alignment—with equidistance being replaced by equal proximity to the superpowers. A problem exists in these views. If India was pursuing a strategy of equal proximity rather than equidistance, given the complex nature of superpower activities in the subcontinent, this would necessarily require intense involvement in superpower politics. True, after 1962, India started to give more attention to its immediate neighbours, particularly Nepal and Ceylon; Burma and Pakistan had always received much attention. However, it does not necessarily follow that giving more attention to its neighbours meant giving less attention to the 'outer perimeter'.

The problem with Brecher's analysis, particularly as it relates to India's security policies, concerns his conceptualization and his assessments. He predicts that the withdrawal from intense involvement in global politics 'will become more marked in the future'. India's NPT diplomacy during 1964–8 suggests otherwise. To correct the errors of assessment, one first needs to correct the errors in conceptualization.

The following model of Indian nuclear decision-making takes a step in this direction. It points to the growth of the influence of the prime minister's secretariat (which is Brecher's point), and it also points to the growth of the influence of the Indian Ministry of External Affairs (which is clearly not Brecher's point) during the NPT debate in Geneva. Our model points to an emerging coalition of civil servants of the Ministry of External Affairs, the Indian Atomic Energy Department, and the prime minister's secretariat, with a prime minister (weak or strong, it does not matter) who is receptive to expert advice so long as the civil servant does not try to obtain credit for the advice rendered. This model suggests that during 1965–7, the effective initiative was in the hands of V.C. Trivedi.

The model suggests that there were essentially four 'decisions' involved: whether India should sign the NPT; whether India should accept weak security guarantees from the United States and the Soviet Union; whether China's missile programme represented an 'immediate' threat to Indian security; and finally, whether India should go ahead with a plutonium bomb programme on a crash basis or instead, continue to develop its nuclear technology. On all points, the formal decisions—not to sign the NPT, not to accept security guarantees, and not to go in for a crash plutonium bomb programme—were inherent in the statements made by Trivedi in Geneva. The central premise in these decisions was that China did not represent an immediate threat to India.

Overall then, during the Shastri era, the sources and the flow of influences bearing on India's nuclear policy appeared to be somewhat as follows. The model is broken into two parts. The first part, which is also the most obvious, concerns the role played by Trivedi. This part identifies three types of targets: (1) the superpowers against whom the Indians were arguing in the ENDC, (2) the Chinese who were not participating in the ENDC but who represented a potential military threat to Indian security, and (3) the 'soft' Indians, who favoured acceptance of weak security guarantees. The second part of the model specifies the efforts by the prime minister and the prime minister's secretariat to explore the possibility of obtaining iron-clad security guarantees. Two hypotheses may be noted: The first suggests that Ambassador Trivedi and L.K. Jha were working at cross-purposes, given the elaborate effort by the latter to secure viable guarantees and given the former's limited attention to this question in the ENDC. The second hypothesis suggests the exact opposite—namely, that Trivedi favoured the insertion of the idea of security assurances by the superpowers in the five-point memorandum presented by Chakravarty to the UN on 4 May 1965 (as described earlier), but both sought to explore the nature and extent of the commitments of the superpowers against China; the second hypothesis, therefore, suggests complementariness rather than competitiveness.

This model has many nuances. Since this is a study about India's nuclear behaviour rather than about the history of Indian foreign relations, the framework is necessarily sketchy. The framework identifies three pillars in India's external policies. These pillars are guides to assess the evolving attitudes of India's political leaders, diplomats, and the heads of the Indian Atomic Energy Commission. The three pillars are the idea of deterrence, the idea of territorial defence, and the idea of giving priority to Indian economic development. The spectrum of opinions within the Indian government during 1947–68 fits into these three attitudinal reference points. Figures 6.1 and 6.2 provide a crude typology of these opinions. The heading 'Nehru and the Consensus' in Figure 6.2 describes the elements that existed in India's nuclear and arms-control policy making during 1947–68. The other headings describe the attitudes of the main actors, and the arrows in the figure indicate the shifts over time.

The framework in which India's arms-control and nuclear policy emerged after 1947 can be identified partially in the words of Warren F. Ilchman. In his thinking, there were essentially two sources of Indian foreign relations—namely, foreign political policy and foreign economic policy. To quote him:

There were throughout the Nehru period two foreign policies: the policy of non-alignment, which was essentially a political policy, and the policy of economic development which contained a foreign economic policy . . . The foreign economic policy, on the other hand, responded to the exigencies of the development process. Its bases were not ideological, but highly pragmatic.[9]

Policy	Argument

Deterrence↑

Jan Sangh Party and pro-bomb lobby: Includes those against a crash bomb programme but for peaceful nuclear explosions and/or nuclear weapons, land or sea-based.

Dr Bhabha: Favours nuclear weapons programme and adoption of deterrence idea by India.

Mr Trivedi: Upheld by Morarji Desai and Y.B. Chavan; eventually approved by the cabinet of Indira Gandhi, 1968. Mrs Gandhi had not been a prime backer of Trivedi due to either factional politics or her lack of expertise in atomic energy.

Nehru and the consensus: Territorial defence is prime goal of security; keep nuclear option open; option has political uses; nuclear weapons should be abolished for all. India should not seek nuclear weapons 'at present', and should avoid military alliances. Collective security through the UN is desirable (that is, Article 51 of the UN Charter is relevant for India). China is not an immediate nuclear threat to India. Indian sovereignty requires national means of defence.

Territorial Defence↑

Shastri: Non-nuclear states ought to have security assurances.*

Indian Economic Development

FIG. 6.1: Overt Arguments of Indian Decision-makers in Nuclear Policy, 1947–68

*For a discussion of the evolution and the confusion in India's approach to this issue, see A.G. Noorani, 'India's Quest for a Nuclear Guarantee', *Asian Survey*, vol. 3, no. 7, July 1967, pp. 490–502.

Source: Compiled by author.

Thus, the criteria for assessing Indian foreign policies is not simply between 'pragmatic' developmental politics and 'unpragmatic' ideological-political external involvement. The framework appears to be broader and more complex in orientation. The framework here has three dimensions: (1) the idea of development as a source of Indian foreign

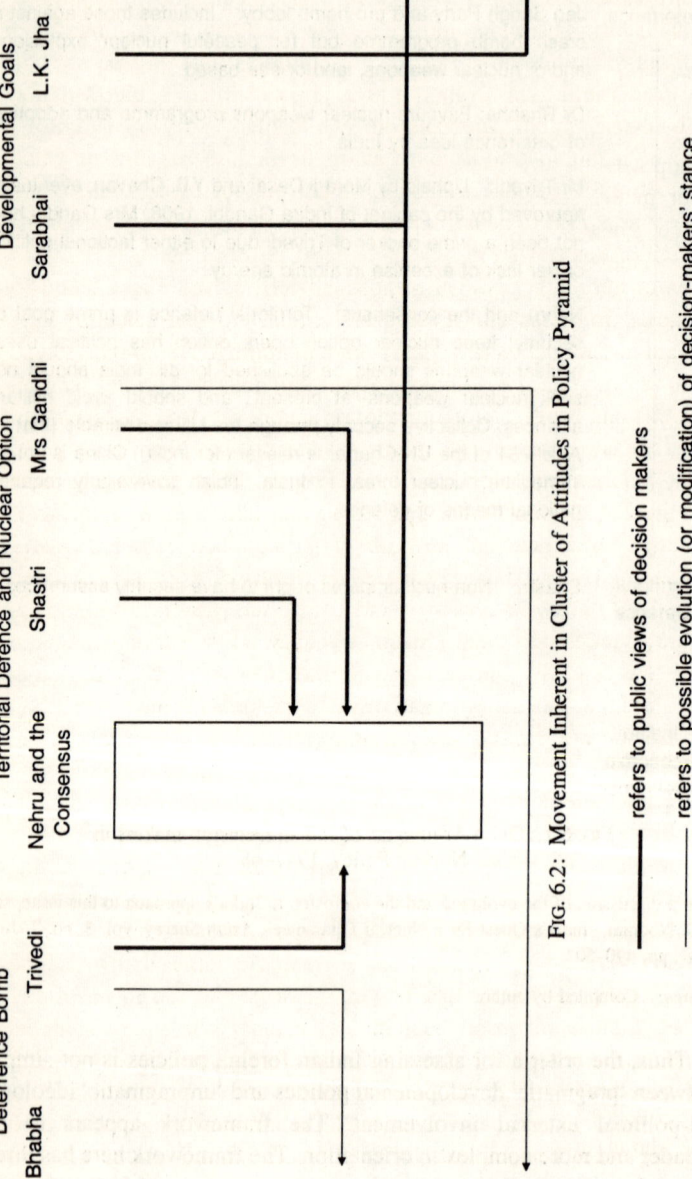

FIG. 6.2: Movement Inherent in Cluster of Attitudes in Policy Pyramid

— refers to public views of decision makers

— refers to possible evolution (or modification) of decision-makers' stance

Source: Compiled by author.

policy; (2) the idea of security—defined as 'territorial defence'—as a source of Indian foreign policy; and finally (3) the idea of deterrence as a source of Indian foreign policy.

The third idea was not accepted by the Indian government publicly until May 1998 when Pokhran II was carried out. On 18 May 1974, India exploded a 'peaceful' nuclear device but claimed no need to develop nuclear weapons. However, the deterrence concept is inserted in our model because Dr Homi Bhabha, the late head of the India Atomic Energy Commission, and Morarji Desai, a senior Indian Cabinet member, both expressed themselves in favour of nuclear weapons under certain circumstances.[10] Moreover, the Jan Sangh party and the unofficial pro-bomb lobby in India had all along advocated the adoption of the deterrence strategy by the Indian government. These pressures shaped the domestic-political context of Indian nuclear decision making.

Attitudinal Prisms in Indian Nuclear Decision-making (1947–68)

According to K. Boulding,

A decision involves the selection of the most preferred position in a contemplated field of choice. Both the field of choice and the ordering of this field by which the preferred position is identified lie in the image of the decision maker.[11]

According to D.J. Finlay *et al.*, 'every decision maker is in part a prisoner of beliefs and expectations which inevitably shape his definition of reality'.[12]

In comparison, Brecher makes the following points. Decision-makers choose alternative paths in accordance with their own perceptions of the world. 'The content of that which they perceive is the Image. The link between Image and Decision is indeed the master key to a valuable framework of foreign policy analysis.' Finally,

the choice among policy options derives from decision-makers' perceptions of their State's environment and its desirable roles in international politics. It follows from this hypothesis that a key, if not the master key, to understanding the Foreign Policy System is the world view of the small coterie of men within each State who make foreign-policy decisions.[13]

A key assumption in hypothesizing such a link is that the subject's public views reflect his/her private beliefs. Images of decision-makers are inferred from the public views of decision-makers, just as these public views are taken to represent the decision-maker's perceptions. But are such inferences valid?

Identifying the real perceptions in the case of Indian decision-makers is hard, if not impossible, because the assessments on which policies are based are not in the public domain.[14] In other words, the speeches of Indian politicians and diplomats cannot be regarded as assessments; these statements usually suggest what ought to be done. Such statements usually do not indicate what the private views of the Indian decision-makers are. They are purposive, that is, they indicate the kinds of activities that ought to be discouraged or encouraged. It is a challenge to the analytical skill of a researcher outside the government to infer the decision-maker's image or perception of the situation from the 'ought' statements that are made publicly.

It is true, as Boulding and Finlay suggest, that images influence or determine the preferences of decision-makers. But a qualification should be added to the Boulding formula, as follows: Ideally speaking, a decision involves the selection of the most preferred position, that is if the power (the capability or the means) to carry out the choice or choices exists. But when preferences exceed the capacity to change the situation or the system, preferences may be of two kinds: the first, where the preferred position or the preferred choice is relative to what the decision-maker thinks can be achieved, and the second, where the preferred choice is relative to what the decision-maker thinks cannot be achieved but ought to be sought in the future.

The model here, therefore, assumes that Indian public statements are purposive but if they reflect only what the practitioners believe can be achieved, then the theoretical implication is that as India's power changes, shifts in public statements about preferred outcomes and threat perceptions should be expected.

In this perspective, three sets of Indian 'images' can be noted. The first expresses preferred position(s) in terms of Indian perceptions of their power to change the environment. The second expresses preferred positions in terms of Indian perceptions of their inability to change the environment. Yet beyond these two sets lies a third set of perceptions and images, which expresses that part of Indian foreign policy that is totally secret, totally beyond the public domain. And it is with respect to this totally secret domain that a non-governmental analyst is unable to specify the operational images and the decisions that flow from them. In other words, our model does not presume that overt activity or public activity in India's foreign policies in general or nuclear policy in particular is simply a linear projections of its images and its decisions. The overt activities can change as Indian capacities change. Neither should the analyst be so rash as to try to identify Indian images and decisions simply by assessing the overt activities.

Overall then, there is a justification for emphasizing the difficulties in identifying the perceptions and images of decision-makers, in the Indian case. It is hard even to identify the decision-makers, let alone the images and perceptions underlying the decisions. As such, the model here is structured on a set of assumptions rather than categorical statements of fact. For the purpose of this model, a 'decision-maker' is defined as a person who actually wields influence, and not necessarily the head of a government or agency who issues the statement. The emphasis is on actual process rather than formal institutions. The assumptions are as follows:

(i) In India, the influence of pressure groups in policy making so far is negligible.

(ii) Disciplined civil servants tend to toe the line of the prime minister, and it is their duty to do so, particularly if the prime minister is strong.

(iii) Theoretically, Article 246 of the Indian Constitution empowers the Parliament to legislate on all aspects of foreign policy, but in fact, the theoretical function remains unfulfilled.[15]

(iv) With some exceptions, the consultative committee of the Parliament for external affairs has not been able to play a significant role in foreign policy making. One such exception was on 10 February 1970, when the foreign minister was forced to examine the possible costs of an Indian nuclear-weapons programme. Similarly, the Consultative Committee for the Department of Atomic Energy was asked on 31 March 1970 to examine these costs.[16]

(v) The standing committee of the cabinet on foreign affairs has not been influential in foreign policy making.[17]

(vi) The Indian cabinet has not functioned, with some exceptions, as the highest collective decision-making body in foreign policy.[18]

(vii) The position of the Ministry of External Affairs has not declined in the post-Nehru era.

(viii) Despite the lack of formal coordination between the External Affairs and the Defence Ministries regarding strategic policies, and, even though the policy planning and review division that was set up in 1966 does not have military specialists on its staff, India's arms-control and nuclear policy has in fact been based on an evaluation of the military and technological implications for India. This is done by specialized civilians rather than military men.[19]

The model here, therefore, challenges the contention in the literature that India's arms-control and nuclear policy was based only on ideological and ethical grounds and that pragmatic and security considerations were ignored. Thus:

In conformity with standard international practice in this respect, the personnel connected with intelligence activities operate both independently and through some of our missions abroad. The information collected through the missions is forwarded to the Ministry of Home Affairs through the head of the mission, and copies of the reports are made available to the Ministry of External Affairs. The Service Attaches send, in conformity with generally accepted international practice, their reports on military developments to the Defence Ministry through the heads of missions; and copies of these reports are also made available to the Ministries of Home and External Affairs.[20]

The above quote indicates that there is ample circulation of information acquired through official channels, but, at best, there may be a lack of coordination of such information. This, however, does not appear to be the problem in the behaviour of actors like Homi Bhabha and V.C. Trivedi. Their interventions in international forums showed that they knew what they were talking about. Therefore, for the purpose of the model here, it is assumed that Indian negotiators involved in the NPT had access to intelligence information of a high quality—indicating the status of the Chinese missile programme and indicating further the nature of the intentions and the mandates of the the US and Soviet negotiators in Geneva. The latter type of assessment probably included information about the priority that Presidents Lyndon Johnson and Richard Nixon and their close advisers really attached to the NPT. The probable effects of Indo–US and Indo–Soviet relations, if India refused to sign the nuclear treaty, were similarly assessed.

In this cluster of views 'at the top' of the policy pyramid, the trends seem to be diverse, or are open to different interpretations (see Figures 6.1, 6.2, and 6.3). One interpretation is that the policy of not deciding in favour of the 'bomb' or nuclear weapons was irrevocable and hence a barrier to the nuclear option. The other interpretation was that the two ideas—namely, no bomb at present and no renunciation of the option at present—were contradictory but that the contradiction was necessary at the time; that is, it was related to the evolution of the Chinese nuclear and missile programme, to India's scientific and material progress, and to developments in India's strategic environment.

Policy	Argument
Territorial Defence	Nehru and the consensus:
	India at present is protected by Sino–Soviet rivalry; China's threat to India is presently of the conventional kind; until China poses a direct nuclear threat to India, a nuclear option is adequate to meet Indian needs.
	Indira Gandhi:
	India will not sign the NPT; India will keep the option open; India will not produce nuclear weapons.
	V. Sarabhai:
	India should rely on collective security; India should rely on nuclear disarmament; nuclear weapons are beyond India's means; India should continue to utilize nuclear energy for peaceful uses; India should keep the option open; security is a prime goal for India.*
	L.K. Jha:
Developmental Goals	Give preference to India's developmental needs and need for foreign aid; sign the NPT if security assurances are available; the cost of an Indian nuclear weapons programme is too high.

FIG. 6.3: Overt Arguments of Indian Decision-makers
in Nuclear Policy, 1964–8.

*The late Dr Sarabhai was the only Indian at the policy level who seems to have changed his views or the emphasis in his views. Originally, he appeared to conform to the Pugwash and Gandhian approach to nuclear disarmament. His public statements emphasized the importance of collective security. His thought that security is a prime goal, which he emphasized in an interview to this author in June 1971, seemed to reflect a reassessment by the Government of India of the nuclear policy in 1970. In short, there is a definite discrepancy between his private and public views—depending on his audience. Confidential sources indicate that Sarabhai did not favour the NPT, and although he was originally against 'the bomb' he subsequently changed his mind.

Source: Compiled by author.

This chapter notes three approaches in the discussions on India's nuclear policy at the time. The first represents a recapitulation of traditional world-order concerns—that is, to make the world safe through nuclear disarmament. The second was more recent, and it represented the late Dr Bhabha's influence and that of the unofficial pro-bomb

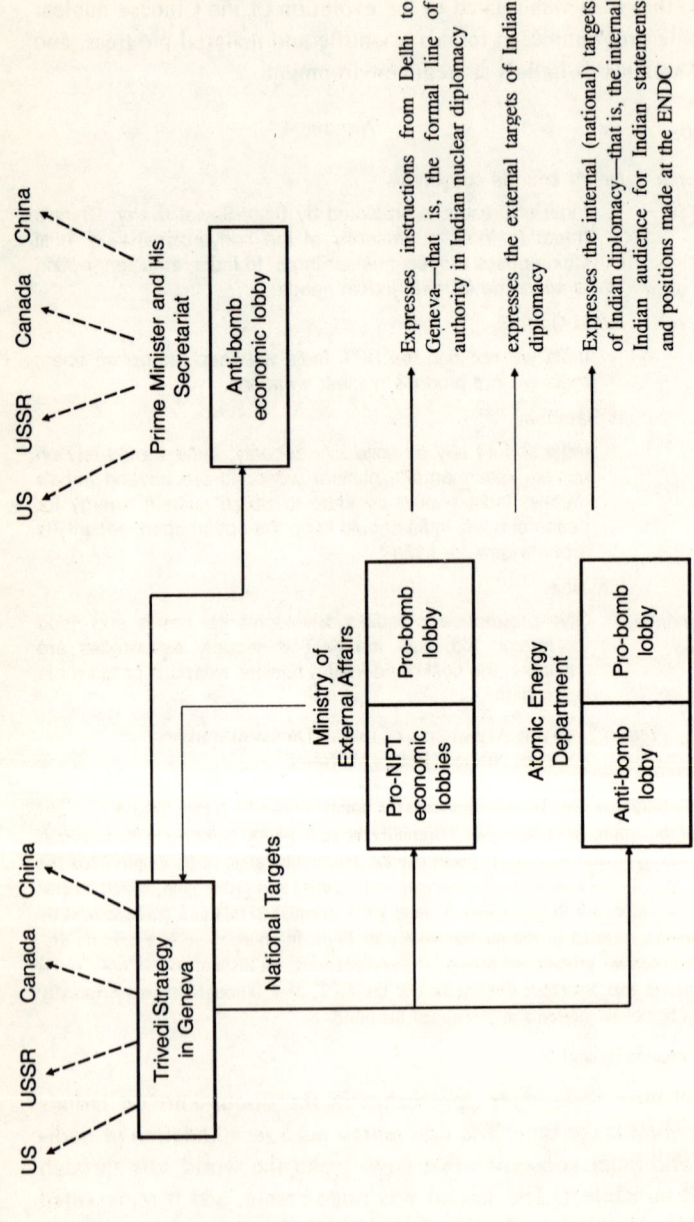

FIG. 6.4: Targets of Indian Diplomacy on NPT

Source: Compiled by author.

lobby in India. This approach sought a radical revision, even repudiation, of the traditional approach to peace through disarmament; it asked for an adoption of a strategy of nuclear deterrence for India. It went beyond the official view that argued that the threats to Indian security were primarily of a conventional kind.

India's behaviour toward the NPT, shown in Figure 6.4, yielded a third approach to Indian security in the nuclear arena in this period. This approach emphasized that it was sufficient to have a nuclear option against the contingency of a Chinese nuclear threat to India. The assessment on which this strategy was based has not been made public.

However, two possible assumptions seemed to be crucial in the third approach. (1) India had the technological capability to launch a well-developed plutonium bomb programme as a last resort, at any time. (2) At the time, there was limited military value in possessing nuclear weapons, but there was a continuing political value in possessing nuclear power—that is, there was a political value in the non-use of nuclear weapons and in the non-use of a visible nuclear option. Even if the Indians perceived that China gained some political and military value from its nuclear-weapons testing programme, the Indians argued that there was also a political value in India's non-adherence to the NPT if this was matched with a demonstration of a will and ability to explode a 'peaceful' nuclear device, as was done in May 1974.

Thus, two points were implicit in Indian views of China's nuclear behaviour. First, there was an expectation that the India–China 'dialogue' may gain momentum and, hence the potential danger of Chinese nuclear activity against India could decline. Secondly, there was an expectation that Moscow would continue to aid Indian security indirectly by aiding India's economic and military development, including space research. Excluded was any expectation of substantial US military aid to India against China. The US aid to the Himalayan 'communications' network was resumed after 1971, but, overall, the US military aid programme to India has been small, compared to what the United States has given many other countries This view developed after 1964 and was reinforced by US behaviour in the 1971 crisis.

This chapter notes a contradiction in the third approach to security. On the one hand, there was the rejection of nuclear weapons for the present; on the other hand, there was the retention of the nuclear option at present. There are two ways of analysing this. The first argues that India's present stance was a step toward a nuclear-weapons capability, with the rate of growth or transformation depending on several factors:

(1) the rate of India's technological progress; (2) the rate of progress of China's missile capacity; and (3) the vulnerability of Indian politicians to persistent professional advice. The second way argues that India's refusal to authorize the manufacture of nuclear weapons was, in fact, a barrier against the nuclear-weapon option. According to this view, keeping the option open was a sop to the pro-bomb lobby in India and nothing else. The first view emphasizes the quality of 'drift' in India's nuclear decision-making and the effect of external developments on Indian strategic perceptions. The second view emphasizes the quality of deliberation in Indian policy planning. It notes the excessively cautious quality that Indian decision-makers have displayed so far in their attitudes toward deterrence planning against China and in their attitude toward the superpowers in trying not to lead an anti-NPT club.

Finally, this chapter highlights the dual thrust in Trivedi's strategy. One aspect of the strategy was to appear to be willing to negotiate if certain conditions were met. The Indian memorandum of 4 May 1965 expressed the five points in terms of which negotiations were possible. Even though Canadian and the US observers tend to argue that India did not appear to be ready to negotiate, in fact there is evidence that suggests that Indians were ready to negotiate seriously before the evolution of US non-proliferation policy.

The Role of Politicized Scientists and Civil Servants

In the Shastri–Gandhi years, the role of scientists and civil servants (not generals) was important in shaping the nuclear decisions. The subtext is that scientists in India (and elsewhere) are not simply leaders in science; they are also political strategists, that is their scientific advice has impact; they are knowledgeable about the external and internal political context of their scientific work and advocacy—be it political or scientific.

The Shastri–Gandhi years increased the politicized involvement of scientists in Indian nuclear work. That is, Indian scientists altered and enlarged the boundary of nuclear science and space research and their advocacy pressured the policy boundary as well, albeit in an *ad hoc* manner, compared to the policy limits of the Nehru era. The following section illustrates the emergence and impact of the *politicized* scientists and the civil servants.

In the nuclear policy process, the original framework, as defined by Nehru, was to use atomic energy for peaceful purposes, but also to leave open the option for possible use for India's 'protection'. The latter aspect was not publicly spelled out by Nehru before he died. Did this mean that Nehru failed to think through the link between atomic energy for peaceful purposes and its possible defence use? Or did it mean that he thought about the link but failed only to articulate it publicly? What was the role of Indian scientists and Indian civil servants after Nehru's death in shaping the policy process?

A linkage between peaceful and potential military uses of atomic energy emerged after 1962. The linkage occurred in response to Bhabha's position on the diplomatic–strategic uses of nuclear energy which differed from Nehru's. Bhabha conceived India's atomic programme under the 'Atoms for Peace' concept, but his commitment to peaceful uses was limited. He never lost sight of the military uses of atomic energy. Because of his realpolitik approach, he did not show much enthusiasm for disarmament beyond the 1960s. Nehru, of course, was committed to disarmament completely, and he talked publicly primarily about peaceful uses of nuclear energy.

A policy shift occurred in the conception and the articulation of a potential link between peaceful and military uses of atomic energy. This occurred no later than the first half of 1964. The change occurred in the context of Indo–Canadian negotiations. Bhabha had submitted a note to the Indian cabinet justifying why India ought to develop its atomic energy programme on the Canadian CANDU technology using natural uranium, rather than on the US technology using enriched uranium. The Canadian CIRUS heavy water reactor had developed a defect in its fuel rods, and the Canadians could not identify the cause of this defect. Dr Braham Prakash of the Indian Atomic Energy Commission rectified the problem by using Indian fuel rods. An Indian scientific journal makes the point.

A notable result of the policy of self-reliance was that Indian scientists learnt the fabrication of nuclear-grade natural uranium fuel for CIRUS. And the fuel was, in fact, better in quality than those initially supplied by the Canadians.[21]

Thereafter, the CANDU design became attractive for India, for political and technological reasons. Canada had been generous in giving blueprints and shop drawings for RAPP I, including access to subsequent developments in CANDU technology. The cost price for this was a mere $5 million, and even this was paid for by the Colombo plan. Access to Canadian technology gave India a chance to move closer to its goal of self-sufficiency since Bhabha's aim was to make India independent after RAPP I and II. Moreover, the Canadian link enabled India to reduce the dependency on the United States and to save foreign exchance that would be spent if India relied on enriched uranium technology. In other words, with Indian scientific expertise, Canadian technology and goodwill, and Bhabha's international reputation and bargaining skill, the foundation was laid for India's atomic energy development with a possible deterrent use of Indian nuclear technology. Given the interesting personal relationship and the fundamental differences in approach between Nehru and Bhabha (Bhabha called Nehru *Bhai* [brother] in his official correspondence), on Bhabha's memo Nehru wrote a note that read somewhat as follows: 'Apart from building power stations and developing electricity, there is always a built-in advantage of defence use if the need should arise.' Thereafter, on 25 October 1964, Bhabha told an All India Radio audience about the need to have nuclear deterrence. This was indeed a major shift in Nehru's thinking and policy.[22]

After Nehru's death in 1964, the focus of atomic decision-making centred on the relationship between Bhabha, Shastri, and L.K. Jha, Shastri's principal secretary. In RAPP II negotiations with Canada, Bhabha wanted the Indo–Canadian agreement to be even freer than the RAPP I agreement. But as a result of the Glassboro conference between President Johnson and Soviet Premier Kosygin, the NPT discussions got seriously under way and the Canadian stance toward India stiffened. L.K. Jha went along with Canadian and American views about the NPT. When Shastri and L.K. Jha visited Canada, Shastri promised to send Bhabha to negotiate with Lorne Gray (who headed the sales side of the Canadian atomic energy department). L.K. Jha pressured Bhabha to go to Canada to negotiate. Bhabha declined to do so. He did not want to negotiate under pressure from Canada and from L.K. Jha. He threatened to buy in the open market from France and calculated that the Canadian industry would pressure the Canadian government to facilitate sales to India.

Bhabha's opposition won over L.K. Jha's views. In November 1965, Bhabha put forward a note on a need for a subterranean nuclear explosion project (SNEP). This project's aim was to produce an underground explosion. In December, Shastri gave his approval to the proposal. His approval was to sanction research up to a point where, once the go-ahead signal was given, it would take three months to have an explosion.

At this time, the story about India's plans to have an explosion started to leak. The *Guardian* (Manchester) had an interview with Shastri around mid-December 1965. The correspondent asked about peaceful nuclear explosions, and Shastri noted that even an explosion could be peaceful. These decisions had a telling effect. On the one hand, Prime Minister Shastri's statement to the Western press leaked India's nuclear intentions. Yet, on the other hand, with SNEP sanctioned, French interest in India gained momentum. A French representative came to India in January 1966 to discuss Indo–French collaboration, and he was in India when Shastri died. As a result of French interest in the Indian atomic energy programme, Canada's Gray also wanted to see Bhabha. Both decided to meet in Vienna around 25/26 January 1966. At this time, therefore, the issue seemed to have considerable momentum, in Indo–French and Indo–Canadian relations. Immediately after Indira Gandhi became prime minister, she sought Bhabha's candid advice, in a meeting around 20/21 January 1966. Unfortunately, Bhabha's plane crashed on his way to meet Gray in Vienna, and the foregoing momentum was lost.

After Bhabha's death, the SNEP story took a dramatic turn. He was succeeded by Dharam Vira, who was also the cabinet secretary. Gray rushed from Vienna to Delhi to see Vira. Vikram Sarabhai then was only in charge of the space programme. There were two immediate problems before Vira: to negotiate RAPP II with Canada and to decide the future of SNEP. Sarabhai and two directors of the Atomic Energy Commission, H.N. Sethna and R. Ramanna, were against SNEP on the ground that they could not carry it out. Dr Prakash, another director, however, favoured preparations for SNEP. One view in the debate argued for the appointment of Prakash as the head of the AEC. Another view argued that no scientist should have independent charge of the AEC. Prime Minister Indira Gandhi, however, took a political view of the question of appointing a successor to the late Homi Bhabha. She wanted to encourage the Gujarat factor, to offset Morarji Desai's influence. (It must be remembered that Mrs Gandhi in 1966 was struggling to consolidate her power against Morarji Desai.) She appointed Sarabhai as the head of the AEC and supported Sethna. J.R.D. Tata was a member of the AEC, and he supported Sethna, arguing that Sethna was Bhabha's man. One can speculate that Sethna's Parsee background aided him *vis-à-vis* Tata (who is also a Parsee). Whether or not Sethna was in fact Bhabha's man is uncertain, but maybe Tata genuinely thought so.

After Sarabhai became chairman of the AEC, he called off SNEP and accepted tougher safeguards on RAPP II. A contrast between safeguards on RAPP I and II is noteworthy, as an illustration of the penetrative influence of Canadian NPT thinking into the Indian bureaucratic process underlying the development of nuclear policy. Needless to say, the penetration was facilitated by the defection of a number of Indian scientists from Bhabha's commitment to SNEP. Since it cannot be argued that Bhabha's successors were better scientists and administrative strategists than Bhabha himself—the record of Bhabha's contribution in putting Indian nuclear science on the world map speaks for itself—one must assume that the defection was motivated by political and personal considerations. The story also reveals that India's campaign against international safeguards on India's nuclear projects was diluted by bureaucratic politics and a shift in senior personnel in the AEC. This affected international negotiations between India and Canada, if not between India and other Western states.

RAPP I, RAPP II, and the NPT

RAPP I included a provision for inspection, by Canada only, and the inspection was restricted to first-generation fissile material. The inspection right was tied to the supply of Canadian uranium. The agreement had a provision for reciprocity. India could inspect Canada's Douglas Point reactor, and the principle of political equality between a donor and a recipient—or a seller and buyer of sensitive materials involving superpower concerns—was preserved.

RAPP II was much tougher. Instead of Canadian inspectors, IAEA inspectors were allowed. The inspection system itself was tougher, reflecting revised Western thinking about safeguards against further nuclear proliferation. The agreement called for safeguards only on all generations of fissile materials unlike safeguards only on the first-generation use, as in the case of RAPP I. Even the use of Indian uranium was safeguarded, which was not the case with RAPP I.

Overall, the contrast was shattering to the Indian nationalists. CIRUS in 1956 had practically no meaningful safeguards. RAPP I had bilateral safeguards, and RAPP II produced IAEA safeguards. Thus, while Ambassador V.C. Trivedi was arguing against international safeguards on the peaceful nuclear programmes of non-nuclear weapon states, his scientific colleagues in Bombay were eroding India's bargaining position. In all this, Prime Minister Indira Gandhi took a political view based on domestic considerations rather than a political view of India's foreign relations.

In the light of Mrs Gandhi's preoccupation with domestic concerns, India came very close to signing the NPT, given the foregoing array of bureaucratic manoeuvres. Senior officials of the Indian Ministry of External Affairs favoured signing the NPT, with some exceptions. Rajeshwar Dayal, Jagat Mehta, and Rikye Jaipal favoured India's adherence to the NPT. V.C. Trivedi and T.N. Kaul were opposed to it, as was S.K. Singh. Sarabhai and some other scientists were ambivalent or favoured signing, but a qualification needs to be added. According to at least one interviewee, in the latter period of the NPT deliberations, Sarabhai seemed to have had second thoughts about signing. P.N. Haksar, then principal private secretary to the prime minister, did not disclose the bent of his own thinking. The original draft of Mrs Gandhi's speech in late November 1967 favoured India's adherence to the NPT.

The rest of India's nuclear story after November 1967 is well known. Mrs Gandhi's final decision was to reject the NPT after the issue was debated in the Indian cabinet. Morarji Desai and Y.B. Chavan were the principal cabinet members who argued against the nuclear treaty, but it is also true that the cabinet was unanimously against the treaty. Yet it should be noted that the decision not to sign was not based on any deep conviction in principle against the NPT. Rather, it was based on a careful reading of Indian public opinion polls. These polls showed that a majority rejected the NPT and favoured an Indian decision toward nuclear weapons. In this instance, public opinion emerged as an ally of those in government who opposed the NPT.

Assuming that the foregoing description of personal politics in the shaping of India's nuclear policy is accurate, the following tentative conclusions are warranted.

First, the personal relations and the political alignments of Indian politicians—as perceived by the Indian prime minister—determined the prime minister's responses to arguments concerning the merits or drawbacks of nuclear policy. This chapter suggests that it is not merely on the basis of the merits of a case that an argument is settled at the policy level in India. The hypothesis is advanced that a foreign policy issue has a domestic use in the hands of a prime minister who does not trust, and is unwilling to give credit to, his or her colleagues even if credit is due and even if the arguments of the colleagues and subordinates are in fact finally adopted by the prime minister.

Second, the hypothesis is advanced that in the foregoing case, several Indian scientists (Sarabhai, Sethna, and Ramana, for example) tailored their commitments to Bhabha's nuclear programme to conform to their perceptions of what the prime minister wanted to hear, given the latter's concern—even primary concern—with her domestic constituents and/or adversaries.

Third, the hypothesis is advanced that if the prime minister is weak (that is, is not sure of support in the cabinet) and if public opinion is perceived and projected by competing members of the cabinet, then the prime minister is likely to be impressed with public opinion and decide accordingly. But once the threat from the prime minister's domestic adversaries passes (in this case after Mrs Gandhi gained a majority in the Indian Parliament), then public opinion is no longer perceived to be a key variable, even if it had been one earlier.

Fourth, attention should be given to another variable: the rate and the scope at which a civil servant and/or scientist is able to educate a political leader about the intricacies of nuclear policy. There is a probable link between the 1962 India–China crisis and the shift in Nehru's thinking as this was reflected in his note on Bhabha's memo in 1964. In assessing interactions between (1) Bhabha and Nehru and, particularly, (2) Bhabha and Shastri and (3) Bhabha and Indira Gandhi, it is a noteworthy hypothesis that the prime ministers were more attentive to Bhabha's security concerns in India's nuclear and disarmament policies after a military crisis—for example, after the India–Pakistan war, in the fall of 1965. A link can be hypothesized between the subtle efforts of Trivedi, Bhabha, and Kaul to educate Mrs Gandhi against the NPT during the period 1965–8. Finally, there appears to be a link between the following. On the one hand, there were Mrs. Gandhi's perceptions of the implications of superpower parallelism in the Tashkent Agreement (1966) and the NPT Agreement (1968), the implications of the US 'tilt' against India during the 1971 Bangladesh crisis, and the problems India had in securing Soviet support during the 1971 crisis. On the other hand, there was her decision in late 1971 and her final decision on or around 15 February 1974 to explode a peaceful nuclear device on or around 16–21 May 1974. The style of superpowers' decision-making in crises in India's strategic environment seemed to affect the prime ministerial perceptions. Inasmuch as a crisis produces a heightened awareness about security, bargaining capability, and reputation, the prime minister appeared to be receptive to arguments about national interests.

Fifth, this and the previous chapter suggests that there is a need to differentiate between the internal and external factors underlying a policy argument and the timing and the context in which the arguments are actually used. Thus, the external factors, (namely the security-diplomatic needs that ought to propel India toward a deterrence strategy) were articulated by Bhabha *vis-à-vis* Nehru, Shastri, and Indira Gandhi, and by Trivedi during the period 1964–8. Yet, it does not necessarily follow that these views prevailed in, say, Mrs Gandhi's decision to explode a peaceful nuclear device on 18 May 1974. India's defence minister, Jagjivan Ram, the second most powerful member of the cabinet, was informed about the test on May 8, but he was not consulted about the decision. India's foreign minister, Swaran Singh, a political lightweight in the cabinet because he did not have an independent political base in the Indian political system, was informed a mere 48 hours before the detonation, thus indicating that the Ministry of External Affairs was totally bypassed in the process. The timing and the manner of decision making suggested that the final decision (February 1974) was taken in the context of Mrs Gandhi's domestic troubles. However, attention should also be given to the role of external factors, namely China and the superpowers, in Indian nuclear decision-making. The decision in late 1971 in fact revived Shastri, Bhabha, and Trivedi's strategy to explode a peaceful device for diplomatic and, potentially, security reasons.

Figure 6.5 indicates the possibility of inferring two distinct (but, to an extent, overlapping) images about the roots and nature of India's nuclear decision-making. The first type of image implied the existence of phasal activity and the content of this image appeared somewhat as follows. (1) Since the late 1940s, Indian prime ministers (Nehru, Shastri, and Indira Gandhi) have all believed in developing the peaceful uses of atomic energy. (2) All three have supported the Indian diplomatic aim of keeping India's nuclear programmes free of intrusive safeguards; and yet have accepted them as a compromise, but only as a temporary expedient. The reluctance to accept international safeguards was a sufficient demonstration of India's intent to develop nuclear weapons in due course. (3) Indian prime ministers have claimed that nuclear energy may be used for a 'state's protection', and its 'defence use' is not prohibited. (4) Even if Indira Gandhi cancelled the decision of her predecessor, Shastri, to have an underground explosion, this may be seen as a temporary delay in the evolution towards nuclear weapons for India in the late 1970s or the 1980s. In short, according to this image, India was moving toward nuclear weapons. Indian declarations that it believed only in peaceful uses and it did not intend to make weapons were not a true representation of the decisions that had been taken or that were implied in the policy stance at the time. The central

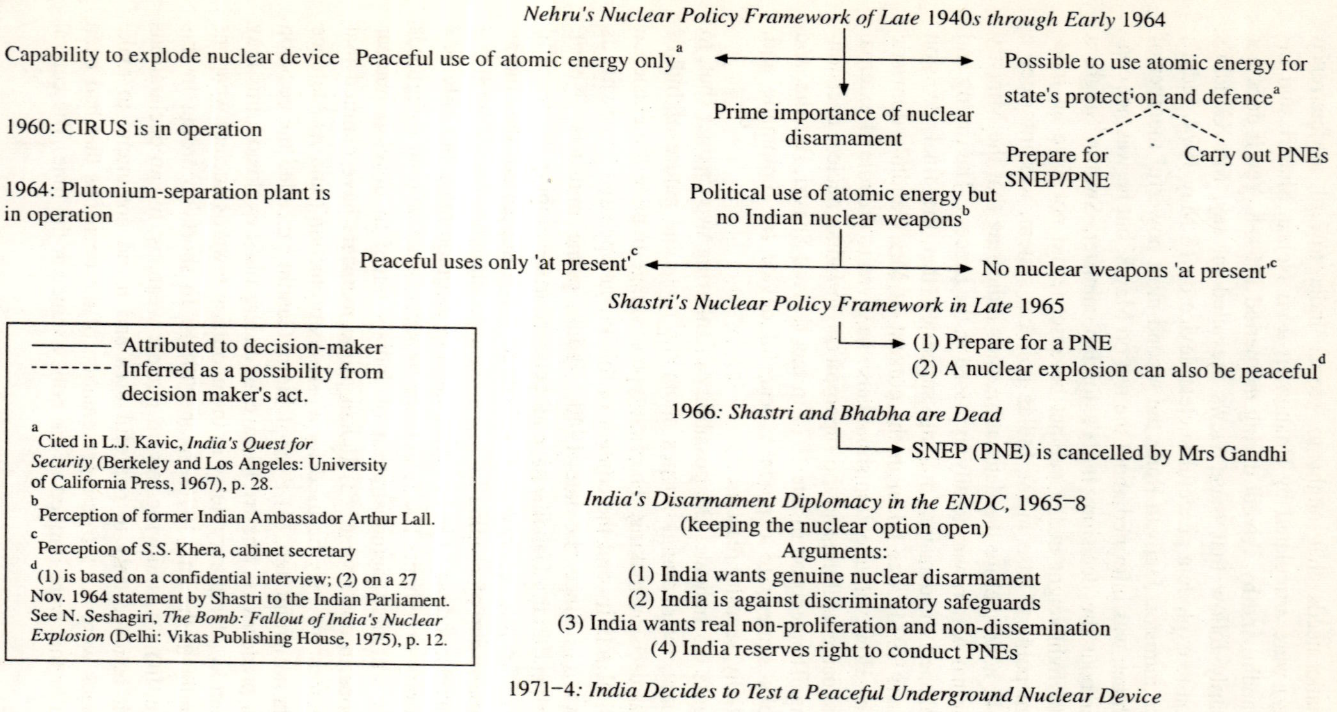

Nehru's Nuclear Policy Framework of Late 1940s through Early 1964

Capability to explode nuclear device Peaceful use of atomic energy only[a]

Prime importance of nuclear disarmament

Possible to use atomic energy for state's protection and defence[a]

Prepare for SNEP/PNE — Carry out PNEs[d]

1960: CIRUS is in operation

1964: Plutonium-separation plant is in operation

Political use of atomic energy but no Indian nuclear weapons[b]

No nuclear weapons 'at present'[c]

Peaceful uses only 'at present'[c]

Shastri's Nuclear Policy Framework in Late 1965

(1) Prepare for a PNE
(2) A nuclear explosion can also be peaceful[d]

1966: Shastri and Bhabha are Dead

SNEP (PNE) is cancelled by Mrs Gandhi

India's Disarmament Diplomacy in the ENDC, 1965–8
(keeping the nuclear option open)
Arguments:
(1) India wants genuine nuclear disarmament
(2) India is against discriminatory safeguards
(3) India wants real non-proliferation and non-dissemination
(4) India reserves right to conduct PNEs

1971–4: India Decides to Test a Peaceful Underground Nuclear Device

---

———— Attributed to decision-maker
- - - - - Inferred as a possibility from decision maker's act.

[a] Cited in L.J. Kavic, *India's Quest for Security* (Berkeley and Los Angeles: University of California Press, 1967), p. 28.

[b] Perception of former Indian Ambassador Arthur Lall.

[c] Perception of S.S. Khera, cabinet secretary

[d] (1) is based on a confidential interview; (2) on a 27 Nov. 1964 statement by Shastri to the Indian Parliament. See N. Seshagiri, *The Bomb: Fallout of India's Nuclear Explosion* (Delhi: Vikas Publishing House, 1975), p. 12.

FIG. 6.5: Shifts in Indian Nuclear Perceptions and Decision-making from Late 1940s to 1974

Source: Compiled by Author.

premise and theme of this image is that India's nuclear behaviour expressed a phasal activity, a gradual movement toward nuclear weapons. Indian nuclear decision-making was seen to mirror that of the other five NWSs. India's nuclear behaviour was seen to be rooted in a nationalistic reaction against the superpowers and China.

The second type of image stresses the theme of retardation, of slower-than-possible progress rather than fast progress in India's nuclear behaviour. The contents of this image contain the following features. (1) While it is true that Nehru talked about the use of atomic energy for peaceful uses and for a state's protection, until early 1964, he did not accept Bhabha's view of the deterrent role of nuclear weapons. (2) While it is true that Shastri sanctioned SNEP (a PNE) after the Indo–Pakistan war in 1965, SNEP was cancelled by Shastri's and Bhabha's successors. (3) While it is true that Ambassador Trivedi in Geneva outlined in 1966 the view that India reserved the right to conduct peaceful nuclear explosions, it should also be noted and underlined that Trivedi was expressing a position that was developed in the context of a political vacuum in New Delhi, namely Mrs Gandhi's tenuous political position in India and the lack of an explicit science-policy preference in India to develop PNEs. Accordingly, the decision to explode a peaceful nuclear device in May 1974 had nothing really to do either with Trivedi's arguments or with Bhabha's suggestion to move India toward a deterrence stance.

In short, the first image traces the roots of the Pokhran I (May 1974) to the late 1940s and particularly to the 1964–5 decisions by Nehru and Shastri. In contrast, the second image traces the roots of the May test to Indira Gandhi's perceptions of the need to improve India's visibility as a consequence of her experience with the great powers, particularly the Soviet Union and the United States during the 1971 Bangladesh crisis. Analytically, therefore, the roots of the decision leading to the May test can be separated, in terms of two distinct time frames: (1) the late 1940s, through 1964–5 through 1971–4 (the first image); and (2) 1971 through 1974 (the second image). The first image attributes influence in decision-making in nuclear policy to the Indian Atomic Energy Commission (Bhabha) and to the Indian Ministry of External Affairs, but the second image does not suggest an input by the ministry. And if in reality the ministry was not involved in decision-making leading up to the May test, the second image asks if the diplomatic aspects were weighed, and if this was done by the Indian prime minister by bypassing the Ministry of External Affairs.

The second image merits a breakdown into two subtypes because there was a gap between the Indian government's statements and informed speculation about the possibilities in India's nuclear behaviour. The first, subtype (a), suggested that the May test was a part of nothing more than a 'scientific experiment', as was stressed repeatedly by the Indian prime minister and other Indian spokesmen. Here the emphasis was only on the development of peaceful nuclear explosives or nuclear explosives engineering (NEE). The rationale for the May test was entirely the development of PNEs, according to this view. A study by an Indian scientist, N. Seshagiri, who worked for the Indian government, stressed exclusively the PNE aspect. It made the following points: The May test was a technological rather than a political decision, and the decision to explode was related to the oil crisis. To quote:

As to the question: What made the Government of India give the final green signal for the underground explosion? One plausible answer might be that, technically speaking, it did not. Even though the government might have asked the scientists to go ahead with the design in 1971 or the following year, a not-so-green signal was flashed in 1973 from the Middle East when gulf oil shot up in price beyond credible limits.

That is,

India had just to wait for the time when the cost-effectiveness index for nuclear technology crossed over that of conventional energy sources. The oil crisis made this possible sooner than we hoped for.[23]

The above noted study makes other points:

Will the bomb be a drain on our resources? Arguments so far have been based on the assumption that the bomb is a war weapon and on building up a nuclear arsenal at the cost of economic development. Often, the cost of the bomb is tied with the cost of a delivery system too ... Such arguments fail if calculations are based on peaceful applications of the bomb. Then bombs are not a drain, but a powerful technological tool that can boost the economy.

India has abjured the production of war bombs preferring peace bombs instead because the country's interest is economic reconstruction and not political power.[24]

Seshagiri made a convincing case along two lines. First, it was desirable to keep an open mind about the potential uses of nuclear explosives engineering in India's economic development and India needed to guard itself against dependence on other advanced industrialized states. Second, his work offered convincing evidence (to a layman at least) that the cost benefits for India of a PNE were better in comparison to those for other PNE states, such as the United States, the USSR, France, China, and Britain. Nevertheless, this study is classed in sub-type (a) because it stresses only the PNE utility of nuclear explosives, and this, of course, was the position of the Indian government at the time.

Yet, there was a reason to conceptualize about subtype (b), namely a strategy that could in due course convert the PNE into weapons use, should the need arise. Seshagiri's work offered an insight into this sub-type. To quote him,

From Kalapakkam to Narora will be another big step leading to almost complete indigenisation. Once this is achieved, India can take up power plant production of the conventional type on a manufacturing scale and perhaps on a war foot-ing.[25]

The foregoing discussion suggested different types of reasons for the reorientation of India's nuclear behaviour in the light of the May 1974 test. Analytically, it was possible to argue that the change was in behaviour rather than in Indian thinking. In fact, Indian speeches provide a sense of continuity—in declarations that India still believed in or preferred nuclear disarmament provided it was universal and non-discriminatory; that India wanted to further the development of peaceful nuclear explosives; and that India did not propose to manufacture nuclear weapons ever.

The reorientation in behaviour was inferred from the unconvincing explanations that the Indian government offered to explain its May 1974 test. The point was not that the focus on PNEs, as a potentiality, was wrong but that the focus was incomplete. A perfectly respectable case could be developed by the Indian government arguing the follow-ing: (1) India at present was not planning to manufacture nuclear weapons because India felt protected by the existing balance of power in Asia. (2) Yet India wished to develop its nuclear option for two reasons: (a) to stay abreast of modern technology in case a later contin-gency required India to manufacture nuclear weapons and (b) to explore the possibilities inherent in the peaceful explosives applications of nuclear energy both for India's economic reconstruction and to explore commercial export possibilities, should these develop later. India as such did not wish to leave the field open to those who had PNE tech-nology. India did not accept the Western logic that it was possible to have PNEs for the NWSs that were parties to the NPT. Such juridical

discrimination was not acceptable to India unless the Western industrialized states themselves renounced PNEs, say in the Strategic
Arms Limitation Talks (SALT). If the argument was that PNEs were at
best a future-oriented activity and their commercial implications should
not be exaggerated, then the logic was that PNEs merited further scientific and theoretical work, nationally and through international agencies.
Thirdly, it was argued, for instance in the NPT Review Conference's
final declaration, that PNE services should be provided by the nuclear-
weapon states. This argument permitted a select group of countries to
continue research and development of PNEs but disallowed others from
getting access to the technology or export of PNE engineering services.
This was objectionable for two reasons. It induced third party dependence on the existing PNE states (nuclear-weapon states) for potential
PNE services. Secondly, it reduced further competition in international
export opportunities that may emerge.

But this was not how the Indian government argued its case. It
stressed points 1 and 2(b) but not 2(a). If Seshagiri's argument (noted
earlier) is taken to reflect the Indian government's posture, the argumentation, taken as a whole, appears to be contrived. The following
overview could, therefore, help present a balanced picture of the various
reasons for the May test of 1974 and the reorientation of India's
strategic stance it implied.

First: Technological determinism obviously underlined the policy
process in India; that is, there had to be a capacity to explode a device
before a government could decide to do so. But it was insufficient as an
explanation for the May 1974 test for the following reasons. (a) If our
preceding analysis of the first image makes sense, and if the work of
the late Leonard Beaton (and John Maddox) about Indian nuclear
developments is acceptable, India had a capacity to explode a device in
the mid-1960s, if not in the late 1950s itself. Yet there appeared to be a
gap in prime-ministerial decision-making during 1966–71. Given this,
two possible explanations are noteworthy. Either the Indian Atomic
Energy Commission was not doing its job or the Indian politicians (particularly the prime minister) did not grasp the scientific trend. Seshagiri
casually dismissed the political aspect of decision-making, but a
reputable Indian scientific journal, *Science Today*, in its issues of June
and September 1974, referred to the question of 'political will'. Thus,
the May test was not an inevitable result of the evolution of Indian
nuclear technology.

Second: Seshagiri also viewed the May test as a response to the 1973 *oil crisis*, which increased the foreign exchange burden on India's oil imports. This aspect merits analysis since India imports two-thirds of its oil, and in the aftermath of the economic effect of the 1971 Bangladesh crisis, the oil crisis posed a real threat to Indian development. Seshagiri states that the decision to test a nuclear device came earlier than expected because the oil crisis offered India the opportunity; that is, the cost benefits of PNEs appeared to become attractive because of the rising costs of importing crude and of developing other conventional power sources. But what this argument really proved was that the study of Indian PNEs became attractive for the Indian Atomic Energy Commission. It also showed that a single test explosion became useful for the Indian Atomic Energy Commission. It may indicate that this was the argument used by the Atomic Energy Commission to the prime minister to justify the experiment. However, the use of a particular argument in the policy process does not prove that the argument was the real one or that it is sound. It only demonstrates that it is politically acceptable.

This review indicates that technological determinism and a desire to find PNE applications for Indian economic development in the coming decade were elements in India's science policy but do not represent self-contained explanations of the entire gamut of Indian nuclear decision-making. Hence attention should be given to other hypotheses, as follows.

Third: The May 1974 test was intended to have *a demonstration effect on the superpowers*; namely, it was meant to signal India's unhappiness with Soviet–US activities that neglected Indian interests—for instance, in the Taskent Agreement (1966) and in the 1971 crisis when India found itself almost diplomatically and militarily isolated from great powers' support. If this hypothesis is valid, the important aspect is that the test occurred after the 1965 and 1971 crises. It was a consequence of Indian perceptions of the implications of an isolated India, given that the great powers' attention was focused primarily on South East Asian and East Asian international relations, and only marginally towards South Asian international relations (except during a military crisis). This hypothesis suggests that even though Nehru sought a lessening of the Cold War, his daughter was concerned about the effect of a détente on third parties like India.

Fourth: This hypothesis suggests that the Indian test was timed before the 1975 NPT Review Conference to remind the parties to the NPT that India's unwillingness to lobby against the NPT, and India's apparent loss of interest in arms control—globally and in South Asia—

did not imply Indian acceptance of a NPT regime. In other words, *the test was a commitment against the NPT*, as distinct from the verbal position India had taken during 1965–8 against the nuclear treaty. As such, the test can be viewed as a climax of India's opposition to the NPT. It was meant to demonstrate that India was not going to behave as if it accepted the treaty. But since India claimed not to need nuclear weapons against China (arguing instead that there was no nuclear threat to India from China), India appeared in fact to interfere with the NPT regime by making its nuclear option internationally visible and technologically demonstrable through the use of sophisticated implosion techniques. Giving visibility to the nuclear option served two purposes: (1) It demonstrated a stronger commitment to nuclear power (explosives capability), thereby revealing a contrast between the Indian position of the 1960s and that of the 1970s. (2) Yet it revealed a difference—a distance—between its nuclear option and a nuclear weapons stance. It is true that the capability for peaceful uses is usable for military purposes, yet, if the explosion signalled a greater commitment to develop the nuclear option, the public declaration against Indian nuclear weapons signalled a non-commitment to a policy of converting the option into a weapons programme. 'Research and development, yes; weapons production, no' seemed to be the Indian messages. In other words, this was a strategy of diplomatic and technological brinkmanship, of letting China make the next move either by staying indifferent to India or by increasing the glacial pace of normalizing India–China relations. In either case, the nuclear factor emerged as a marginal factor in India–China politics. Only the rate of Indian nuclear development seemed to rest on progress in the bilateral relationship once the new thermal reactor in Trombay and the Kalapakkam reactor come into operation.

This hypothesis, however, contained one ambiguity. How much of the timing of the Indian test before the NPT Review Conference was meant to catalyze the arms-control-oriented 'world community' and how much of it involved Indian use of arms-control arguments as a platform to signal to China? If Indian practitioners did not expect meaningful arms control to take place in the SALT dialogue, then Indian demands for real nuclear disarmament were based on an aspiration and did not reflect an expectation. Thus, the Indian logic about horizontal proliferation being a 'consequence' of vertical proliferation required spelling out. If Indians did not expect the USSR and the United States to disarm (Indian statements only suggest that they ought to), surely it was wrong even to imply that India could or would undertake nuclear-weapons production just because there was a Soviet–US nuclear arms race. This type of linkage made little sense because the superpowers did not pose a military threat to India (except in the instance of the coercive naval diplomacy of the *Enterprise* in the 1971 crisis). Also, even if the superpowers did, India could hardly deter them in a credible manner. Rather, *the residual interest of India in arms control centred on the effects of the superpowers' strategic arrangements on China, and the effects of a Chinese nuclear missile build-up on India.* Without attempting to resolve the foregoing ambiguity, we should say that the effect of India's first test was to catalyze disarmament diplomacy to an extent. The test was very much on the minds of official delegates to the NPT Review Conference in May 1975. At the same time, it contained the inherent possibility of Indian weapons development and production *vis-à-vis* China if the strategic environment altered to India's disadvantage in the future.

Whether or not Mrs Indira Gandhi and her advisers actually followed the foregoing logic is not clear, and even with archive material, our speculations may be hard to verify since Indian strategic decision-making appears to be mostly oral. But this review makes one point clear. The May 1974 test was not simply the result of technological determinism, and it was not simply an activity sanctioned only by the Indian AEC. A highly personalized and politicized system such as that in India required the highest political approval, whether this is obtained by the nod of a head or through an elaborate performance in a cabinet meeting to ratify decisions already taken. If the analysis in this chapter has some merit, it indicates that Indian nuclear decision-making is a product of a coalition of political and scientific czarism.

ENDNOTES

1. Pupul Jayakar, *Indira Gandhi*, (New Delhi: Viking Penguin Books India, 1992) is a revealing account of Indira Gandhi's personality and insecurity.

2. For the legislative history of Article III, see Arnold Kramish, 'The Watched and the Unwatched: Inspection in the Non-Proliferation Treaty', *Adelphi Papers*, no. 36 (London: International Institute for Strategic Studies [IISS], June 1967). Also see *International Negotiations on the Treaty on the Nonproliferation of Nuclear Weapons* (Washington, DC: US Arms Control and Disarmament Agency, January 1969); hereafter, *International Negotiations*. On 24 August 1967, the superpowers agreed on a

draft treaty, except for Article III. On 7 December 1967, the ENDC reported substantial progress to the General Assembly and the Disarmament Commission. W. Foster noted (*International Negotiations*, p. 92) that the 'public record did not give a full picture of the progress that had been made'. The United States appeared to believe that a treaty would emerge and prove 'widely acceptable to other countries'. In confidential interviews conducted in early November 1967 in Washington, DC, this author gained the distinct impression that some senior US officials felt that India would sign the NPT because of its dependence on US foreign aid. Agreement on Article III was reached on 18 January 1968.

3. These approaches are identified in Trivedi's speech of 26 October 1965, in US Arms Control Disarmament Agency, *Documents on Disarmament, 1965* (Washington, DC: US Government Printing Office, 1966), pp. 492–5.

4. Confidential interviews, New Delhi, July–August 1973.

5. George Quester, 'India Contemplates the Bomb', *Bulletin of the Atomic Scientists*, January 1970, p. 16.

6. The opinion of the Indian navy is, however, interesting. Admiral A.K. Chatterji noted, on 9 January 1972, as follows: 'Thus, there is likely to be the start of a rapid growth of nuclear power towards the end of the decade. We may also willy nilly become one of them. In the course of time, the navy will thus acquire an additional strategic role of ability to deliver the nuclear bomb.' (Cited in J.V. Schall, 'India Joins the Human Race', *Worldview*, New York, August 1972, p. 34.)

7. The Tripartite Draft Security Council Resolution on Security Assurances (submitted to the ENDC on 7 March 1968 and approved by the Security Council on 19 June 1968 with a vote of ten for, none against, and five abstentions, including India) offered assistance to the NNWSs that signed the NPT. Such assistance was to be 'in accordance with the Charter'. Here the emphasis was also on the 'obligations' of the 'permanent members' of the Security Council.

8. Michael Brecher, *Nehru's Mantle: The Politics of Succession in India* (New York: Praeger Publishers, 1968), pp. 105, 106, 110, 120, 126, 127, and 188. Most of Brecher's interviews (in this particular study) were with politicians, prime minister's secretariat officials, some Indian academics, at least one Indian general, some members of the Indian press, and some foreign correspondents. There is little or no evidence that Brecher was able to discuss India's nuclear policy with officials in the Atomic Energy Department or with Foreign Ministry officials—in India or abroad—who had the responsibility for atomic energy. Moreover, in view of the distortions that appeared in Brecher's analysis of his interviews with Krishna

Menon, it is an open question if the Ministry of External Affairs officials felt the need to discuss matters candidly with Brecher. Brecher's special interest in India's attitudes in Middle Eastern politics, and particularly toward Israel, is well known, and this aspect did not appear to endear him to the Delhi bureaucracy. These observations are based on confidential interviews, New Delhi, June 1971, and in Ottawa during 1968–9.

9. Warren F. Ilchman, 'Political Development and Foreign Policy: The Case of India', *Journal of Commonwealth Political Studies*, vol. 4, no. 3, 1966, pp. 220–1. Ilchman's footnotes have been deleted from this quote.

10. On 25 October, 1964, Bhabha broadcast the following statement over the All India Radio:

One must remember that [no] object . . . is intrinsically good or bad, but the use that is made of it. A minimum supply of nuclear weapons coupled with an adequate delivery system confers on a State the capacity to destroy more or less totally the important cities and industrial centres in another State. There appears to be no means of totally intercepting such an attack, and if even a small fraction of it gets through, entire cities and regions may be totally devastated. The only defence against such an attack appears to be a capability and threat of retaliation. [Cited in A.G. Noorani, 'India's Quest for a Nuclear Guarantee', *Asian Survey*, vol. 7, no. 7, July 1967, p. 490.]

Morarji Desai's views were as follows:

I have often said that nuclear weapons are not weapons of defence; and it is not necessary to have nuclear weapons or a nuclear umbrella for us to get our territory vacated by China. Vacation of territory can be effected by relying on the strength of our conventional army . . . I do not believe in nuclear weapons or nuclear umbrella of any sort. If, however, I were to make a choice, I would rather have my own nuclear weapons than to seek the nuclear umbrella of any outside Power. To ask for such umbrella would merely make us dependent on others, and our independence would be diluted.' [Cited in B. Chatterjee, *The Mind of Morarji Desai* (Bombay: Orient Longmans, 1969), pp. 90–1.]

11. K. Boulding, 'National Images and International Systems', *Journal of Conflict Resolution*, vol. 3, no. 2, 1959, p. 121.

12. D.J. Finlay, Ole R. Holsti, and Richard R. Fagen, *Enemies in Politics* (Chicago: Rand McNally, 1967), p. 96.

13. Michael Brecher, *The Foreign Policy System of Israel* (New Haven, Conn.: Yale University Press, 1972), p. 229 and pp. 4–5; and Michael

Brecher, *India and World Politics: Krishna Menon's View of the World* (New York: Praeger Publishers, 1968), preface, p. vii.

14. This point was repeatedly made by Indian sources in confidential interviews.

15. Points 1 to 3 are from J. Bandyopadhyaya, *The Making of India's Foreign Policy* (Bombay: Allied Publishers, 1970), pp. 123, 125, 131–2, and 137.

16. Ibid., pp. 134–6.

17. Ibid., p. 140.

18. The decision not to sign the NPT was formally a cabinet decision. Confidential interviews, New Delhi, June 1971; also Bandyopadhyaya, The Making of India's Foreign Policy, p. 147.

19. Ibid., pp. 171 and 179.

20. Ibid., pp. 179–80 and pp. 197–8.

21. *Science Today*, September 1974, p. 12.

22. According to R.K. Karanjia's interview with Nehru, the latter's final assessment of India's nuclear policy was as follows:

Q: Then what would be our answer to a Chinese nuclear explosion?
A. I would intensify our campaign for the abolition of everything that has anything to do with the nuclear bomb—all tests, including underground tests, and, of course, the abolition of nuclear warfare by common agreement between the two great powers of America and Russia. Next, I would call Dr Bhabha and ask him to go ahead more vigorously with out projects for the peaceful use of nuclear energy. We are more advanced in nuclear science than China, a fact which should provide our campaign for the outlawing of nuclear war with a great deal of prestige and moral backing.
Q. In any case, would not a Chinese nuclear attack upon India, if it ever comes about, precipitate a global war?
A. Naturally, it would bring about a world catastrophe which is quite unthinkable in modern times. [See R.K. Karanjia, *The Philosophy of Mr. Nehru* (London: George Allen & Unwin, 1966), pp. 161–2.]

23. N. Seshagiri, *The Bomb: Fallout of India's Nuclear Explosion* (Delhi: Vikas Publishing House, 1975), preface to Part I, pp. 14–15.

24. Ibid., pp. 67 and 85 respectively.

25. Ibid., p. 122.

7

Factors and Issues in the Development of Indian Strategic Independence with Nuclear Explosives, 1974–98

Introduction

Between 1974 and 1998, the internal dynamics defined the pattern and process of Indian nuclear decision-making with regard to the military aspect of the nuclear question. This was an uncertain period and Indian decision-making oscillated because of the unstable Indian economic and political conditions. The 1974 test reflected Indira Gandhi's familiarity with the Nehru–Bhabha philosophy on the nuclear question, but difficult internal political and economic conditions subsequently distorted the style and direction of prime ministerial nuclear decision-making. The existence of Western sanctions and the threat of sanctions meant that Indian prime ministers—Indira Gandhi, Rajiv Gandhi, Narasimha Rao, V.P. Singh, Deve Gowda, and I.K. Gujral—did not want further trouble from the West. The fear of Western pressures induced self-restraint in the nuclear and missile decision process. This was a sign of weakness which was nonetheless projected diplomatically as Indian self-restraint—Indira Gandhi had wanted to test again in 1982, and Rajiv Gandhi had an emphasis on delivery systems and had pushed the missile programme. Indian scientists and military experts recognized that India had a political and a diplomatic philosophy about Indian political and strategic independence, but India was losing its independence because it did not possess nuclear explosives for military use. The philosophy provided the base for Indian diplomatic speeches and the theme of autonomy, but the internal political and economic conditions as well as Western pressures and sanctions created a pattern and a process of distorted decision-making. The posture suggested independence of thought; the actual behaviour however, indicated weakness in will and action. The latter condition frustrated the Indian scientists who believed that independence without nuclear explosives was a myth. It was dangerous because it undermined the material (expressed by developed nuclear weapons capability) as well as the psychological (expressed by a cohesive political organization and political will) basis of independence. It was dangerous also because the disconnection between 'independence' and nuclear explosives was based not on Indian (Hindu and Muslim) political and military organization and philosophy since ancient times, but it was rather based on the development of a political culture of foreign-linked Indian factional politics in the strategic sphere after India became independent in 1947. The problem was one of organization of India's nuclear strategy and it was not one of scientific means. It was one of missed opportunities in the development of the explosives base of Indian nuclear strategy.

In this perspective, the issue is not simply about bombs and nuclear non-proliferation. The issues are cultural, strategic, economic, and political. The *cultural and strategic* issue is whether it is possible to have national independence without an infrastructure of chemical–nuclear explosives capacity that is well understood by India's public and by her enemies as well as allies. A related cultural issue is whether it is possible to settle international disputes without armed strength. Is armed strength necessary to organize and settle power struggles among nations? Was G.B. Tilak right in his view that Indian nationalism required armed strength to sustain itself? The issue is also *cultural and political.* On the one hand, it is arguable that economic and technological modernity will help the growth of a stable and peaceful Indian democracy, that is, democracy without property is a sham and a prescription for social and economic instability and possibly a revolution. But on the other hand, Indian democracy allows the proliferation of multiple and foreign-linked coalitions and points of leverage which appear to work against Indian interests, that is, if the development of Indian explosives capability is seen as a national interest. The issue is as well *cultural and economic* in the sense that work on the frontiers of science and technology is essential to gain credibility; and a country usually gains and benefits from technology from abroad if it possesses a credible indigenous base and a record of technological and scientific accomplishment. The US is a superpower not because its political leaders are all bright, but because it possesses a significant scientific and an economic edge, and on this basis it has a military edge. Historically, the US has had an edge in the atomic, space, and electronics spheres, and historically, especially since 1945, the US has tried continuously to discourage or stop others from developing high technology. The issue becomes cultural, strategic, and economic when some Indian economists and journalists push politics that emphasize consumerism and peaceful development and oppose nuclear weapons and missile development. A 'guns versus butter' debate or 'hard statist security versus human security and NGO power' polarity is loaded with cultural, strategic, and economic implications. In this context, the World Bank and IMF agenda is not simply good economics if the message is to leave high technology development and frontier science education in the hands of the 'developed' powers, while the 'developing' societies are encouraged to concentrate on acquisition of borrowed technology and consumerism. So there is a direct connection between say, atomic energy (high technology) and economics if the expectation is realistic that an Indian scientific edge will revolutionize Indian industrial capability.

The issue can also be examined in terms of the problem of a perpetual potential for harassment for a country which lacks the scientific, industrial, and the military means to pursue an independent policy. The French General, Pierre Gallois, made three points forcefully.

It is obvious that the risks involved in the perspective of a nuclear exchange are such that, against a nuclear power, no nuclear guarantee (that is no deterrence) can be given by an 'ally', and this, independently of its strength, stockpile, etc. . . . compared to the strength of the would-be aggressor. No military alliance can be trusted if new weapons may be used.

False protection by an (or two) atomic Powers has always to be paid very heavily. Against what cannot be 'protection', the 'protected' country has to give up a part of its independence, politically, diplomatically and economically. But what it gives is patent while the 'protection' it is supposed to obtain is theoretical and probably vain. You are right to say that the 'so-called guarantees are of theoretical value and, in practice, would place Indian defence in serious jeopardy'. But you could add reduce the freedom of action of your country and impose upon her a policy which may be contrary to her interests.

. . . by their very nature, the new weapons have no other signification than the defence of the national territory against a direct and total menace. They are defensive weapons. On the contrary, it is with conventional ones that the nuclear nations, already secured at home because they possess the new arsenal, are fighting 'local' wars outside their territory, to increase their influence, acquire new interests or protect what they have already obtained. If they want to carry on their hegemonistic designs, they must keep the 'A' and 'H' weapons for themselves, prevent proliferation in such a way that they can always use their conventional forces in the rest of the world. These forces are the instruments of 'continuation of policy by force' and without risks for they know that no local conflict can degenerate and reach their soil for they are atomic and they are, each one, a 'sanctuary'.[1]

The literature argues that liberal democracies do not engage in war with each other.[2] However, even liberal democracies engage in economic warfare in peacetime. For example, the US and Canada, and the US and Japan are military allies and they are democracies. Still, they often use trade pressures and counter-pressures to harass each other. The US and Canada have maintained a sanction policy against India because of Pokhran I (1974) and Pokhran II (1998), even though India is a democracy. The US did the same with the PRC as a part of its policy to contain and isolate the communist regime. The sanctions policy, however, was relaxed when the PRC emerged as a strategic partner of the West from the 1970s onward. Strategic interest rather than democratic ideology appears to explain the difference in behaviour.

In other words, independence in the atomic energy and missile sphere is essential to acquire a deterrent capacity in the military sphere; as well it helps to minimize the harassment potential of sanctions in the sphere of dual-use technology and industry. In this context, arms control and disarmament arrangements are simply a method to stabilize military relationships or relationships of conflict; they are a method to preserve a country's scientific, technological, economic, and strategic edge and to diminish the potential edge of a rival state. So arms control and disarmament arrangements should be assessed for their potential to create a political as well as a technological discrimination. Arms control and disarmament arrangements and proposals are usually double games and with one set of rules for the US and its strategic partner(s); and another set of rules for others. The latter usually creates a line of pressure or harassment potential for the duration of the arms control/disarmament arrangement.

During 1974 to pre-May 1998, Indian nuclear and missile activity and decision-making was shaped by a complex internal and international environment.

(i) Indian governments were *weak coalition governments* (for example

Narasimha Rao, V.P. Singh, Deve Gowda, and I.K. Gujral) and they were elitist and secretive regimes that were vulnerable to foreign-linked factional political and manipulative influences and to international pressures (for example Indira Gandhi and Rajiv Gandhi).

(ii) *International arms control arrangements*—NPT, MTCR, CTBT, Fissile Material Production Ban—were taking shape but they were *politically and technically discriminatory*, and they revealed the emergence of a system of four strategic worlds. The US was the top player. The other members of the P-5 group made the second tier of international strategic players who participated in bilateral and collective strategic bargaining that accommodated and protected their strategic interests, international status, and military capacity. The third tier had three members—Israel, India, and Pakistan. The members of the first and the second tier were the nuclear haves; their nuclear weapons status was recognized by the NPT, an international treaty. The others—members of the third tier and the members of the fourth tier, the 'audience' discussed below, lacked a nuclear weapons status, either because they renounced it, or because they did not claim it. The third tier consisted of regional powers who were not a part of the strategic bargain which was implied in the coexistence among members of the first and the second tiers.

The analogy of the theatre is relevant in discussing these four tiers. The P-5 nuclear states were the principal and secondary characters on the world stage. These were the regime-builders. The audience and the cheer leaders consisted of the majority of the non-proliferation regime members—most of who either lacked nuclear expertise or an ambition to acquire it, or who lacked a need to go nuclear. These were like pigs who either could not fly, or who lacked the need to do so. They were the regime followers who, having gained something materially in the form of aid and diplomatic support from the P-5 states, renounced a desire to function independently in world and regional affairs, and who willingly cast their votes as members of the 'international community' in favour of the regime builders.

(iii) *China and India were diplomatic and military rivals* in South Asian (including the Indian Ocean) and world affairs. This rivalry was likely to continue because both represented two historical civilizations. This rivalry became inevitable and exacerbated by the clash of personalities: J.L. Nehru, Mao Tse-tung, and Chou En-lai saw themselves as great leaders and their egoism affected their behaviour *vis-à-vis* each other. Territorial issues, namely the boundary dispute in the Himalayas and Chinese possession of a part of Kashmir, along with the PRC's refusal to acknowledge Indian sovereignty in Sikkim and Arunachal Pradesh, gave the rivalry a geopolitical focus, as did the possibility that China saw Nepal and the Himalayan kingdoms, in addition to Tibet, as a part of its sphere of influence. This rivalry ended in a military conflict in 1962, but sophisticated Indian strategic planners note that a Sino–Indian military conflict is not inevitable in the future if India possesses a deterrent capability. However, competition between the two in Asia is inevitable and to manage this competition, a level playing field of conventional and nuclear strength is essential to keep the Sino–Indian military gaps manageable. During the 1971–98 period, successive Indian governments, beginning with Indira Gandhi and Rajiv Gandhi, sought to find a diplomatic way to ensure that rivalry did not end in military conflict. The Indian mind, therefore, made a distinction: rivalry was a part of human culture and civilizational difference; it was necessary for progress in different statist and societal spheres. But on the other hand, civilizational differences and rivalries need not necessarily lead to military conflict; and the task of diplomacy and military strategy was to manage the rivalry and to avoid violent conflict if possible. In other words, the China factor had cultural, as well as strategic, importance in Indian thinking during this period. Nevertheless, the Sino–Indian competition was kept under the table; it was not in the open until May 1998.

The scope of Sino–Indian rivalry was enlarged during the period by the establishment of Pakistan's nuclear weapons programme (1972 to present), and by the growth of a special military supply relationship between China and Pakistan since the 1960s; the latter acquired a nuclear and a missile content in the 1980s and the 1990s. By its military supply relationship, China was able to give Pakistan the military capacity to pressure India, to raise the costs of Indian defence, and to keep India locked into the Indo–Pakistani balance/parity paradigm and to push other foreign policy goals.[3]

The scope of rivalry was also enlarged by China's entry into Myanmar in the 1980s, especially after 1988. Myanmar was India's eastern strategic flank. China's ethnic, economic, and military presence in Myanmar and the Bay of Bengal had the potential to undermine India's strategic interests in the region. The development of China's influence in India's western and eastern flanks, along with the continuation of its military presence and contentious claims in the Himalayan region, meant that the rivalry had moved and deepened—from the ideological and the diplomatic arena of the Afro–Asian world to India's strategic neighbourhood: in the north (Himalayan kingdoms and Kashmir), west (Pakistan), east (Myanmar), and the south (the Indian Ocean/Bay of Bengal area). The rivalry was now provocative because it engaged tangible Indian interests in the military, nuclear, missile, and naval spheres, and they challenged India's prestige in the subcontinent as well as in Asia and the non-aligned world.

(iv) The fourth element in the Indian environment was inherent in the history and culture of Indian atomic and space science and governmental organizations. As previous chapters show, since the 1940s, Indian scientific establishments projected a culture of autonomy from political interference in the determination of the research agenda; and the history of Indian nuclear and space science showed an incremental growth of Indian capacity to acquire explosive capability in the atomic sphere, and delivery capability in the space/missile sphere. The constraint against demonstrating an explosives and delivery capability was political, not scientific after the late 1950s. This culture and history was ably helped by India's diplomatic culture, formed and protected by the Indian Ministry of External Affairs; it ensured that Indian atomic establishments did not fall prey to full scope international safeguards and inspections. So even though some Indian nuclear facilities came under Canadian, American, and IAEA safeguards and the Western governments maintained a sanctions regime against India, and the international arms control arrangements had a harassment potential, the *Indian diplomatic culture protected Indian legal and political boundaries, while India's scientific culture enlarged the research boundaries. The two were mutually supportive. During this period, despite the volatility of Indian politics, despite or because of the intensification of pressure on Indian strategic interests by the growth of international arms control arrangements, and despite or because of the growing provocation by China in India's strategic neighbourhood, there was never a discontinuity in Indian efforts to develop nuclear explosive technology since 1974.* The fault line was between the political leadership culture which advocated a triple 'no' stance (no Indian nuclear weapons; no NPT; and no Indian nuclear tests) and India's scientific culture which developed the nuclear explosive technology.

(v) Finally, *Indian military behaviour from 1974 to 1998 revealed a profound shift towards the use of conventional military power to deter and contain Pakistani and Chinese military pressures and to study the nuclear question in the context of India's security environment and In-*

dian strategic planning. Table 7.1 gives a chronology of Indian military attentiveness to the nuclear question even though the official policy was to reject Indian interest in nuclear arms and to reject nuclear deterrence as a basis of national security. The defence-deterrence dilemma existed in Indian thinking in this period. Internal and international conditions up to the 1990s did not allow the Indian government to resolve this dilemma. However, a military culture emerged during this period; it took the armed forces to the margin or the sideline of the Indian nuclear question. The suggestion is *not* that the Indian armed forces became participants in an advocacy to build the bomb or to demonstrate an atomic explosive capability. The armed forces remained preoccupied with the development of the Indian defence mechanism in relation to Pakistan, China, and the Indian Ocean. Rather the suggestion is that this period saw the incremental embrace of the idea that the fear of punishment induced caution in the enemy's mind, and demonstrable conventional and nuclear strength was therefore essential to check the interventionist impulses of the enemies. Indian defence budgets and annual reports of the Indian ministries of defence and external affairs up to 1997 showed a preoccupation with conventional defence capabilities and threat perceptions. But in hindsight, this period saw the growth of thinking within the Indian armed forces about the implications of the nuclear question for Indian security. The conventional defence versus nuclear deterrence dilemma was settled by Pokhran II, but the process or the preparation for this outcome took shape during the 1970s to 1990s period. Note, however, that the scientific, diplomatic, and the military cultures were functioning generally in a compartmentalized manner. There is no public evidence to indicate coordination between the Indian armed forces and the Indian atomic organizations on the nuclear question in the 1970s and the 1980s. There is, however, evidence of coordination between the Indian diplomatic and atomic agencies in activities in international organizations, for example in the IAEA in particular. Only in the 1990s did signs emerge of coordination between the armed forces and missile development work because the latter has been under the auspices of the Minister of Defence.

Figure 7.1 recaps the parameters of the complex Indian decision-making environment before May 1998.

Between 1974 and May 1998, the internal dynamics of Indian nuclear decision-making occurred in the context of Figure 7.1. Five themes or factors shaped the post-May 1974–pre-May 1998 Indian nuclear decision process.

TABLE 7.1
Indian Military and the Nuclear Question

Period	Action in Response to the Nuclear Questions
1974	Indian defence laboratory involved in assembly of the nuclear device (Pokhran-I).
'Soon after' the 1974 test	The Indian Army made the 'initial foray' into nuclear planning, targeting, and doctrine. The first unofficial manual on the use of nuclear weapons was introduced by General K. Sundarji, later the Army Chief.
1978–81	Pakistan started uranium enrichment.*
May to August 1981	Indian College of Combat (Mhow) under General K. Sundarji published two major papers on nuclear deterrence (see source below).
1987	Pakistan acquired and advertised its nuclear weapons capability.
1988	Indian Air Force began test bombing exercises.

*According to Dr. A.Q. Khan, the head of Pakistan's nuclear weapons programme, 'The first enrichment was done on 4 April 1978. The plant was made operational in 1979, and by 1981 we were producing substantial quantities of uranium. Until 1982–3 we were producing low-enriched uranium and from 1983, weapon-grade uranium which is more than 90% enriched.' Interview with Chief Weapons Scientist, 31 May, *the Observer,* UK, 31 May 1998, reprinted in *Disarmament Diplomacy*, London, UK, no. 26, May 1998, p. 14.

Sources: 1. A.K. Mehta, Major-General (retired), 'Dialogue Seen As Best Way to Avoid a Nuclear Conflict', *India Abroad*, New York, vol. 14, no. 38, 19 June 1998, p. 2.
2. 'Effects of Nuclear Asymmetry on Conventional Deterrence', Combat Papers No. 1, College of Combat, Mhow, India, May 1981, 94 pages.
3. 'Nuclear Weapons in Third World Context,' Combat Papers No. 2, College of Combat, Mhow, India, August 1981, 72 pages.

(i) *Indian political leaders were weak,* because of weaknesses in domestic economic and political conditions within India, and because of weakness of political will and confused strategic thinking.[4] *Indian political leaders were reluctant to develop and articulate a public policy that saw the connection between Indian independence and explosives capability in the fields of conventional and nuclear armament.* (ii) *During this period, the harassment potential of discriminatory international arms control arrangements was increasing. Indian experts*

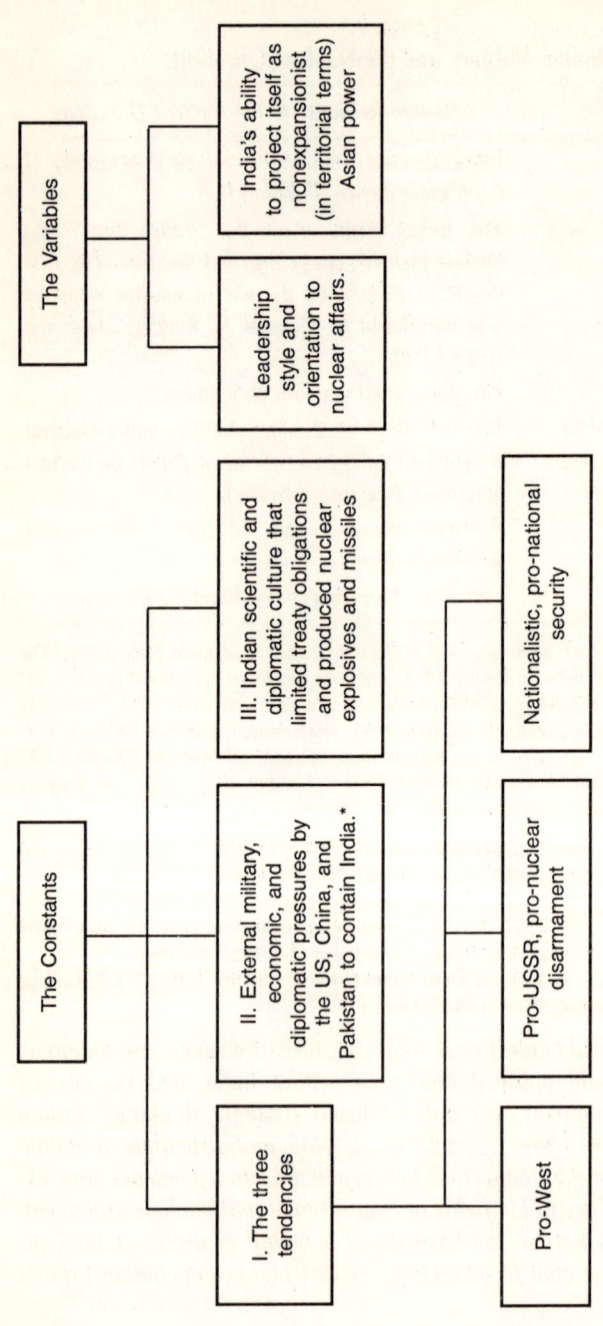

FIG. 7.1: Recapping the Historical Parameters of Indian Nuclear Decision-making, 1947–74

*Containment of India meant that the 'Indo-Pakistan military and diplomatic balance/parity was the norm, and India was to be recognized only as South Asian state'. Containment implied a limitation of India's military capacity to defend its regional and global interests, and to limit its prestige within the subcontinent and globally.

recognized the elements of discrimination and harassment. They com-plained about it in international conference diplomacy, but they did not alter India's 'no-nuclear weapons' stance to challenge the international trend to corner India. The NPT and associated arrangements in the non-proliferation regime were openly discriminatory. The Treaty validated the legality of five nuclear weapons states and it legitimized their right to bear nuclear arms; conversely, it delegitimized the sovereign right of others to use all military measures for self-defence. The NPT was politi-cally discriminatory because it created two different sets of obligations and rights. The non-nuclear weapon states got the obligations to disarm and the obligation never to seek nuclear arms except when supreme in-terests require a renunciation of NPT obligation with three months notice. The nuclear weapons states got the rights; their obligation to move towards nuclear disarmament was vague, it lacked a time frame, and it was contrary to the declared military doctrines and the national interests of the five nuclear powers. The NWSs had an obligation under the NPT not to assist non-nuclear powers to acquire nuclear explosives capability. But there was no independent mechanism to verify such as-sistance in cases where the NWS either provided such help to their al-lies or looked the other way. There was no mechanism for the so-called 'international community' to enforce the NPT rules against the nuclear-weapon P-5 states. There was, however, a mechanism, through the IAEA, to apply the NPT rules against those non-NWSs who voluntarily accepted the treaty obligations of the NPT. Those who did not were nevertheless subjected to bilateral and international pressures to comp-ly. The full meaning of the harassment potential of international arms control arrangements was revealed in the manner of UNSCOM's end-less 8-year-old campaign to disarm Iraq, the inconclusiveness of this campaign, and the unwillingness of the United Nations Special Com-mission (UNSCOM) to bring closure to the issue because UNSCOM was actually a cover for the US spies, and spies require prolonged cover rather than closure to an issue. In other words, harassment is inevitable in an arms control arrangement which relies on international inspection and mistrust of independent minded nations.

The CTBT was the second major international arms control arrange-ment which was formulated during the 1974 to May 1998 period and it was finalized in 1996. This agreement avoided the problem of political discrimination of the NPT but raised the issue of technical discrimina-tion. A permanent ban on testing of nuclear explosives except in laboratory conditions had the effect of freezing the NNWS on the technological curve on the date the CTBT came into effect (on or after 30 September 1999). For India, the harassment potential came from two directions: (a) if India continued its refusal to accept this treaty, then an international conference was expected to formulate measures against the 'rogue' nation(s) because India's adherence was required by the CTBT's Entry into Force clause; (b) even if India signed on, it was inevitable, in the aftermath of the Iraqi experience with the UNSCOM, that international inspectors and spies would descend on Indian military and scientific establishments to verify Indian compliance with CTBT obligations. Those who have made a career of arms control and international inspections are expected to promote their personal and institutional interests; they are not expected to close the file and legislate themselves and their constituents out of existence. This is elementary bureaucratic politics. One should think of international arms control organizations as employment agencies—with a long shelf life like the deadly plutonium.

(iii) *The China factor grew in importance in Indian strategic calculations during this period but India avoided engaging China in an open competition; it did not challenge the PRC's provocative activities against Indian strategic interests and it did not create a situation whereby the PRC had to take India seriously.* China pursued a deceptive strategy *vis-à-vis* India in this period. Its public line highlighted the importance of a foreign policy of peace because China sought peaceful economic development and claimed it wanted peace in its neighbourhood; its military modernization, it claimed was its lowest priority. With India, it claimed to want a tranquil border and good neighbourly relations. Since the late 1980s, it engaged India in border talks and the two sides agreed that the concept of the Line of Actual Control (LAC) should be the basis of a border settlement. Both sides also signed agreements concerning border trade, economic, and scientific cooperation in 1996–7.[5]

But other realities impacted the Indian strategic psyche. China had a thirty year old friendship with Pakistan, which started in the mid-1950s when China declared that it had no conflict with Pakistan but it had one with India. This friendship included a solid military supply relationship, involving tanks and aircraft, since the 1960s. Taking into account the history of the Indo–Pakistani military conflict and diplomatic rivalry and the prospect of a long-term rivalry with India, despite its acceptance of the NPT and its desire to follow the MTCR guidelines, China continuously helped Pakistan build its nuclear and missile capability. What was China's motive in doing so *vis-à-vis* India?

The China factor impacted India's strategic psyche from two other directions. Beginning in the early 1980s, China developed its diplomatic, economic, and military links with Myanmar. Chinese Yunnanese moved into northern Myanmar and developed a commercial and ethnic presence. Chinese military personnel were active in road building in strategic parts which was justified in terms of building roads for Chinese and Burmese commerce, but which also had the potential to impact on the Indian north–east border areas where China had territorial claims. Finally, Chinese naval personnel were active in developing radar and low frequency communication facilities in the Bay of Bengal, which were close to Indian naval facilities. As well, it had an agreement (not implemented thus far) to build a submarine base in a Burmese island. The China–Myanmar ethnic–commercial–military–naval axis was emerging in the context of China's belief that India should not become an Indian Ocean power, and that India posed a danger as a regional hegemon. In short, this period revealed China's increasing encirclement of India by diplomatic and military means, and by the build-up of a PRC–US–Pakistan coalition—with support from the 'international community'. As before, the aim was to corner India in subcontinental, as well as global affairs.[6]

(iv) *Even though Indian political leaders were reluctant to embrace nuclear deterrence as a strategic necessity for India in response to the trends in international non-proliferation arrangements and in China's India policy after Pokhran I (May 1974), there was nevertheless ceaseless scientific activity in Indian nuclear energy and space/missile establishments.* The aim was to acquire an indigenous explosive capability in the nuclear sphere. Table 7.2 shows the pattern of scientific activity. At the same time, diplomatic work by the Ministry of External Affairs ensured that India remained relatively free of international treaty obligations and multilateral arrangements that could limit the Indian development of explosive and missile capabilities. During this period, India's diplomatic posture remained anti-NPT, pro-general nuclear disarmament, and it opposed the P-5 and G-8 strategy which supported and sought nuclear *reductions* by the nuclear powers rather than a realistic plan or a commitment to *eliminate* nuclear weaponry. India also opposed the US–Canada–China–Pakistan strategy to find ways to cap, roll back, and eventually eliminate India's nuclear weapon and missile programmes. The pattern of scientific activity and the thrust of Indian

TABLE 7.2
Pattern of Indian Scientific Activities in the
Nuclear and Missile Spheres

Scientific Activity	Year	Weapons Capability	Safeguards Status	Foreign Collaborator
Nuclear weapons production in covert manner occurred	1974–7 and 1986	Yes	Nil	Nil
Plutonium–uranium mixed oxide fuel was fabricated	1979	Potential	Nil	Nil
Heavy water plants established	1980s	Potential	Nil	Swiss, French, West German companies
Space launch	1980	Potential	Nil	
Tarapore reprocessing	1982–4	Yes	Partial	Nil
Purnima II experiment set up using U-233	1984	Potential	Nil	Nil
FBTR using plutonium and natural uranium	1985	Potential	Nil	Nil
Dhruva experiment set up using heavy water/natural uranium	1985–8	Potential	Nil	French aid
Kamini II and Purnima-III used U-233	1988	Potential	Nil	Nil
Uranium enrichment work started	1984	Potential	Nil	Nil
Missile testing (i) Prithvi (ii) Agni	1988 1989	Yes	Nil	Nil

nuclear diplomacy indicated the emergence of nationalistic scientific
and diplomatic cultures. Their attitudes and institutional interests converged even though the two cultures were compartmentalized in the organizational charts. However, despite the emergence of a strong
bureaucratic coalition, these nationalistic cultures were vulnerable to

decisions by confused and weak Indian politicians and to, domestic as well as international, pressures on the political leaders and the Indian bureaucracy. This vulnerability revealed the vitality of foreign-linked factional activity in the nuclear sphere during this period. The factional activity was represented by anti-nuclear Indian and international NGOs and by Indian and international economic reformers. The reformers were anti-nuclear. They advocated the primacy of an interdependent global economy where economic gain and international economic cooperation was more important than nuclear nationalism. Figure 7.2 outlines the competition and the balance of power of these diverse forces during the period, that is, before the series of Indian tests in May 1998. Figure 7.2 indicates the contention between two coalitions. The first coalition comprised (A), (B), and (C). The second comprised (D), (E), and (F). The two coalitions had radically different policy positions. The first sought India's nuclear disarmament. The second, a bureaucratic coalition, sought India's nuclearization—either overt bomb and missile development or, at the least, preservation of the Indian nuclear weapons option. Both coalitions pressed the 'weak' Indian political leaders to adopt their respective positions. We emphasize here the necessity to examine the interface between shifting alignments and balance(s) of power within India, and between the Indian and outside powers. Here the standard 'domestic politics' and foreign policy' distinction or level of analysis is considered meaningless in our analysis because in this case international politics is seen to affect Indian politics and Indian politics is seen to affect external relationships.

(v) Historically, the Indian armed forces maintained an arms-length approach to the nuclear question. In part, this was the result of their preoccupation with the modernization of Indian conventional armament in the aftermath of the debacle with China in 1962, and in response to Pakistani military activities in the border areas. In part, India's political culture since the Nehru years, and the organization of the Indian defence machinery after 1947, precluded military initiative and participation in the decision process unless it was called upon to offer military advice on a military question. Nehru was personally anti-military even as he was enthusiastic about the role of atomic energy in India's development; and as noted earlier, he recognized its built-in defence use 'if necessary'. Between 1947 and May 1998, the 'defence use' was not deemed to be necessary; hence, the formal participation of the Indian military was not required. These are the reasons that India's

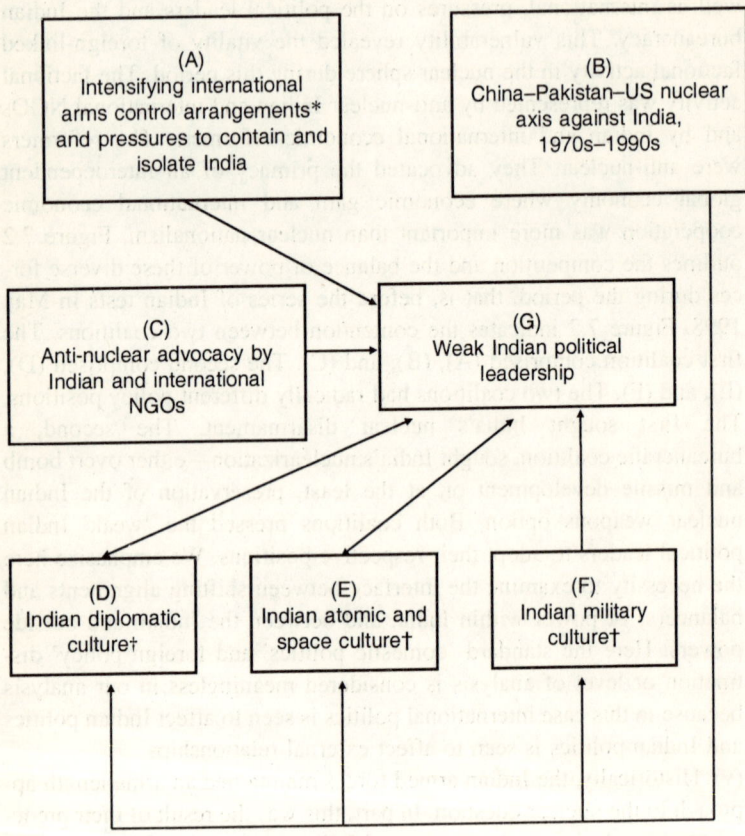

FIG. 7.2: The Setting and Framework of Indian Nuclear Decision Process, 1974
to pre-May 1998

⟶   Pressure

⟷   Interactive influences

*(a) Growth of NPT Regime; (b) Indefinite NPT Extension; (c) CTBT agreement.
†'Culture' in each case refers to a philosophy and policy that favoured India's nuclearization and that opposed international nuclear controls against India.

nuclear debates (which were in-house and secret in the 1950s and became public since the 1960s) involved economists, political leaders, civilian governmental and academic strategists, NGOs, atomic scientists, and foreign governments, but there is no public record of active participation in the Indian debate by members of the Indian armed forces. Since the Nehru years and up to May 1998, the nuclear question was a diplomatic and a scientific issue; hence, the input of the Indian military agencies was not sought by Indian political leadership, and it was not offered, or volunteered, by the Indian military. Pokhran I brought the Indian defence establishment into the picture in the sense that the engineering of the device took place in a defence laboratory, while the designing was done by Indian atomic scientists. However, the decision to test was political. Because it was a 'peaceful test' the input came from the Indian Atomic Energy establishment, not the Indian military. Even the Indian Ministry of External Affairs was not consulted by Prime Minister Indira Gandhi about the necessity, the timing, and the diplomatic preparation to manage the diplomatic fallout of Pokhran I.

The Indian military became engaged with the nuclear question, and specifically with the question of nuclear deterrence, in the early 1980s. This occurred in the context of nuclear developments in Pakistan (1970s onwards), the emergence of the Sino–Pakistan military supply relationship, and the tolerance of Pakistani nuclear weapons activity by the US because of Pakistan's frontline status in the Afghanistan war in the 1980s. Table 7.1 outlined the chronology of Indian military actions in response to the nuclear question; the Indian military's assessment of the importance of nuclear deterrence is outlined in a following section. Note that the Indian military's actions took place despite the rejection in public of nuclear deterrence as a doctrine and policy of the Indian government.

The development of the Indian military's interest in the nuclear question informally enlarged the decision-making structure and process. It also revealed the rising importance of a military culture in Indian deliberations on the nuclear question. Although this military culture was compartmentalized from the diplomatic and the scientific cultures—there was no formal coordination between the military establishment and the scientific and diplomatic establishments—it nonetheless broadened the bureaucratic base of the support for Indian nuclear weaponization.

In Figure 7.2, the weak Indian political leadership was vulnerable to international pressure to maintain a non-nuclear weapons position (that is, to decide against nuclear testing) and to curb the testing and deployment of the Prithvi and Agni missiles. These pressures were cast in a US government formula, articulated publicly by the US ambassador to India, T. Pickering, that the US expected India to first cap its nuclear programme, then roll it back, and eventually eliminate it. Figure 7.2, like Figure 7.1, had three contradictions. First, although India advertised its nuclear weapon option before and after Pokhran I, successive Indian political leaders insisted on a 'no testing', 'no weapons' policy. Without testing and eventual production and deployment, a nuclear weapons option was practically meaningless as an instrument of statecraft. The second contradiction was between the Indian government advocacy of the importance of total nuclear disarmament and the existence of diplomatic, scientific, and military cultures within India that debated the importance of maintaining a nuclear weapons option (keep it but do not use it and do not provoke the great powers) on the one hand, and exercising it through overt Indian weaponization activity ('use it or lose it' and do not bother about great powers' hypocritical reactions) on the other hand. The third contradiction was between Indian governmental insistence that a global approach was required to deal with the nuclear question and the pattern of Indian diplomatic and scientific activities since the Nehru years which highlighted the 'built-in defence' use of nuclear weapons option against regional enemies. The involvement of the Indian military since the 1980s highlighted the importance of regional imperatives and a regional approach in dealing with the nuclear issue. These contradictions were not addressed in the 1974 to pre-May 1998 period until the indefinite extension of the NPT (1995) and the CTBT agreement (1997), along with regional nuclear developments, precipitated a shift in the Indian debate.

It is debatable whether the CTBT by itself forced India into the Pokhran II tests. We judge it to be the 'final straw which broke the camel's back'—the other straws being the challenge to Indian strategic interests posed by China's India and Pakistan policies, by Pakistani nuclearization, by the US tolerance of Sino–Pakistani nuclear arrangements which contradicted the non-proliferation regime rules, and by the general indifference of the 'world community' to Indian strategic dilemmas. Our analysis hypothesizes that the balance of bureaucratic power was shifting during the post-Pokhran I and pre-May 1998 period. The shift acknowledged the utility of nuclear deterrence in the context of a fluid strategic neighbourhood whose inner circle included China, Pakistan, Myanmar, the Bay of Bengal, and whose outer circle included

Central Asia, South East Asia, and the sea lanes from the Persian Gulf to the South China seas. In both circles, the US and China were key players. Their engagement required stable political institutions, economic and conventional strength, as well as nuclear and missile power. In other words, *while the contradictions were not dealt with in a proactive manner by the weak Indian political leaders, the internal balance of power had shifted towards the nuclear deterrence school during this period.* The CTBT agreement—whose main hidden agenda was to isolate India—and the rise of the pro-nuclear, nationalistic BJP became the two immediate causes of Pokhran II but the story was bigger than these two precipitating events.

The Military's Changing Attitudes on the Nuclear Question and Space Developments

The shift in the internal balance of power on the nuclear question was facilitated by the injection of professional Indian military opinion in the Indian decision process, and by the familiarity of the BJP leadership with the complexities of the nuclear question and its implications for India. Before he became the Prime Minister, Vajpayee was a part of a special parliamentary team that dealt with atomic energy. He knew the nuances of Indian atomic affairs. He obviously knew about the BJP's position and interests and the spectrum of opinion on the nuclear question among Indian political parties. Moreover, with many sympathizers in different branches of the Indian government (for example intelligence services, home ministries, and the armed forces), the BJP had a sense of the mood of the Indian public.

The story of the projection of Indian military opinion in the Indian nuclear debate and decision process was a part of the hidden dynamics of the 1974–98 period. The Vajpayee/BJP side of the story also took shape in this period and it burst on the national and the international stage with the Vajpayee decision to conduct the tests in May 1998. These two tracks emerged in a parallel manner during this period in the context of the parameters outlined in Figure 7.2. They came together in May 1998 in the form of the Indian tests and the articulation of India's position as a nuclear weapon state and a new recruit to the doctrine of nuclear deterrence. The role of the attitudes of the Indian military about the nuclear question is extremely important in India's nuclear history. Since 1947, atomic energy was a diplomatic issue which was managed by the Ministry of External Affairs and by the Prime Minister's Office because of Nehru's personal interest in the subject. Since 1947, it was also a scientific question which was addressed in the Indian Atomic Energy Commission where Bhabha pushed the nuclear agenda with Nehru's strong support. But at this time, the issue did not engage the Indian military, because the military was engaged with the problem of defence against Pakistani ambition in Kashmir, and later with the question of military defence against China. The Indian military agenda was dominated by the issue of conventional defence. Since the 1960s, Indian scientists developed the agenda regarding India's space activities but this did not engage the Indian military for the reason given above. Hence, Indian space development during the 1960s and the 1970s was essentially a programme in the hands of civilian scientists but it had a dual use, that is, it had civil as well as potential military applications. Thus, the Nehru philosophy about the built-in defence use of the nuclear programme applied to the Indian space programmes as well. The Indian military became engaged in the nuclear question in the 1980s after India's conventional defence mechanism had been modernized and the Indian military felt secure about its ability to wage conventional war against Pakistan and China, and after China's and Pakistan's nuclear developments and their implications for Indian security developed a salience in Indian professional and public opinion.

General K. Sundarji stands out as the key articulator of the views of the Indian military officers on the nuclear question. As Commandant of the College of Combat (Mhow), Lt. Gen. Sundarji initiated a 'seminar by post' inviting commentary by members of the Indian armed forces. The seminar findings were published in May and August 1981. The problem was defined in the following way.

Statement of the Problem

General	A state with no aggressive designs, i.e., a *'status-quo* power,' generally opts for a Strategy of Deterrence. A non-nuclear weapon *status-quo* power relies on a Strategy of Deterrence with conventional forces, in the field of Military Strategy.
The Problem	Does a situation of Nuclear-Weapon-Asymmetry degrade the effectiveness of Conventional Deterrence? If it does, how can the non-nuclear-weapon state, minimise or eliminate such degradation?[7]

Although a small minority of seminar participants felt that conventional deterrence was possible in a situation of China–India and Pakistan–India nuclear asymmetry, the majority concluded as follows:

How does a nation maintain *status-quo* on the military field? It is by having such weapons as your adversary has. And whether it is a 7.62 mm rifle or an atom bomb, it is just a weapon. Certainly, the chariots and swords of the past cannot be a match to the tanks and guns of today. The same rule is applicable to conventional and nuclear weapons. If your adversary has these weapons, you have no choice but to have them too. It is only in such a case that *status-quo* can be maintained. If you do not want your adversary to use nuclear weapons, have nuclear weapons yourself. This will be a proper deterrence. The aim of deterrence is not only to deter the adversary, but also to 'teach a lesson' if he ever ventures to be belligerent. But in case of nuclear asymmetry, 'no lesson can be taught'. The fear of nuclear weapons with the adversary, will deter one from launching an offensive. Deterrence is not measured in *your* capabilities alone, but it also takes into account the projected or estimated strength of the adversary.[8]

This became the received wisdom in the Indian armed forces. It produced a major shift in the internal balance of power in the decision process as per our outline in Figure 7.2. After he became the Army Chief, General Sundarji remained active in the nuclear debate and in India's decision process. After his retirement and before the May 1998 nuclear tests, Sundarji outlined the foundation of an undeclared Indian nuclear deterrence posture under an ambiguous nuclear cover. He specified the following points in a public way.

The absence of a visible strategic nuclear force, or an articulated doctrine, or elaborate C3 does not mean that a force capable of carrying out a first or second strike is not yet ready on the minimum deterrent scale.

The fact that no massive reorganisation of conventional forces has taken place or no revised doctrine has been articulated does not mean that nuclear weapons have not yet been fielded.

The fact that no physical testing has gone on does not mean that nuclear weapons are not yet ready to be fielded, or that they would be ineffective if fielded.[9]

No Indian political or military leader questioned Sundarji's comments on the nuclear question.

Indian Space Developments

Today India possesses missiles but it is important to recognize that, originally, the initial emphasis was on the development of satellite launch and communications capability. The aim was to use satellites for mass communication and education. There is no denying that once a country acquires space launch capability, it also gains missile launch capability. So the Indian programme had a built-in missile dimension. Three features defined the Indian space programme. In its origins, it was open rather than a secret programme. Secondly, it moved from satellites to missiles. Thirdly, the programme has had limited foreign input. In contrast, China's programme started as a missile programme and was built on Soviet rocket technology. Chinese space/missile launches laid stress on the payload and the recovery capability, which are the inherent components of missiles. It moved from missiles to satellites. Today, China's missile programme and satellite programme are ahead of India's because of a larger budget and a heavy input of foreign technology at the outset. Japan too is ahead of India in the space/missile sphere. It benefited from its alliance with the US and the transfer of the US rocket technology. Despite these differences, the Indian space strategy was to emphasize the acquisition of communications and remote sensing capacity in its space work. The Indian progress has been good. Having developed its space capability, India moved into the missile sphere but it did so without *much external* help. So the pattern of Indian space and missile development during the 1970s and the 1980s shows a strategy to develop dual-use capabilities in Indian hands. For example, remote sensing technology helps geological work but it also provides surveillance capability. The latter ties in with the concept of open skies and arms control verification. Rocket engines and technology are needed for geostationary launches, and these are big business. This ties in with the concept of free trade, and secondly, it also ties with the utility of such technology in missile development. Table 7.3 shows the pattern of Indian space developments.

TABLE 7.3
Pattern of Indian Space Developments

Year	Developments
1972	The Department of Space and the Space Commission set up by the Government of India to promote the development and application of space science and technology for identified national socio-economic tasks. Professor Dhawan takes charge.
1972–6	A number of airborne remote sensing experiments conducted for surveying earth resources. Several indigenous sounding rockets were tested and flown for scientific experiments. A number of elements of solid propulsion, propellant, and avionics systems developed on laboratory scale. Development of a launch range at Sriharikota begun. Tracking station experiments with liquid propulsion including a major technical know-how arrangement with a French company made.
1975	The first Indian satellite, *Aryabhata*, launched on 19 April 1975 from the Soviet Union.

(Contd.)

Table 7.3 contd.

1975–6	The first major space application programme, the Satellite Instructional Television Experiment (SITE) conducted during August 1975 to July 1976 using the US satellite, ATS-6.
1977	The Satellite Telecommunication Experiments Project (STEP) carried out from the middle of 1977 to 1979 using the Franco-German satellite, *Symphonie.*
1979	The second Indian satellite, a satellite for earth observations, *Bhaskara-I,* launched on 7 June 1979 from the Soviet Union.
1980	SLV-3, India's first satellite launch vehicle, puts the *Rohini* satellite into a near-earth elliptical orbit from Sriharikota on 18 July 1980.
1981	India's first experimental geostationary communication satellite, APPLE, successfully launched by the European Space Agency's (ESA) *Ariane* launch vehicle from Kourou, French Guyana, on 19 June 1981. India's second satellite for earth observation, *Bhaskara-II,* launched from the Soviet Union on 20 November 1981.
1983	The second developmental flight of SLV-3 successfully conducted from Sriharikota on 17 April 1983 and RS-D-2 satellite orbited. INSAT-1B, India's multipurpose domestic satellite, launched on board the US space shuttle, *Challenger,* on 30 August 1983. A major national seminar to define National Natural Resources Management System (NNRMS) conducted, arriving at a national consensus preparing ground for the government decision on NNRMS made in early 1985.
1984	The first joint Indo–Soviet manned space mission launched on 3 April 1984. Professor Dhawan retires at the end of September 1984 and Professor U.R. Rao, who was Director, Indian Space Research Organization (ISRO) Satellite Centre, takes over the same unitary structure from 1 October 1984.

Sources: 'Atomic Energy and Space Research: A Profile for the Decade 1970-80', Atomic Energy Commission, Government of India, 1970; Y.S. Rajan, 'Management of the Indian Space Program', *Sadhana,* Academy Proceedings in Engineering Sciences, vol. 12, Part III, March 1988, pp. 289–305, especially pp. 290–1; Y.S. Rajan, 'Development of Space Technology: Indian Experience and Future Prospects', *Current Science,* vol. 62, no. 8, 25 April 1992 (reprinted as a pamphlet, 16 pages).

India's Technical and Decision-making Strength Compared

This review of India's nuclear and space activities shows a pattern and process of incremental development of a nuclear weapons and missile delivery capability. The review also indicates the emergence of the Indian military's voice in nuclear affairs, albeit as a low-key analytical voice rather than as an activist in the Indian nuclear debate. The interest of the Indian military in the military uses of atomic energy and space-launch capability created the basis of coalition-building involving the Indian atomic science, space, diplomatic, and military constituencies. This coalition consolidated and enlarged the political space within Indian body politik for the nuclear weapons option policy, and it created the basis for the subsequent conversion of the covert nuclear weapons option policy into the overt nuclear weapons demonstration and development policy. But the latter change was not a given in the post-Pokhran I and pre-Pokhran II period.

Instead, the period revealed two stories. There is no doubt that India's nuclear and missile/space programmes faced internal inefficiencies and delays caused in part by external sanctions and pressures. Nevertheless, a delayed programme implementation was one side of the Indian nuclear and space/missile story. The technical base of the Indian nuclear and missile/space activities grew from a zero level in the early 1950s to a sophisticated, broad-based programme in about forty years. That is, the technical achievements show development and strength. However, on the other hand, Indian nuclear decision-making shows a pattern of vacillation and weakness. This was the other side of the story. This is evident from a number of signs. Since the mid-1960s, there was an ongoing internal nuclear debate that oscillated between the pressures and advocacy to join the international non-proliferation regime and the pressures and advocacy to go nuclear overtly. The nuclear posture remained poorly articulated with an emphasis on nuclear disarmament/anti-discriminatory strategies in Indian diplomacy. The posture showed an over-emphasis on the value of a global non-discriminatory non-proliferation regime and an under-emphasis, indeed, limited public emphasis on Chinese, Chinese–Pakistani, US/Western–Pakistani nuclear activities and relationships that negatively affected Indian diplomatic and military interests. These signs did not indicate clarity and strength in the decision-making. The issue here was not that of secrecy. China and India are both secretive in their decision-making processes. But in nuclear affairs, China's nuclear posture and decision process demonstrates strength in the acquisition and maintenance of a minimum nuclear deterrent and in the articulation of a posture of no first use. The Government of Indian remained publicly evasive about the real determinants of its nuclear policy during this period, but the situation was dynamic behind the scene.

The pattern of Indian activities in the nuclear, space, and missile spheres point to four separate conclusions concerning this period. Even with a nuclear armed China in India's strategic environment, India was unwilling to pay the price of going nuclear overtly, partly because of the fear of the US and Soviet pressures, and partly because of the lack of bureaucratic consensus about the strategic value of an overt nuclear status. Here, the ongoing internal debate suggested organizational disunity, and/or weak political leadership in strategic affairs, and/or honest differences of ministerial and bureaucratic judgements about the nature of India's security problem and the value and form of a nuclear response. On the other hand, India was unwilling to abandon its nuclear weapons option. Here India's nuclear, space, and missile history revealed technical and decision-making strengths to develop and to maintain the weapons option without a formal declaration. This position enjoyed bureaucratic and ministerial support and consensus.

When the Indian policy elite was confronted by signs of Pakistani nuclearization (1979 onwards), of US tolerance of Pakistani nuclearization (1980–6) with significant help, via exports of sensitive Western equipment and technology, in the Pakistani enrichment sphere, and Chinese aid to Pakistan in the nuclear and missile spheres (1980s to the present), India showed technical and decision-making strength by quietly developing the means to form a small nuclear arsenal. The Indian military joined and strengthened the Indian bureaucratic coalition that sought a credible response by nuclear and missile activity to counter the challenge to Indian power, interests, and prestige in the military and the diplomatic spheres at the regional and international levels.

Another strategy was to publicize the issue and to induce US involvement and pressure on Pakistan in the context of the US non-proliferation laws. But note that only the Pakistan dimension of the nuclear equation was attacked and publicized. The China dimension was not the focus. This differentiation may be by design and showed the pattern of Indian diplomatic tactics. Even though China's strategic orientation and pattern of military modernization, as well as the Sino–Pakistani special military relationship remained the object of Indian suspicions and long-term planning, still, there was an expectation that China and Pakistan were not permanent adversaries. Even as Indian diplomatic practitioners and political leaders attacked the US policy which effectively tolerated Pakistani nuclear weapons activity, other Indian practitioners remained interested in a regional peace process. Thus, General Sundarji argued:

Pushing or pressuring India in the NPT is an exercise in futility. What the USA should attempt to do, is to reduce the chances of war by miscalculation, which might lead to a nuclear exchange between China and India or India and Pakistan. It should attempt the prevention of nuclear arms racing among the three countries. Given that minimum or proportionate deterrence is what all three countries are talking about, it should not be impossible for an agreement on the kind of stockpiles that the three will need for the purpose. With transparency, agreed verification procedures and with the assistance of the USA acting as an honest broker, this should be possible. Credibility will be greatly enhanced by the USA's national technical means reinforcing verifications and inspection which have been mutually agreed to by the three. As confidence builds up, mutually agreed conventional force reductions, of forces deployable against each other can also be undertaken. It is for this kind of result that a four-power conference can be thought of with China, India and Pakistan included as active participants, with the good offices of the USA available. I am not sure whether the presence of Russia is necessary and what purpose it would serve. Till the final disposition of strategic and tactical nuclear weapons in the erstwhile Soviet Union is decided, it will be difficult to take a view on the credentials of Russia, for attending a conference of this nature. I do not think India should attend any meeting, in which China's role is confined to that of one of the referees and the substantive discussions are restricted to Indo-Pak nuclear issues.[10]

In sum, Indian practitioners were using different diplomatic tactics with the concerned audiences in public, and as well were developing a pro-nuclear and pro-missile bureaucratic coalition. The diplomatic activity and publicity about Pakistani nuclearization created the cover to move towards missile delivery work via the development of the Prithvi and Agni missiles. These missiles were potentially useful against Pakistani and Chinese targets respectively. Furthermore, once the US government was tied to the application of the Pressler process against Pakistan in 1990, the object of Indian diplomacy changed. The new frontier was to induce US attention to the China factor in India security calculations. This strategy appeared in the bilateral talks between India and the USA that followed up the Nawaz Sharif proposal (June 1991) to have a multilateral regional nuclear arms control arrangement.[11] This phase of Indian diplomatic strategy was ineffective because the US and the PRC saw themselves as strategic partners in Asia-Pacific and in South Asia. The polarity was between China–Pakistan–US *vis-à-vis* India because both the US and China saw India in the context of their Pakistan policies, and both fashioned their Pakistan policies in the context of their idea that regional stability required an Indo–Pakistani balance. In this approach, it was up to India to accommodate Pakistan and to make peace with it. The Indian diplomatic strategy to project China as a part of the problem rather than a part of the solution was initiated during the last year of the Bush presidency and it was pursued with the new team of Asia and arms control specialists in the Clinton administration. The Clinton administration's position hardened with India because of President Clinton's inexperience and relative lack of interest in foreign affairs, including South Asian affairs, and because the State Department's South Asia policy was in the hands of hardliners, especially Madeleine Albright (Secretary of State), Thomas Pickering (Undersecretary of State), and Robin Rafael (Assistant Secretary of State) along with hardliners in the Arms Control and Disarmament Agency like its director, John Holum. These practitioners felt that India was internationally isolated. With continued western nuclear sanctions and diplomatic pressure on the nuclear front, the weak Indian political leaders could be pressured and manipulated to avoid overt nuclearization. They could also be pressured to act by the NPT rules and to respect the international norms. Here the norms were expected to be a good alternative where a country was unable to accept the formal treaty obligations. In these circumstances, India's external processes were twofold: 'keep developing the weapons and delivery capability' and 'keep talking' to develop a security and arms control agenda, in relation to India–Pakistan, India–China, and India–US.

The CTBT: The Straw that Broke the Camel's Back

The problem with the Western and Chinese hegemons is that they do not know when to stop pushing, and they are not open to persuasion by diplomatic means. In the US–China–Pakistan versus India nexus during the 1990s, the US saw itself as a global hegemon, the winner of the Cold War following the USSR's self-destruction. China saw itself as a potential global power and as an Asian hegemon. Pakistan felt it had powerful patrons. It saw itself as an extension of the power of China, Talibanized Afghanistan, and Saudi Arabia in Indian subcontinental international relations; it functioned as a line of military–diplomatic pressure against India. The USSR had protected Indian interests in the past in subcontinental and global affairs, but after its breakdown, its countervailing influence was not available to India. In this changed international situation, and given the two major preoccupations in Indian diplomatic history and Indian politics—viz., the desire to be taken seriously by the major powers and to eliminate the opportunities of outside intervention and harassment of India in diplomatic, military, and economic affairs—the loss of the USSR connection and the increased outside pressures that appeared to take advantage of India's vulnerabilities led Indian strategic thinkers to an important conclusion: India was pretty much on its own. This conclusion was emerging among Indian 'nationalist' strategic thinkers at the time that the US–China–Pakistan group and their allies, in parallel but necessarily in a coordinated way, became overconfident about their ability to contain and isolate India's nuclear power and its diplomatic prestige and to redefine or delimit the scope of Indian strategic interests and power to the Indo-Pakistani sphere.

Ideally, the end of the Cold War and the decline of the Indo–USSR special relationship during the Gorbachev era should have (a) removed the major impediment to real normalization in Sino–Indian relations and (b) there should have been a reduction in direct military threats to Indian security. But such logical possibilities did not materialize. Instead, during the 1990s, (1) insurgencies in Punjab and Kashmir continued, (2) Chinese nuclear and missile supplies to Pakistan continued and intensified, (3) the PRC's military modernization continued, (4) China's commercial and military push into Myanmar and the Bay of Bengal intensified, and (5) the PRC continued to deny India a position as an Indian Ocean power. In this context, Sino–Indian relations had the quality of a ceasefire. The purpose of normalization talks was to extend the ceasefire, pending a stable political settlement. The Himalayan border was stable because the two armies faced each other suspiciously, but the list of disagreements on territorial and other issues remained long, and the Sino–Indian Joint Working Group was not able to bring closure to any of the outstanding issues. Note that multiple channels of Sino–Indian discourse do not exist. There is nothing comparable to the multifaceted Indo–Pakistani channels since 1947, and inter-German channels during the Cold War. In these hostile pairs, communication channels between journalistic, business, family, intelligence, diplomatic, and military sources existed. In the absence of tangible signs that the PRC took India seriously as a player in Asia–Pacific (especially in South East Asia and the Indian Ocean area) and in international conference diplomacy, the shadows in Sino–Indian relations in the 1990s continued to grow ominously.

With over-confidence came smugness and a lack of curiosity in the US, the PRC, and Pakistan about the likely consequences of developments within the Indian boxes (Figures 7.1 and 7.2). The history of these boxes showed the emergence of a critical mass of players and

issues that were bound to affect Indian decision processes. The overconfidence and smugness was heightened by the ease with which the US
and its partners (the UK, Canada, and Australia) were able to secure the
indefinite and unconditional extension of the NPT (1995) and later to
secure the acceptance of the CTBT by the UN General Assembly
(1997).

In sum, there were three major contextual elements in play in the
1990s that shaped the CTBT and India's reaction to it. First, the
ominous nuclear and military shadows in Sino–Indian and Indo–Pakistan relations were growing following the end of the Cold War; and US
inattention to Indian representations added to the Indian sense of isolation and insecurity. These were the *regional security imperatives.*

Secondly, there was a subtle and a fundamental process of redistribution of power and authority within the Indian system as per the shift
from the structure and process outlined in Figures 7.1 and 7.2. Here the
new *bureaucratic* and *Indian political systemic imperatives* showed a
major change that highlighted the salience of an emergent coalition of
Indian atomic and defence scientists, the armed forces, and the
diplomats. Earlier, the Indian service chiefs had promoted their respective interests. The military had sought tanks and other means of land
warfare; the airforce sought aircraft and other means of air warfare; and
the navy wanted ships and other means of naval warfare. With the
growth of Pakistani and Chinese nuclear and missile capabilities, and
with increasing signs of their collusion, Indian inter-services competition for limited budgets found common ground in the sense that nuclear
and missiles projection and defence activities would require the involvement of all the three services.

Third, and finally, the adherence of France and the PRC to the NPT
indicated the emergence of a P-5 strategic bargain that solidified the
discriminatory NPT regime. The emphasis was four-fold: (i) securing
horizontal non-proliferation by non-P-5 states, especially the incipient
regional nuclear powers; (ii) working towards nuclear arms *reduction*
by the P-5 nuclear powers; and (iii) developing an international stance
and a policy of *avoiding* any discussion of *elimination of nuclear
weapons* by the P-5.

The fourth emphasis was to cap the nuclear weapons development
by the P-5 powers through a *non-comprehensive* ban on testing of
nuclear explosives but to maintain the option to restart nuclear weapons
tests if the 'supreme national interest' so required. This was a remote
possibility, but it kept open the political option and the legal right to do

so if the international strategic conditions deteriorated. The indefinite and unconditional acceptance of the NPT Extension indicated that the majority of countries and NGO groups were comfortable with the new orientations in P-5 strategic diplomacy. Mention may be made of the destruction of nuclear armament in several former Soviet Union states, like Kazakhstan. This was real disarmament, which was used in P-5 pronouncements as a sign of commitment to nuclear disarmament. In our judgement, however, the latter projection is pure propaganda (a lie meant to deceive) given the orientation of the P-5 non-proliferation diplomacy outlined above. In other words, the post-Cold War era also revealed the emergence of a P-5 strategic bargain that significantly diminished the prospect of nuclear disarmament and that significantly heightened the right of the P-5 states to decide on action against the nuclear rogues and indeed to define who the rogues were. We label this as the P-5 *orchestrated imperative* in international conference diplomacy. This reflected the changing distribution of economic and military power and the changing pattern of relationships among the P-5 powers.

These imperatives had crystallized and were in play when the CTBT negotiations started in Geneva at the Conference on Disarmament. By summer 1995, it became clear to Indian negotiators that the scope of the proposed treaty was basically a P-5 bargain, just as the NPT's scope was basically a US–USSR bargain. It also became clear to them that the CTBT was being projected by all the P-5 countries, and especially by the UK, as a non-proliferation measure and not as a disarmament one. The Indian concern was shared by many third world participants but they were not able to effectively challenge the authority of the P-5 powers. Many of them were beholden to them for military, economic, and diplomatic support. Their ability to act independently had been compromised by the deals they had made with the US and other P-5 powers and their influential allies, such as Japan and Canada. Several members of the Non-Aligned Movement (NAM)—South Africa, Indonesia, and Egypt being prime examples—had spearheaded the break-up of NAM unity in the NPT Extension Conference in 1995. They facilitated the NPT's unconditional extension, and having done so, they thereby lost the leverage in future NPT meetings in their call for nuclear disarmament. India's CTBT behaviour in 1995–6 was driven by the three imperatives noted earlier, viz., (1) the regional security imperative, (2) the bureaucratic and Indian political systemic imperative, and

(3) the P-5 orchestrated international non-proliferation imperative. NAM and the third world were no longer relevant.

The Indian ambassador to the Disarmament Conference in Geneva, Arundhati Ghose, had several major concerns. These became the basis of India's rejection of the CTBT in Geneva and the subsequent blockage of a consensus agreement in Geneva. Her concerns are shared by many practitioners and, therefore, should be spelled out, as follows.

(i) The CTBT's basic parameters and orientation are outlined in Article 1. It is tied to the maintenance of the nuclear weapons status of the P-5 powers. This Article reveals a permanent legal linkup between the provisions and philosophy of the NPT and the CTBT. Article 1 of the CTBT is the bridge between the two international treaties which solidifies the nuclear weapons status of the P-5. The treaty has a structure of impermissibility, i.e. all nuclear tests are banned but it also has a structure of permissibility, i.e. non-explosive tests are permissible. These include computer simulation, sub-critical tests, laser tests, and exchange of technical data by the P-5 nuclear powers and among themselves. The NPT is politically discriminatory because it created a legal distinction between nuclear weapon states and non-nuclear ones. The CTBT avoids this problem. But still, it creates an opportunity for technological discrimination in the sense that the permissible activity in Article 1 of CTBT favours the technologically advanced nuclear powers of which the US is the leader. The CTBT would freeze the US's technological edge over all other P-5 nuclear powers, as well as India, Pakistan, and Israel. For India, the issue does not concern the technological gap between India *vis-à-vis* the US, France, the UK, and Russia. The concern is about the effect of the technological gap between China and India once the CTBT comes into effect, given the uncertainty about the nature of PRC's strategic intentions and capabilities in the 2000–2010/2020 time frame when the PRC's military modernization is scheduled to be completed. The question for India is both scientific and military. Can Indian scientists maintain a manageable gap in this time *vis-à-vis* China with the degree of permissibility and impermissibility under Article 1 of the CTBT? The nature of the PRC's future strategic intentions and capabilities is a question for Indian military practitioners to address. This involved professional military assessments, which are beyond the professional competence and mandate of Indian nuclear and defence scientists. Scientists cannot make a political judgement about the strategic environment, now and in the future. Even diplomats can at best offer a partial assessment of the security environment.

(ii) The CTBT international monitoring system is meant to catch tests over 1 kiloton capability. Zero to one kiloton clandestine testing is supposedly filtered by national means, e.g. by satellites. Does India possess such national means or would it have to depend on the US? Suppose the PRC or Pakistan tested in the 0–1 kt range? What is the guarantee about the timeliness, the quality, and the scope of US intelligence input to India in a moment of crisis? This is a serious and a practical question for India, who is not a US ally, and there are no formal inter-governmental intelligence sharing arrangements. This question is relevant because Japan, a US ally, has had doubts about the timeliness, quality and scope of US intelligence input to Japan when North Korea sent its missiles over Japan in August 1998. Following this episode, Japan was determined to enhance its national intelligence acquisition capability *vis-à-vis* North Korea.[12]

(iii) The CTBT has a built-in potential of harassment of a non-P-5 country by a P-5 power. The experience of UNSCOM inspections of Iraq shows how even intrusive and prolonged international inspections are inconclusive, how an international agency can become a vehicle for spying by a major power (in this case, the USA) and how a UN-mandated inspection activity can become a cover for both spying and harassment, without any prospect of closure. Imagine a Richard Butler making daily pronouncements that India is hiding something and his team has evidence (based on US and other national means) that India is doing something in apparent violation of CTBT rules. The Iraqi experience is a chilling reminder of the harassment potential of an international treaty where sensitive national strategic interests and sensitivities are involved. The CTBT has an intrusive on-site inspection system and it is quite likely that the P-5 powers will harass the non-P-5 ones because the P-5 states have a common interest to check the non-P-5 states. As permanent members of the UN Security Council, the P-5 states enjoy the veto and they possess nuclear weapons; they themselves cannot be harassed against their will.

(iv) Article 14 of the CTBT concerns the requirements for the Entry into Force (EIF). The EIF clause requires that 44 states including all P-5 nuclear powers, as well as Israel, India, and Pakistan must sign and ratify the treaty before it comes into force. The UK, Russia, China, Egypt, and Pakistan insisted on EIF. Russia would not agree to the CTBT unless the PRC did, and the PRC would not agree until India did, and so on. The US initially did not insist on this particular formula for

EIF, but it faced a dilemma, and it agreed eventually with the formula as it was finally adopted.

These four major objections indicate that the critics of the treaty see it as a way to co-opt India into the non-proliferation regime. It is a control mechanism for those who are not members of the NPT. Indian critics of the CTBT, including Ambassador Ghose and Indian Prime Minister I.K. Gujral, saw it as a way to corner India because Israel and Pakistan enjoy US and PRC strategic protection respectively, and only India was exposed. Hence, India's hardened stance against the treaty during 1995–6, and the eventual refusal to agree to the consensus at the Disarmament Conference in Geneva in June 1996.

Summing Up

The discussion points to two kinds of problems in Indian nuclear decision-making during this period. First, the distribution of decision-making authority had been dysfunctional since the Indira Gandhi days. Figure 7.1 shows three aberrations. (1) Forces outside India—the USA, the PRC, Pakistan, key players in international conference diplomacy (for example Europeans, Canada, and Australia), and international organizations (for example IAEA and the UN Disarmament Affairs division)—were able to continuously influence decisions within India on key issues such as nuclear testing, missile testing, and deployment of Indian missiles within India. (2) The Indian military was marginal in the decision-making process even though the issues (for example CTBT, NWFZ, missile development, the future of Chinese and Pakistani strategic intentions and capabilities) had military implications. Instead, the emphasis was on the diplomatic (externally), political (internally), and economic (to generate nuclear energy for civil use and to develop space capabilities for educational and economic purposes) uses of atomic and space sciences. The militarization of Indian science was condemned by the international governmental and non-government organizational forces and by Indian non-governmental organizations (NGOs) and peace activists. Here the peace activists preferred the marginalization of Indian military's input into the nuclear debate and decision-making. (3) A combination of external, international pressures and internal (within India) polarization produced the third aberration. Upto the ascendancy of the BJP-led government in early 1998, successive Indian leaders, including Indira Gandhi, revealed that indecisiveness was the main characteristic of their approach to the issue of the militarization of Indian science. Their actions were protected by official secrecy.

The combination of the three aberrations produced a dysfunctionality in the Indian nuclear and missile decision process because Indian nuclear policies (on nuclear weapons and missile production and deployment, maintenance of its nuclear option, the role of nuclear disarmament in Indian security, the value and timing of nuclear testing, the importance of the NPT regime and the way to deal with it, and so on) were inconsistent with Indian nationalism and public opinion. It had favoured the development of the Indian bomb since the 1960s. There was an inconsistency also between India's declared wish to be taken seriously as a major non-expansionist power in regional and international affairs and its unwillingness to make the necessary decisions. While regional and international changes required an Indian nuclear and missile response, the behaviour of Indian political leaders sent confusing signals. However, limited functionality was maintained in this period by the ceaseless scientific activity to acquire the means to make and to deliver nuclear bombs, and by the diplomatic activity to keep India free of intrusive multilateral inspections and harassment. In other words, India continued to gain the technical strength to become a nuclear weapon state, but it lacked the decision-making strength to become one. The latter problem was self-inflicted, and it fed the perception of outside agencies who felt that India obviously did not believe its own rhetoric because Indian policies during this period showed restraint in the nuclear and missile spheres *vis-à-vis* the so-called China and Pakistan strategic threats. The signals being given by India's behaviour in these spheres during this period differed from the official rhetoric. The involvement of the Indian military in the nuclear and missile spheres and the doctrinal discourse shifted the bureaucratic balance of power in this period, but it did not, nor could it, change the problem of weakness and indecisiveness in the leadership style of successive Indian prime ministers since the days of Indira Gandhi up to April–May 1998.

The ascendancy of the Indian military as a source of input into India's nuclear debate was nonetheless significant. It changed the structure, process, and quality of the internal intra-governmental and intra-societal debate. Historically, since the Nehru days, a major part of the internal problem that produced the dysfunctionality in the decision process was that the Indian political leaders, the civil bureaucracies, and the social pacifist constituencies sought to locate the nuclear issue and nuclear decision-making in political–bureaucratic–scientific hands.

They sought also to maintain the marginalization of the Indian armed forces in questions of decision-making concerning war and peace issues. This was easily accomplished because Nehru himself was anti-military and distrusted the Indian military officers. This kind of attitude, rather than a fear that the Indian military was likely to upset the Indian constitutional equation of civilian supremacy in strategic affairs, produced the marginalization of the military in nuclear affairs.

The Indian military's poor performance in the disastrous campaign with China in 1962 and the criticism of Nehru's policies were the decisive events that recognized the Indian military as a legitimate agency that deserved better state and social support. Its performance in the 1965 and 1971 military campaigns and in other crises established the military as a credible force in a hostile neighbourhood; and its refusal to take sides in the political fray or to usurp political power, as in the case of Pakistan, made it a legitimate and a responsible institution. So the Indian military's decision to study the nuclear question and its implications for India, and to provide input into strategic affairs was a logical build-up of its increasing legitimacy and authority in subcontinental affairs. (The Sri Lanka peacekeeping operation was not an Indian military defeat because, against its will, the Indian military was asked to function as a political force in a problem which was basically political and psychological. The use of armed intervention to deal with such a problem was a bad political decision by Indira and Rajiv Gandhi.)

If dysfunctionality in the Indian nuclear and missile decision structure and process was the result of a lopsided distribution of power and authority as per Figure 7.1, the second problem was that the distribution of power and the pattern of strategic relationships were changing in Asia-Pacific even before the Cold War ended, but India seemed to be out of the loop during the Cold War and following its official end in 1990. From an Indian perspective, not only was the *Indian decision-making space* occupied by outside forces, and until the Indian military got into the act in the 1980s, the 'military' box was empty, but furthermore, there was 'unredistributed power' in Asia–Pacific since 1945. This idea comes from the assessment of a distinguished American scholar, Owen Lattimore. In a remarkable book, he argued in 1949,

Current [1946] American thinking about the power situation resulting from World War II starts from the assumption that America and Russia, in that order, have become the two most powerful countries in the world—so powerful that they can and must divide the world between them . . . The trouble with this thinking is that it does not begin at the beginning. It is not the *absolute* but the *relative* power of both America and Russia that counts. Both countries have grown in relative power because of the enormous power lost by Germany and Japan, and the almost equally great power lost by Britain, France, and, in the colonial world, Holland. Some of the power lost by these countries has been transferred directly to America and Russia, with America acquiring far more than Russia; but much of it has not.

This unredistributed power is as important and critical in Asia today as is the power of America or Russia. Some of it may come into American or Russian hands. In China, India, and colonial Asia, however, most of it has already been taken by parties and movements which vary in their ideas of social and economic revolution, but are alike in their intense nationalism.[13]

Lattimore argues that Asia has been out of control since 1945, and the distribution of power and the pattern of relationships have been in a redistributed mode since 1945. In this context, during the Cold War and following its end, the strategic situation in Asia–Pacific has repeatedly created an imperative for India to participate in the creation of a new and stable balance of power in Asia. The US and Chinese scholarship and policy pronouncements emphasize the importance of a US–China strategic partnership in Asia–Pacific. The expectation is that the PRC would be the main Asian power, and the US and the PRC would be the core players in the region. This is not a realistic idea because the future of China and its economic, social, and military base is not assured and neither Japanese nor Indian strategic thinkers believe that the PRC is likely to emerge as the sole Asian power. What is more likely is Paul Dibb's (a senior Australian professor with an intelligence background) analysis about the emergence of an Asian balance of power that involves the US, the PRC, Japan, India, and Russia.[14] The process of 'redistributing power' has been taking shape since 1945, and it is still evolving.

To sum up, the post-May 1974 to pre-May 1998 period was an extremely dynamic and important one. There was a fundamental redistribution of power within the Indian bureaucratic and political system. India had many opportunities to go nuclear before and during this period. With a nuclear China and a militant Pakistan as its neighbours, it had the *motive* to go nuclear. It also possessed the *capacity* to go nuclear since the late 1950s or at least the early 1960s, but it lacked the decision-making strength to do so. During this period, the Indian decision-making space was occupied by weak Indian leaders; a divided bureaucracy and powerful and well-organized international forces worked effectively at the Indian political–bureaucratic levels; and a third of the bureaucratic space which would, in any major country, normally belong to the armed forces was unoccupied. From the early 1980s, however, the Indian military gradually took its rightful place in the bureaucratic set-up but the outside pressures on the Indian political will and on the definition of India's strategic agenda remained intense during this period. Secondly, the regional security changes were dynamic. They showed the importance of regional and international traditional–statist geopolitical considerations rather than the non-proliferation norm. They indicated that the rivalries were active and growing in the subcontinent, especially between China and India, India and Pakistan, and the US and India. Each conflictual relationship had a historical baggage as well as negative futuristic implications.

This chapter relies on two core concepts. The first, 'redistributed power', applies to the entry of the Indian armed forces into the nuclear debate and decision process. This enlarged the political space of the three pillars of the Indian bureaucracy, viz., scientists, diplomats, and the military within the Indian decision-making structure. During this period, the space taken by international forces in the Indian nuclear decision-making sphere remained intact because India's political leaders were weak, confused, and indecisive, and they were vulnerable to conflicting advice from different sources. Consequently, the tension and suspicion between the international non-proliferation forces and the Indian nationalist forces in the bureaucracy remained high, and the Indian political leadership at the centre remained weak, confused, and indecisive. *Our first hypothesis is that in such circumstances, the process of redistributing internal power is likely to remain incomplete that is, the increase of space and decision-making authority by professionals in the bureaucracy will not be matched by a reduction in space and decision-making power or a veto by international forces, but if the leadership style becomes decisive, then the space and power of the international forces will likely shrink.* The hypothesis has a zero-sum game quality. It requires a reduction in the space and authority of the international forces, and it expects that the latter will likely face dilemmas in dealing with the new coalition. So the redistribution process is triangular and dynamic. The process involves 'deadly', not 'ritualistic', confrontations because the stakes are high and they concern the personal, institutional, and national interests of all the players.

The second core concept refers to 'unredistributed power'. Recall that our premise is that the US and the USSR were not successors to the European empires in Asia–Pacific after 1945. The existence of nationalism in many parts of Asia made it impossible for the two Cold Warriors to divide Asia between themselves. But, on the other hand, the internal economic, military, and political weaknesses of many Asian states made it impossible for the nationalist countries to effectively acquire a part of the *un*redistributed power in the Asia–Pacific region. *Our second hypothesis is that a combination of nationalism and economic/military planning is necessary to participate in acquiring a part of unredistributed power in Asia–Pacific. Re*distributed power assumes that the decision-making space is finite or limited; that is, a critical and dense mass of players (international and domestic), issues, interests, and capacities exists, and entry of a new, powerful player such as the Indian military requires the development of a winning coalition and a winning strategy; here there are clear losers. *Un*redistributed power, on the other hand, assumes that a dense, critical mass of players, issues, interests, and capabilities has not emerged in a regional subsystem such as Asia–Pacific. It is in a process of forming. A new entrant to the power game has an opportunity to enlarge and modify the geographical as well as the systemic scope and characteristics of a regional subsystem. Hence, in our second hypothesis, the new entrant is redefining the strategic agenda in staking a claim to participate as a new member of an existing geopolitical system. This refers to a defined regional or subregional geographical sphere where the movement of political/strategic ideas, economic goods, and military activities is being organized by the powers.

India lacked the means or the political will to make a claim to the unredistributed power in Asia during the period 1974 to pre-May 1998. However, this period witnessed the process which redistributed power *within* the Indian nuclear decision-making process. The decision by Prime Minister Vajpayee to authorize nuclear testing in April–May 1998 was the outcome of this redistributed power. For a discussion of the consequences of this decision, on the unredistributed power in Asia, we now turn to Chapter 8.

ENDNOTES

1. Pierre M. Gallois (Retired General of the French Army), private communication to Professor M.L. Sondhi, 18 December 1970. The author thanks Prof. Sondhi for permission to use this letter. The first and the second point highlight the problem of 'false protection' of a so-called

nuclear guarantee and the loss of independence in action. The third point shows the harassment potential of conventional means of statecraft in a situation of nuclear asymmetry, that is, where 'A' possesses nuclear means and 'B' does not. A corollary to the Gallois formula is that the harassment potential exists in another form of nuclear asymmetry, that is, where both 'A' and 'F' possess nuclear capability, but 'F's nuclear capability is limited compared to that of 'A', 'B', 'C', 'D', 'E' (the P-5 NWSs), its development is frozen on the technological curve as a consequence of the CTBT, and the P-5 NWSs come together to harass 'F' because of the latter's refusal to join the NPT regime, and because of major differences in the strategic purposes and policies of 'F' in comparison to the dominant member(s) in the P-5 NWSs club.

2. M.W. Doyle, 'Kant, Liberal Legacies, and Foreign Affairs, Parts I and II', *Philosophy and Public Affairs*, vol. 12, no. 3, Summer 1983, pp. 205–35, and vol. 12, no. 4, Fall 1983, pp. 323–53 respectively.

3. By the mid-1960s, the PRC was supplying military aid, military aircraft, and tanks to Pakistan. See Y. Vertzberger, *The Enduring Entente, Sino-Pakistani Relations, 1960–1980*, The Washington Papers/95, vol. 10 (New York: Praeger, 1983), p. 44. After 1971, the PRC became Pakistan's main source of arms; see Vertzbenger, p. 53 and ch. 7. For a summary of China's basic aims *vis-à-vis* India that had regional, Asian, and global implications, see Vertzberger, especially pp. 25–6. For the nature of PRC nuclear and missile aid to Pakistan, see Ashok Kapur, 'China and Proliferation: Implications for India', *China Report*, vol. 34, nos. 3 and 4 (New Delhi: Sage), pp. 401–17.

4. See Appendix B for the tenure of each Indian Prime Minister. Our comment refers to the 1974 to 1998 period, that is, the Prime Ministers in items 6 to 15. Appendix B shows a trend towards political instability measured by one indicator, that is, the total length of tenure of each government.

5. See A. Kapur, 'China and Proliferation', p. 402, note 4.

6. 'Can the Chinese Army Win the Next War', Beijing: Central Military Commission, 1993, p. 6 (unpublished paper). Vertzberger, The Enduring Entente, especially ch. 2. M.B. Zingger, 'The Development of Indian Naval Strategy Since 1972', *Contemporary South Asia*, vol. 2, no. 3, Abingdon, UK, 1993, p. 354 for the nature of Sino-Indian rivalry in the Indian Ocean.

7. 'Effects of Nuclear Asymmetry on Conventional Deterrence', The College of Combat, Mhow, India, Combat Papers No. 1, May 1981, The Problem Statement, no page number is given.

8. Ibid., p. 94.
9. General K. Sundarji, 'India's Nuclear Options 1992', *Trishul*, Defence Services Staff College, Wellington, India, vol. 5, no. 1, July 1992.
10. Ibid.
11. Nawaz Sharif's proposals were outlined in the Prime Minister's address to the National Defence College of Pakistan on 6 June 1991.
12. See A. Kapur, 'Japanese Worries', *Frontline*, vol. 16, no. 7, Chennai, India, 27 March–9 April 1999, pp. 64–5.
13. Owen Lattimore, *The Situation in Asia* (Boston: Little Brown, 1949), pp. 36–7.
14. *Towards a New Balance of Power in Asia*, Adelphi Paper 295, IISS (Oxford: University Press, 1995).

8

Pokhran II and After: The Reactions, Debates, and Consequences

Introduction

Two expert opinions express the themes of this chapter. Writing in 1949, in a book full of practical insights, Owen Lattimore, an American, argued that Asia was out of control; nationalism was the major elemental force in Asian societies; the major powers including the US had to negotiate with the Asians and they could not dictate to nationalistic peoples in Asia.[1] Writing in 1998, Thérèse Delpech, the Director of Policy Planning at the French Atomic Energy Commission, argued as follows:

... for the past 50 years, a rather patronizing attitude towards India has prevailed, despite its growing importance on the world stage. Analysts and statesmen have also stubbornly limited their view to the India–Pakistan context.

With so many forecasts of a multipolar world, it should have been clear that India would have a significant place in it. But little analytical work has been done on the emerging poles and even less on the potential relations among them. From a strategic standpoint, however, this is a crucial issue. International relations, like nature, abhor a vacuum: the Soviet empire's disappearance inevitably had further consequences. China was the first country to perceive the advantages to be derived from the radical changes in its security environment at the end of the Cold War. But China will not stand unchallenged on the Asian stage. The clearest challenge was not issued by China's potential rival Japan, which is experiencing an alarming—hopefully temporary—decline on the international scene. It came from India, still poor and weak. If the fall of the Berlin Wall signalled the end of an era, the India tests could be an early warning of the new times at hand. The twenty-first century has begun.[2]

Both views highlight the theme of multipolarity in Asia–Pacific (rather than bipolarity or unipolarity). Dibb, like Delpech, sees Asian international relations as a five-powered exercise.[3] Both analyses imply that a new bargain will have to be struck between India and other powers. There is, of course, a difference in these views. Lattimore was dealing with the struggle between Asian nationalism and the behaviour of the Cold War successors to western imperialism in Asia after 1945. Lattimore was asserting that the 'part played by Asia in regrouping the complex of international relations between Asia, Europe, America, and Russia may prove to be more decisive than the parts played even by America and Russia'.[4] Delpech and Dibb are dealing with the problem of restructuring a multipolar Asia following the collapse of the USSR. The Sino–Indian controversy or the clash between the two nationalisms was not prominent in Lattimore's analysis. However, it is consistent with his emphasis on the key role of nationalism in the organization of Asian international relations. Nationalism, not communism, was the elemental force in Asia. Delpech, on the other hand, locates the Indian nuclear issue in the context of nuclear proliferation in Asia. This is the trend. To quote her:

Nuclear trends in Asia are moving in the opposite direction. Asia contains the only nuclear-weapon state that is increasing its arsenal of nuclear and ballistic missiles (China); the two states which have recently chosen to declare their nuclear capabilities (India and Pakistan); the third and now unique 'threshold' country (Israel); and the two countries found guilty of violating their non-proliferation commitments (Iraq and North Korea). In addition, South Korea and Taiwan ran military nuclear Programmemes in the 1960s and 1970s; Iran has long been suspected of activities prohibited under the NPT; and Japan is recognised as having a latent capability to produce nuclear weapons quickly. Lastly, the US and Russia are major Asian powers as well. Asia therefore comprises more nuclear powers or nuclear-capable states than any other region in the world.[5]

Secondly, she located the nuclear issue of India and other powers in the context of the international debate between the Abolitionists and the Marginalists. What is a 'reasonable level of nuclear arsenal?' is the question for the nuclear powers.[6] 'What are the requirements of minimum credible nuclear deterrent?' is the question before the Indian practitioners.

This chapter is divided into two parts. The first section examines the international reactions to the Indian tests in 1998, and argues that the official reactions were irrelevant as well as confused because they did not connect with or engage the key parameters of the shift in India's nuclear behaviour, that is, the impact of Asian multipolarity, the role of nuclear weapons in Asia, and the dual trend towards a military modernization by unilateral means and confidence building through bilateral and multilateral diplomacy.

The second section examines the debate among Indian scientists and the political elite. It argues that the debate is intense and it reveals the importance of debate among Indian scientists and the Indian political class. This debate deals with scientific issues such as yields of Indian tests, the costs of weaponization, and the number of weapons required for the development of a credible minimum deterrent in the coming decade(s). But this debate is narrow because it does not deal directly with the China issue, the issue of Asian multipolarity, and the role of Indian diplomacy as well as strategic power in the context of Sino–Indian rivalry. So, it is argued that the core question of 'what are the scientific and technological and military ingredients of a minimum credible nuclear deterrent' can only be addressed in the context of the international Abolitionist–Marginalist debate among the P-5 powers. The devil here is not in the detail about the Indian requirements of a minimum deterrent. The devil instead lies in the international (especially Asian) context. Where India lies on the technological and military curve *vis-à-vis* China depends on where China finds itself or wants to be in the future on the technological and military curve *vis-à-vis* its adversaries especially the US, Japan, Russia, and Taiwan. Secondly, it depends on where China's strategic behaviour (not speeches) projects China's policies and ambition (nuclear as well as diplomatic) in the Abolitionist–Marginalist debate.

The second section points to the dysfunctionality between, on the one hand, the narrow Indian nuclear debate after Pokhran II and, on the other hand, the China question. Unless the nuclear and the China debates are brought together, India's post-Pokhran II debates are likely to remain intense and narrow, and they will lack the ability to engage the strategic community. Debates with narrow parameters tend to be intense and repetitive, and unless all points of view and a variety of issues are brought on to the table, a discourse is not likely and 'debate' will likely remain a dialogue of the deaf that goes around in circles. In such a case, the expression of opinions is not a debate because the issues have not been joined; there is no engagement among the parties. In such a case, pressure and manipulation are strategies to manage international conflict, whereas dialogue or discourse may be the better method to understand the causes of conflict and to find solutions.

The consequences of India's tests may be briefly noted here. The consequences affected Indian domestic politics; it strengthened the link between nationalism and the nuclear question. India's strategic relationships with its immediate neighbours (Pakistan and China) gained a competitive edge; while tensions increased, so did the negotiating opportunities. The process to restructure the distribution of power and the pattern of strategic relationships in Asia–Pacific was invigorated; international experts began to consider the relevance of Asian multipolarity and the Sino–Indian question in their approach to the nuclear question. Finally, the international Abolitionists versus Marginalists debate was joined. India's tests tilted the balance towards the Marginalists. It showed up the dilemma, the poor tactics, and the hypocrisy of the Abolitionists. They faced huge problems: nuclear disarmament of, say, Kazakhstan was not in fact a step towards nuclear disarmament of the P-5 nations as the Abolitionists argued. Nor was nuclear arms reduction by the P-5 powers really nuclear disarmament. When it was accompanied by military and nuclear modernization, calls for nuclear disarmament by the US generals were totally insincere; they would enhance the US's conventional military superiority, and cap or eliminate the nuclear weapons capability of the enemies or political enemies. The Abolitionists had nowhere to hide after the Indian tests. They had failed to secure real nuclear disarmament before the Indian tests. They had failed to use the window of opportunity between the signing of the NPT (1968) to its indefinite extension (1995) to secure real, meaningful nuclear disarmament. After the Indian tests, the P-5 powers needed to maintain, as well, their nuclear weaponry against nuclear 'upstarts' like India and Pakistan and other nuclear 'rogues' like Iraq and North Korea.

International Reactions to Pokhran II

The international reactions to the Indian nuclear testing in 1998 had a number of characteristics. First, despite the public condemnation by the P-5 and G-8 countries, there was a *deep division among the P-5/G-8 governments about ways to deal with the new situation*. Some countries (for example the US, Canada, Japan) imposed economic sanctions against India. A few (Canada and Australia) imposed a ban on ministerial-level talks with India as a sign of their displeasure. Others (especially the US, France, Russia, and the UK) sought diplomatic engagement with India based on two parameters: non-proliferation and Indian security. The Jaswant Singh–Strobe Talbott talks were a sign of this approach that sought to fence off the US commitment to non-proliferation from other issues, viz., seeking Indian nuclear restraint as a *de facto* nuclear weapon country in return for recognition of Indian security imperatives *vis-à-vis* China and Pakistan and an appreciation of India's role as a constructive force in South East Asia and the Indian Ocean area. These interlocutors (except the US) did not even bother to impose economic sanctions against India. The US did so in part because of a mandatory legal requirement, and in part because of its diplomatic culture that believes in a carrot and stick diplomacy. As it became apparent that the stick of sanctions was not likely to alter India's nuclear and missile behaviour, and that it hurt US economic businesses in India as they hurt the Indian ones, the American enthusiasm for sanctions diplomacy lost its force.

Secondly, the international reactions showed *the emergence of a strange democratic–authoritarian combination* in Asian international relations. Canada and China combined in expressing the most extreme position against India. Both sought to ban India's quest for a seat at the UN Security Council. Both sought unconditional Indian acceptance of the NPT and the CTBT and Indian roll-back of its nuclear and missile programmes. In effect, both sought to contain India and leave it naked in the nuclear and missile spheres. That Canada joined the Chinese communist cause to contain India was taken by Indians as a sign of Canadian ministerial bias because of Foreign Minister Lloyd Axworthy's personal crusade against Indian (but not against other P-5) nuclear arms. It was also seen as an example of bad Canadian political judgement, that is, to reinforce Chinese demands against India when China was a part of the problem because of its nuclear and missile supply to Pakistan and because of its threat to Indian strategic interests in the Bay of Bengal and Tibet. The bad judgement was inherent in Canada's refusal to acknowledge that the issue was not simply about the future of the 'global non-proliferation norm' (which was an abstract idea); it concerned other tangibles such as: India's strategic well-being; China's strategic intentions and position on different aspects of the nuclear question such as the role of nuclear weapons following the end of the Cold War in 1990; the role of strategic and tactical atomic weapons for war-fighting in addition to deterrence; China's desire to be the sole superpower in Asia, that would exclude Japanese and Indian membership of the UN Security Council; and lastly, the place of India in an evolving structure of a multipolar Asia. Was Canada ill-informed about this aspect, or was the Canadian government single-minded about the non-proliferation issue only, or was it biased specifically against Indian security, or was its policy one of indifference towards India because Canadian interests in India were mainly in the area of immigration, visas, and refugees? The emergence of the Canada–China coalition following the Indian tests became bad news and good intelligence for the Indian experts.[7]

Thirdly, the international reactions showed a split between, on the one hand, non-governmental organizations who adopted a proactive, action-oriented, and forward-looking stance and, on the other hand, those who were preoccupied in over-analysing Indian motives and were more interested in blaming the Indians rather than in taking a balanced overall perspective. On this point, a comparison between the commentary of Harald Müller (Peace Research Institute, Frankfurt), Cathleen Fisher (Stimson Center, Washington DC), and Marcus Raskin (George Washington University and Institute for Policy Studies, Washington DC) is instructive:

Müller makes two broad generalizations ((a) and (b) below) and one critique of American policy ((c) below).

(a) The events in South Asia have changed the parameters of world politics, and in particular those of nuclear non-proliferation and disarmament, fundamentally. They are as significant as the fall of the Berlin Wall nine years ago. Unfortunately, they point us in the opposite direction: away from cooperation, arms control and disarmament, towards confrontation, arms racing and, eventually nuclear war. The world community must make its utmost efforts to stem this fateful tide.[8]

(b) It is essential to see the trigger to the events in the fundamentally changed character of the present Indian government—a precarious coalition headed by the Hindu nationalist Bharatiya Janata Party (BJP). These nuclear weapons are not for security, status or prestige in the first place, as is all too often assumed. They are instruments for political power, for dominating the subcontinent and achieving equality with China. They are instruments for increasing the tensions with Pakistan, so that the more radical elements within the BJP can enhance their influence within their party and in India at large. To expand the electoral basis beyond the tiny 26% of the last ballot, the BJP needs increased hostility with Pakistan. For this reason, a nuclear arms race is inevitable as long as this government prevails.[9]

Müller's criticism of the USA's opportunistic policy is as follows:

(c) At the top, the lone superpower, the US, is oscillating between a pragmatic continuation of past (pro-arms control) policies and the attitudes of Congressional conservatives (with some followers in the Pentagon and the Labs) that are the moral equivalent of rogue State views: contempt for multilateralism and international organizations, an opportunistic attitude to international law that is abused when it is convenient, and refused if it demands compromise, a complete reliance on unilateral military strength, and the relentless pursuit of the national interest—egocentrically defined—without regard to the claims and interests of others.[10]

Whether or not the Indian tests are as significant as the collapse of the Berlin wall, they undoubtedly changed the nature of the international non-proliferation game as well as the structure of international security, especially Asian security. It undermined the smugness of the 'international community'—more than 170 states and the P-5 nuclear powers—which felt secure in the belief that the NPT with its indefinite extension had put the nuclear proliferation issue to rest in the world. India's testing was a rude shock to those who felt that further proliferation could be contained by aggressive non-proliferation measures. India's tests brought out the reality that the Western attitude of marginalizing India in world affairs was wrong, as well as patronizing and arrogant, and nuclear testing as well as nuclear weaponry was still a currency of international power and prestige. The fault line all along in the NPT system was that the treaty was publicized as a bargain between renunciation of nuclear arms by the non-nuclear states and the eventual disarmament of the nuclear powers. Given a choice between nuclear disarmament and nuclear deterrence, the P-5 powers were inevitably likely to choose the latter, and use the fig leaf of nuclear arms *reduction* as a sign of a move to 'eventual disarmament'. India's tests exposed the fraud inherent in the public relations of the P-5. So even though India's test did not alter the distribution of military power between, say, India and the USA, it exposed the carefully orchestrated architecture of deceptive Western diplomacy which had accompanied the projection of non-proliferation as a shared value and interest of the 'world community'. By creating a new situation, India's tests enlarged the number of nuclear weapon states. The new ground reality became a source of permanent friction with the provisions of the NPT. By openly challenging the NPT norm against further proliferation, India also showed that the nuclear taboo against further proliferation—which had lasted from 1964 to 1998—could be broken by a poor, marginal, post-colonial state. The outrage in international reactions reflected an understanding of the psychological impact of the Indian challenge to the authority of the P-5 nations. At issue in the condemnatory international reactions was the ability of India to *revisit* the international non-proliferation agendas by widening the cracks in the existing fault lines. Furthermore, India was rewriting the strategic agenda through bilateral negotiations with the US, China, Pakistan, and others. Here the emphasis was on a 'security dialogue' rather than the 'global non-proliferation norm'. India was not rejecting non-proliferation. It was insisting that Indian nuclear restraint could not be taken for granted, and it could not be achieved unless Indian strategic interests were accommodated by the P-5 states, especially China and the US. This way, India was reaffirming nuclear non-proliferation but it was also making it difficult for the P-5 states and their associates (for example Canada and Japan) from fencing off security interests of others from the global non-proliferation norm. Thus, the outrage in international reactions reflected the discomfort the practitioners felt about being boxed into a set of two dilemmas: (1) the deterrence–disarmament dilemma; and (2) the global non-proliferation–national security dilemma. The international reactions showed the struggle in dealing with these dilemmas.

One set of reactions showed a preoccupation with the building of a global non-proliferation regime. This is a favourite activity and a source of employment for many western arms controllers who have life-long investments in this area, and hence have personal and institutional stakes in non-proliferation and proliferation. Another set of reactions, especially by China, showed a preoccupation with the breakdown of its carefully laid strategic plan to contain and encircle India and to win without fighting.

The proactive, forward-looking international reactions as well as the negative reactions pave the way for our assessment of the real impact of the Indian tests. These elements make up the balance sheet. This is emerging as the basis of the strategic discourse between India and the powers, and among Indians. The P-5 and the G-8 condemnations are not the last word on the subject from the world community. The negative reactions could not undo the reality of two new nuclear powers. At the same time, the negative reactions created an opportunity for India and her international interlocutors to fence off the nuclear bomb controversy and to find ways to secure Indian (and Pakistani) nuclear restraint. In this sense, the negatives and the positives should not be viewed as polarized dichotomies. The two polarities were interactive and dynamic. The likelihood of a shift in the balance from the negative to the positive side of the equation depended on the strategic interests and the skill of the Indian and foreign practitioners. Our review of the negatives and the positives is based on this perspective.

The first negative was the public condemnations by the P-5 and G-8 countries and some NAM countries (especially South Africa) of India's tests. This revealed that international opinion did not have a positive view of India in general and it lacked an understanding of Indian strategic problems and dilemmas. Even though India had a good case for its nuclear and missile tests in view of the Pakistani, Chinese, and American provocations *vis-à-vis* India, and even though the 'world community' had failed in the past fifty years to achieve real nuclear *disarmament* (as opposed to arms reductions), the negative effects of regional and international developments on Indian security were either ignored or they were dismissed or downplayed. A contributory element to the build-up of the negative international stance was that the Indian diplomacy and Indian information service did not develop an effective public relations strategy since the Nehru years. Indian diplomatic and political practitioners constantly spoke about peace, disarmament, and non-violence rather than military power and economic strength as the twin pillars of Indian security. By overplaying the theme of Indian utopianism in international relations and by overemphasizing the importance of NAM, the Third World, and North–South issues, India effectively dealt itself outside the global power game. The world routinely ignored the Government of India's utopian rhetoric because it lacked the power to engage and to ensure acceptance of Indian security goals and methods. Nehru and his successors had wrapped themselves in the legacy of anti-imperialism and the Bandung spirit. This was projected not only in speeches at the UN repeatedly as a ritualistic mantra, but it appeared as well in proclamations about India's China policy. This was surprising because China and India were (and are) rivals in Asian and international affairs. There were (and are) fundamental conflicts of interest involving territory, distribution of power, and prestige in the subcontinent and in the regional neighbourhood that included Afghanistan in India's west, Tibet and the Himalayan kingdoms in India's north, and Burma (Myanmar), South East Asia, and the Indian Ocean area in India's East; and finally, the two had fought a war and were engaged in military modernization with an eye to each other's activities and motives. Still, the ritual mantra of peaceful coexistence since the Nehru years, and the quest of normalization after 1962, has been kept in the diplomatic rhetoric of India. What exactly is normalization, and is it a vital goal in interstate relations? As a minimum, it refers to an exchange of ambassadors. It does not necessarily mean a relationship of peace and harmony. If the existence of ambassadorial-level relations is the minimum requirement of 'normalization', then it does not say much about the nature of the relationship. It could be a relationship of long-

term conflict or it could be a difficult relationship. In the latter circumstance, the search for 'normalization' is neither a real goal nor a
good tactic because 'normalization' becomes a rhetoric which masks
the mistrust, the animosities, and the conflict of interests. At the same
time, if normalization expresses a search for normal international
relationships and approaches, then one must recognize that usually there
are four types of normal relationships or approaches in the systems of
states: hostile, difficult, friendly, and indifferent. Which of these expressed the Indian quest for normalcy with China (and Pakistan)? The
Indian Ministry of External Affairs should clarify this point.

Indian diplomatic rhetoric and diplomacy was also ignored by the international community because India could not engage the world in the
absence of an ability to either harm the interests of the major players or
to facilitate their agenda. Nehru talked about an independent policy,
defined as possessing the right to independence in thought and action
in diplomatic affairs. But this public stance masked India's dependence
on foreign goodwill as well as resources. Nehru and his successors were
also dependent on foreign input because of the absence of independent
national means to acquire hard diplomatic and military intelligence. As
India was dependent on friendly powers for its economic sustenance
and military security, these dependencies reduced India's wriggle-space
or manoeuvrability and capacity to achieve real independence in
thought and action. The Indian problem during the 1947–98 period was
that India neither had the means nor the will to establish a specific
strategic agenda and a strategic plan; and real independence requires a
demonstrated pattern of actions and decisions that would reveal India's
strategic agenda and plan. In sum, the ritual mantra about India's independent policy was belied by the lack of economic and military power
and leverage to engage and to bargain with the outside powers. As Dasgupta points out:

The point to be stressed is that foreign policy is finally [1999] pursuing a
defined Indian agenda. Since the Pokhran tests, the US administration has kept
up sustained pressure on India to toe the line. Apart from the insistence on NPT
and CTBT, there has been a torrent of gratuitous advice from Washington for
Delhi to rapidly mend fences with Islamabad. It was a sensible suggestion that
Americans never believed India was capable of carrying through. Therefore,
when Vajpayee took up Nawaz Sharif's pre-arranged invitation to bus his way
to Lahore, it was the American lobby that was stunned into incomprehension.
It is, for example, bewildering that there has been few encouraging noises from
the Track-II wallahs [types] who routinely burnt candles at the Wagah [an Indo-

Pakistani border post, border. Why is there not even a squeal from the great theological activists who were so miffed by Indian 'hegemonism' after the Pokhran tests and who have lobbied the US Congress and the European Parliament to pass strictures against India?

Their silence is a bit like the dog that didn't bark. As long as Indian diplomacy was mired in effete Third Worldism and neighbourhood sabre-rattling, there was a certain predictability to life. The moment a government refined its priorities and began conducting itself in a manner befitting its nuclear status, there is deathly silence.[11]

In other words, a connection is being suggested between the lack of seriousness by the world community about India's strategic agenda and a self-inflicted Indian problem: India's political leaders themselves repeated the ritual mantras rather than focus on a strategy of action and decision that revealed India's strategic agenda and methodology. In other words, India was not taken seriously by outside powers because India's political class itself did not take India's strategic interests seriously.

If the diplomatic rhetoric is ritualistic and repetitive and if it is not backed up by a specific strategic agenda and plan of action, such rhetoric is dangerous: it projects false expectations (which only fooled the Indians) and it projects high ideals. They did not force others to take India seriously because the ideals were expressed without any sign of a commitment to back them up by military and economic measures; the signs of commitment and power were absent. A policy and a strategy is required continuously to engage and to contain the enemy, to develop pro-India international coalitions, to find ways to convert enmities and difficult relationships into neutrality and better still, into friendship, to find ways to transform neutrals into friends, to expose secret enmities, and generally not to convert important neutrals into enemies. Without this, if the diplomatic rhetoric appears to be successful, that may be the result of lucky circumstances rather than diplomatic and military skill. For example, Nehru claimed that India was protected by the international balance of power. India was protected by international circumstances up to a point, that is, until China decided to attack and to militarize the frontier. Up to 1962, Nehru was lucky, not skillful. That is, a successful strategy requires a combination of military, economic, as well as political (psychological warfare) strategies that rely on skill rather than simply luck. Nehru and his successors up to 1998 did not change many minds in India's favour—either among India's immediate neighbours or on the world stage—because the leadership lacked strategies that effectively engaged the outside world in terms of specific Indian interests rather than the mantras. The change started with the BJP-led government in 1998. Then the Indian strategic agenda began to crystallise and the world started to notice India and take Indian interests seriously. The approach of the BJP coalition since 1998 has been to emphasize military and economic security and to discard the traditional emphasis on NAM, the 'Third World' and North–South dialogue. Two conclusions follow. *The first is that the world did not take Indian interests seriously until Indian leaders started to take themselves seriously. Secondly, there is a connection between the world's negative view of India and India's poor psychological warfare strategy.* A shift or improvement in the latter, whose beginning we date to the rise of the BJP-led government in 1998, produced a polarization in international and Indian reactions to India's new strategic agenda. This linked India's strategic activism to Indian strategic interests. It shed the Nehru–Gandhis' utopianism in favour of a policy of engagement of the external environment on the basis of military and economic strength. However, a caveat is in order. This major cause of negativity in India's relationship with the outside world (that is, India's poor strategies as discussed above), is now changing in the Indian body politic even though the Congress party and ex-Congress party types still cling to the old rhetoric. The speeches by Natwar Singh and Mani Shanker Aiyer reflect the old rhetoric and a faith that rhetoric equals strategy. They are still prisoners of their past. There is now a polarity between the BJP and the Congress party approach to Indian strategic interests. *The caveat is that the change is ad hoc, not systemic. It is driven by the pragmatic personality and temperament of the Indian Prime Minister A.B. Vajpayee, rather than a broad-based recognition in Indian party politics about the importance of psychological warfare in reducing the negativity about India in the international environment.*

The second negative was that the emergence of two declared nuclear powers in the subcontinent gave credence to the theory that Pakistan's nuclear and missile development was an equalizer to India's edge in conventional armament. According to this view, India lost its advantage in conventional armament *vis-à-vis* Pakistan because Pakistan's demonstrated nuclear and missile capability degraded the perception of India's advantage in conventional armament. The perceived change in the distribution of military power between India and Pakistan meant that the rise of the nuclear factor was likely to dampen the use of Indian conventional armament *vis-à-vis* Pakistan. This change was thought to be an Indian problem because it was a *status quo* power. Pakistan was anti-*status quo* and a revisionist power. India needed the edge in conventional military arms because a strategy of active defence requires a clear margin of strength in favour of the practitioner of a defensive strategy. The core premise is that a *status quo*-oriented defender must be able to fight at a time and place of the enemy's choice—as happened in the case of the armed infiltrators from Pakistan who occupied strategic places on the Indian side of Kashmir in May–June 1999. Conventional superiority is required to mount a successful active defence. Asymmetry in conventional arms favoured India before the Indo–Pakistani nuclear tests, but this was negated after the tests. The new situation after May 1998 became a positive for Pakistan and a negative for India according to this argument.

The third negative was that the Indo–Pakistani tests reinforced or entrenched the 'no prospects of a peace settlement, and the perpetually troubled ceasefire' situation between India and Pakistan and between China and India. The argument is that a 'no war, no peace' situation is inherently unstable; it lacks equilibrium. At best, the protagonists can seek and achieve a ceasefire, or to extend it, in the diplomatic and military battlefields, while the psychological warfare continues ceaselessly in the 'no war, no peace' situation. Being a *status quo* power, India's strategic interest *vis-à-vis* Pakistan was to take steps to enlarge the ceasefire envelope in the diplomatic, military, economic, and cultural spheres; that is, to develop the existing multiple points of discourse between India and Pakistan. This meant that the interventionary and revisionist impulses of Pakistan could be curbed if India took the view that the enmity with Pakistan was not permanent. Conversely for Pakistan, an anti-*status quo* power, its interest was the exact opposite, that is, to degrade the depth and scope of the fabric of the 'ceasefire' envelope, to shrink its diplomatic, military, economic, and cultural content, to avoid a peace settlement, and to seek diplomatic and military escalation with a view to changing the parameters of the military confrontation and the diplomatic discourse. The aim here is to secure concessions from the enemy (India) by means of military and diplomatic pressure. The negative here is not that the May 1998 tests caused Pakistan to adopt this strategy. This was historically the Pakistani strategy since 1947. Rather, the negative was that the Indo–Pakistani tests created a further Pakistani incentive to continue its revisionist policy with the added confidence of its nuclear and missile capability. This explains the Pakistani military adventure across the Line of Control in Kashmir during January to July 1999.

The fourth, and final, negative was that the Sino–Pakistani supply relationship in the nuclear, missile, and conventional arms areas was likely to continue as long as the two had a common enemy, India. The argument is that, historically, China has thought of India as a rival, and this was not likely to change. To quote from a high-level secret Chinese military document,

The Indian military is not as large as the Chinese one, but its quality may be superior. The Indians are obviously superior to the Chinese with regards to equipment for navy and airforce, fighting capacity on the blue water, and military fortifications at the borders.

At present, the direct threats of the Indian military to China are mainly medium-range missiles and fairly advanced fighter airplanes. . .

The main reason for listing India as a potential adversary is that India's strategic focus is still on the Indian Ocean and Southeast Asia. India has never changed its request for Chinese territory and still occupies a large block of Chinese territory near China's southwest border.[12]

Given this, China's public diplomacy towards India is in a deceptive mode. The Chinese ambassador in India has been giving two kinds of signals. The first one emphasizes the importance of good neighbourliness and peace. To quote:

India is China's most important neighbour, and the two countries share a 2000 kilometres long common border. As two largest developing countries in the world, China and India exert important influence in the affairs of South Asia and Asia as a whole. Sino-Indian relationship is an important component of China's foreign policy of neighbourliness. In the past 40 years or so since the establishment of diplomatic relations between China and India, the Chinese leaders of three generations have all along been for developing neighbourly and friendly relations with India on the basis of the Five Principles of Peaceful Co-existence and have made sincere efforts to achieve this goal. Chairman Mao Zedong expressed the hope that 'the two nations of China and India continue to unite and work hard for peace'. Mr. Deng Xiaoping pointed out, 'China and India are the two most populous countries and as well as close neighbours. It will do the two countries no good unless they understand each other and be friendly with each other'. While visiting India at the end of 1996, President Jiang Zemin and the Indian side agreed to establish constructive and cooperative partnership towards the 21st century on the basis of the Five Principles of Peaceful Co-existence. Therefore, it has proved that China has been sincere and remained unchanged in developing friendly relations with India.[13]

The second one publicly emphasizes the importance of Indian nuclear and missile disarmament or denuclearization. In a provocative statement, China's ambassador Zhou Gang outlined the Chinese strategic agenda *vis-à-vis* India. To quote:

Is China willing to accept India as a nuclear power today? *Does Beijing consider it necessary for India to sign the CTBT and the NPT to improve Sino-Indian ties and before China signs the same?*

In accordance with the provision in the 7th and 13th executive paragraphs in the UN Security Council Resolution 1172, *India should abandon its nuclear weapon development Programmeme and accede to CTBT and NPT immediately and unconditionally.* There, China's position on this issue is very clear. It *is wrong to regard the nuclear issue of South Asia as an issue between China and India, which is in fact an issue between the international community and India.*

As is known to all, Resolution 1172 was unanimously approved by the UN Security Council through consultations. *According to the United Nations Charter, the Security Council represents the international community. For India's part, the only option in solving the nuclear issue of South Asia lies in fully complying with Resolution 1172.* China, as a permanent member of the Security Council, participated in the Security Council's consultation. China has no other option but to abide by Resolution 1172.[14] (Emphasis added.)

The second public signal shows the importance China attaches to its P-5 status and its power. As well, it shows that India, China's rival, must be negated and contained by Chinese diplomatic and military means. Since the Nehru years, China has been thinking strategically. Its interests and activities in Pakistan (since the 1960s) and Myanmar (since the 1980s) indicate that it has an undeclared strategic policy to encircle India. Obviously, China does not want war with India; hence, its emphasis on peaceful, good neighbourly relations. So its first public signal that China wants peace, that is defined as absence of war or negative peace, is correct in the context of the narrow definition of negative peace. But this definition hides the significant core of China's broader strategy. It is to block India's power and influence across the board: in terms of its quest for nuclear and missile power *vis-à-vis* China and Pakistan; in its quest for a UN Security Council seat; in the development of the Indian naval presence in the Indian Ocean area, especially in the Bay of Bengal area and eastward towards the South China Seas; and lastly in terms of India's position as a non-expansionist, regional leader (a benign hegemon) which can insulate the region against external interventionary impulses.

China's strategy of encircling India strategically and diplomatically gained ground because of subcontinental circumstances. Nehru was sleeping and he was not a visionary in the strategic sphere. He did not understand the mind, the ambition, the calculations, and the diplomatic–military tactics of the Chinese leadership. Even today, Indian Leftists, many Indian Sinologists, and many Congress party leaders are still sleeping and dreaming about Sino–Indian friendship and normalization. Their understanding of the strategic base of China's India and Pakistan policies is superficial. However, the BJP-led Indian government has shown that it is realistic about China's strategic capabilities and motivations. This is why George Fernandes, India's defence minister, declared that China was India's 'potential threat' number one.[15] The Sino–Indian rivalry has been a long-term systemic or structural negative but this negativity has been reinforced by bringing the rivalry into the open with the emphasis on the China and the Sino–Pakistani factors in Indian nuclear diplomacy since May 1998. The argument is that negativity exists if China continues with its strategic support of Pakistan, and if it tolerates or encourages Pakistani warlike activity *vis-à-vis* India, the common enemy. On the other hand, if China restrains Pakistan and curbs its interventionist impulse *vis-à-vis* India, the negativity can be reduced.

The Indian Debate After Pokhran II

Pokhran II triggered a debate in Indian scientific and political circles. The debate was intense but it was also narrow and fragmented. It did not connect the Indian nuclear issue with the nature and implications of China's strategic orientation and the impact of the Sino–Pakistani strategic relationship on Indian security. Nor did it locate the Indian nuclear question in the context of the historical debate (since the 1940s) about India's role in the changing balance of power in Asia and about the mix of diplomatic, economic, and military–nuclear strategies that India must employ to gain its objectives. The post-Pokhran II Indian debate also did not connect with the Abolitionist versus the Marginalist or the Disarmament versus Deterrence debate at the global level. Our contention is that to manage international reactions to India's strategic agenda and its strategic behaviour, India must accept the responsibility to formulate an integrated strategic plan. This should bring together the question of Indian security with the question of the balance of power in Asia–Pacific and the future of nuclear weapons or nuclear disarmament in the international system. This section examines first the scope of

India's nuclear debate, and then highlights the real issues in the Indian debate.

India has gone through many strategic debates. The preceding chapters have discussed the nuclear history up to the 1980s. The emphasis in this chapter is on the nuclear debate in India in the immediate context of the CTBT, and in the general context of US policy. The latter concerned US efforts—which went back to the negotiations concerning enriched uranium supply to Tarapur in the 1980s—to obtain a confidential assurance from India that it would not conduct a test. This was an intergovernmental debate which was carried out in secrecy. An intense public debate, however, took shape in the context of the international CTBT negotiations during 1995–6. The issue here was: what did the CTBT involve for India, given the reality of the indefinite extension of the NPT?

The Indian debate revealed a variety of Indian points of view. Praful Bidwai, who is much admired in the West, argued for unilateral Indian nuclear disarmament. M. Dubey, former foreign secretary of India, opposed the CTBT but felt that India could not stay out of it presumably because of international pressures. Others sensed the danger of the likelihood and negative impact of international economic and diplomatic sanctions against India if it tested and if it rejected the CTBT. Bidwai and the American disarmament lobby in India was vocal but it was isolated from the mainstream Indian intelligentsia and the press. The unilateralists like Bidwai and Kanti Bajpai could not make their case in India because their advocacy was not connected in an analytical way with the history of Indian security dilemmas.[16] During 1995–6, the dilemmas grew in scope and intensity. The 1995–6 dilemmas could be summarized in the following way.

(i) Was it advisable to abolish Indian nuclear arms or were they necessary to secure Indian nuclear deterrence *vis-à-vis* China and Pakistan?

(ii) Was it advisable to continue with the rhetoric of global nuclear disarmament or was it better to gatecrash into the nuclear club given that the P-5 nuclear powers and permanent members of the UN Security Council were not likely to give up their international status and diplomatic privilege that depended on possession of nuclear weaponry?

(iii) Should India continue to practise non-weaponized deterrence and to accept the CTBT (as K. Subrahmanyam advocated) or was it advisable to 'use it' (by testing) rather than 'lose it' (by not testing, and by accepting the CTBT and later the fissile material production ban)?

(iv) Was Pakistan the main strategic problem for India rather than China, and if so, was it in India's interest that Pakistan should not take a clear and demonstrable action to reveal its weaponized capability in response to an Indian test? In this case, was the traditional Indian policy of 'extended nuclear ambiguity' sound?

(v) If Pakistan actually possessed nuclear weapons and missiles capability, and if it was able to maintain it, like Israel, under these circumstances did nuclear ambiguity favour Pakistan? Was there conclusive evidence on this point? (Indian AEC Chairman Homi Sethna and M.R. Srinivasan felt that Pakistan was bluffing and they questioned the press reports.)

(vi) Was Indian testing necessary to attract US and Chinese attention? Or was it better to let sleeping dogs lie?

The Indian CTBT debate (1995–6) ran parallel to the Indian debate about nuclear ambiguity. The latter had two essential elements. On the one hand, it meant a commitment to pursue an *independent and principled opposition to the discriminatory NPT and 'NPT equivalent' international arms control arrangements* such as the CTBT. Secondly, it meant the *continuous exercise of conditional self-restraint*—where India held the line against nuclear testing. The conditions for self-restraint included the following: that there were signs of movement towards nuclear disarmament; that India was not pressed to join the NPT formally; and that external military pressures on India were containable.

The self-restraint had a history going back to the Nehru years. The Nehruvian base of India's nuclear orientation was peaceful. Nehru did not take any political (within India) and diplomatic (outside India) steps to make India a nuclear-weapon state even though the capability to do so became available in the early 1960s with an 18-month time frame. Nehru's approach was to do nothing to shorten this lead time. This element held during Nehru's prime ministership (1947–64); the Nehru line not to shorten the lead time held against the advice and pressure of Indian scientists, especially the physicists. Prime Minister L.B. Shastri shortened the lead-time from 18 months to 3 months but he died before India's policy establishment could effect a change. Shastri was succeeded by members of the Nehru dynasty. Once again, the political decision-making authority was located in the Prime Minister's office. The Nehru–Gandhis again decided not to shorten the lead time for nuclear testing. This line held until May 1974, that is when Pokhran I occurred. In the decision leading to Pokhran I, the Indian AEC was ridden by factionalism and by internal quarrels. Indira Gandhi's decision to conduct a 'peaceful nuclear explosion' was *ad hoc*; it was not meant to be a trend. Indira Gandhi clearly indicated after May 1974 that there would be no more testing and that India did not seek a nuclear weapons status. The fear of diplomatic and economic sanctions was real in the Indian government's political and bureaucratic apparatus. Consequently, the Indian government was deterred from further nuclear testing and India reverted to a policy stance of nuclear ambiguity. Some prominent Indians like K. Subrahmanyam, Jasjit Singh, Raja Mohan, and General K. Sundarji had lobbied against nuclear ambiguity in the post-Nehru period. They argued that nuclear weapons and missiles were cheaper than tanks and modern aircraft but their position on overt nuclear weaponization was unclear. However, the Indian armed forces as an institution did not lobby the government, and hence the Nehru line against nuclear testing and in favour of a long lead time was maintained.

Indian scientists started to lobby the government from 1983 onwards and, when they succeeded in May 1974 and again in May 1998, they emerged as the fathers of the Indian bomb programme. This lobbying was internal; it revealed the vitality of the scientists–politician dynamics. In the context of the scientists' lobbying the Indian political hawks brought in the issue of China as a long-term strategic problem for India. The interactions between the Indian nuclear scientists and India's political leadership, and between the Indian scientists and Indian political hawks on the China question is an under-researched topic in Indian academic circles. A reason for this lacuna is that Indian Sinologists usually do not assess the strategic dimension of Sino–Indian relations; they are content to define the relationship in terms of bilateral normalization and the boundary dispute. So one must turn to the analysis of the Indian political hawks on the relationship between the China question and the nuclear question rather than to the Indian Sinologists. The latter, by and large, have neither the inclination nor the training to make this crucial connection.

This spectrum of India's strategic debate and dilemmas was the context in which the BJP-led government of A.B. Vajpayee decided in early 1998 that India should conduct another set of nuclear tests to get American and Chinese attention. The premise behind this decision was that India would do well if it took a stand and revealed its core strategic interests and priorities rather than repeat its old diplomatic rhetorical mantras. The targets in Indian calculations were the American and the

Chinese political minds. NAM, the Third World countries, or the UN Secretary General were irrelevant in Indian calculations. If nuclear proliferation and nuclear non-proliferation rhetoric is like a political theatre, then the NAM countries, the UN Secretary General, and small European countries as well as the NGOs are the cheerleaders and the audience. The political act revolves around the major and minor nuclear powers. The passive audience consists of the vast numbers of countries who do not possess nuclear weaponry, who do have a strategic reason to possess it, and who make the vocal majority of the so-called world community which is ritually against nuclear proliferation. To put it in crude colloquial terms, what does it matter to the elephants, the major and the minor nuclear powers, if the dogs, the noisy anti-proliferators in the NAM and the powerless small European states, bark!

What was the structure and quality of the Indian debate pre-Pokhran II (1995–6) and post-Pokhran II (1998–)? The advocacy of India's (mainly New Delhi's) intelligentsia and the press in major cities may be assessed in terms of the parameters in Figure 8.1.

The fault lines or contradictions exist in the A–D and B–C relationships in this figure. At the same time, harmony also appears in philosophical and political terms in the A–B, A–C, and B–D relationships. However, the harmony in A–B existed only so long as the P-5 states did not take steps to (through the NPT indefinite extension and the CTBT) practically close off the diplomatic space and the technological base of India's nuclear weapons. So the A–B harmony was of finite duration. It was handcuffed by international arms control developments in the 1995–6 period. Parallel to this process was the process of encircling India in the 1980s and the 1990s by a combination of Chinese, Pakistani, and US policies that affected India's strategic position. Hence, the Indian strategic debate and the Indian perception of acute dilemmas in the 1995–8 period reflected a fear of global handcuffing as well as regional encirclement. The former pointed to the US's strategy; the latter to China's strategy. And the Indian fear was that both had emerged as strategic partners in Asia–Pacific and in the UN Security Council, and both, therefore, were driven by their strategic interests rather than those of India. In this scenario, India was on its own.

Figure 8.2 outlines the framework of the debate within India, and between India and the major powers. On one extremity is the view of K. Subrahmanyam that Indian nuclear tests in May 1998 have taken care of Indian security concerns, and India should sign the CTBT now. A variation is a view of the Institute of Defence and Strategic Analyses

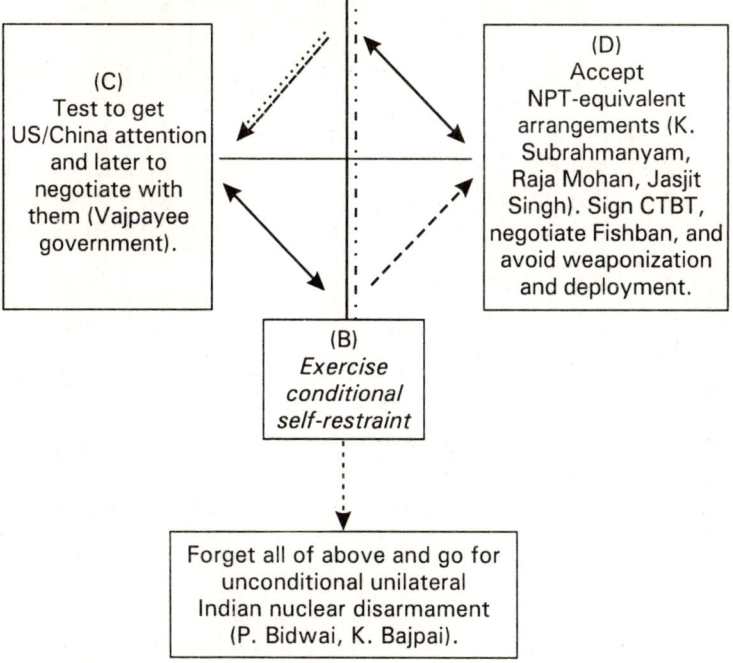

(A)
Pursuit of Independence: oppose discriminatory arms control arrangments, i.e. NPT and NPT-equivalent treaties. This has been the Indian (Nehruvian) government's line and the majority view of Indian intelligentsia.

(C)
Test to get US/China attention and later to negotiate with them (Vajpayee government).

(D)
Accept NPT-equivalent arrangements (K. Subrahmanyam, Raja Mohan, Jasjit Singh). Sign CTBT, negotiate Fishban, and avoid weaponization and deployment.

(B)
Exercise conditional self-restraint

Forget all of above and go for unconditional unilateral Indian nuclear disarmament (P. Bidwai, K. Bajpai).

◄──► Contradiction in Indian intelligentsia thinking.

· - - · · Harmony in Indian policy and social thought up to May 1998.

· · · · ► The rocky road that goes into the Indian political wilderness. This is the US lobby in India.

═══► Trend in Indian government thinking and policy, 1968–99.

- - - · The positions are convergent or harmonious.

FIG. 8.1: Parameters of India's Nuclear Debate

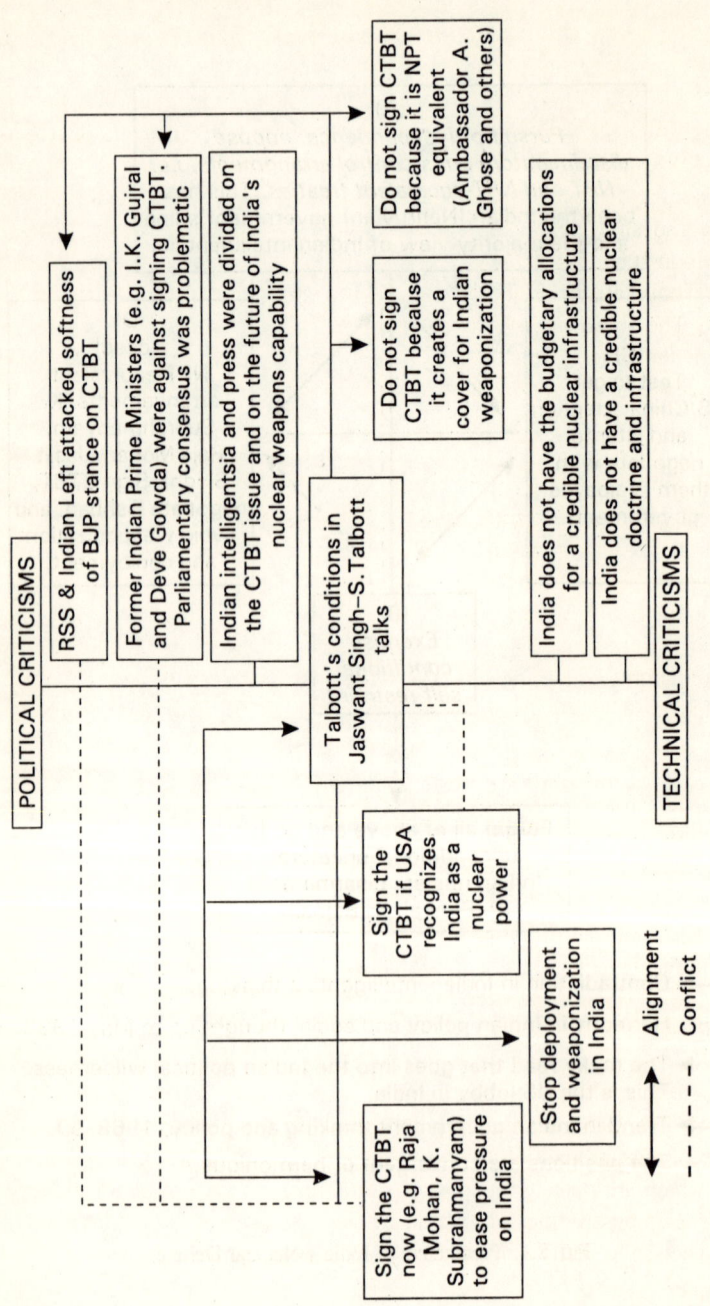

FIG. 8.2: The Post-Pokhran II Indian Debate

(IDSA) leadership that after Pokhran II, India should exercise restraint; it should induct nuclear weapons capability into Indian security planning but it should avoid its deployment. Another variant is the view of India's AEC chief, Chidambaram, and the missile programme chief, Abdul Kalam, that India possesses weaponized nuclear capacity, and it can vacate any foreseeable nuclear threat. The view here is that India can and should sign the CTBT if the US recognizes it as a nuclear weapon state. The other extremity questions the value of the CTBT (an NPT equivalent) because it negatively affects Indian security and prestige. The objections of Ambassador A. Ghose are relevant in this debate. Here the critics argue that India should maintain a position of independence and principled opposition to the NPT and NPT-equivalent arms control arrangements and it should reject the CTBT.

To recap, the objections to the CTBT highlighted the following: (1) The scope of Article 1 was not comprehensive; it allowed weapons development and testing in laboratory conditions. It created a technological discrimination in favour of the technologically advanced states. It permitted the P-5 states, especially the USA, to maintain their technological advantage in the nuclear sphere. At the same time, this article capped other states who are lower on the technological curve by eliminating their right and opportunity to test and to manage the gap with the states higher on the technological curve. (2) It was a corollary of the NPT regime and it was projected by the P-5 states as a non-proliferation, not a disarmament, measure. (3) There is no time-bound schedule for nuclear disarmament in the CTBT. (4) It affected Indian security because it choked the test route to the development of nuclear explosive technology; and it narrowed the window of opportunity to the development of non-explosive technology under laboratory conditions. In rejecting the CTBT in 1996, the Gujral government emphasized the importance of national security and the Indian nuclear option in the Indian decision on the CTBT.[17] (5) The other objections concerned the harassment potential and the Entry into Force requirement that placed India on a collision course with the USA and China, among others. (6) Finally, the endgame is not CTBT, but the Fissile Material Ban (Fishban). This ban would be even more demanding than the CTBT because it prohibits production of fissile material for those weapons, purposes of which are outside international safeguards. This too, like the CTBT, opens up possibilities of harassment because it requires measurement or inspection to verify *new* production. A determination of what is new and prohibited (after the treaty enters into force) and what is old and exempt would require physical inspection of Indian nuclear facilities.

Between the two extremities, there is a soft, intermediate core. It was soft, partly because of the US pressure and partly because of Indian criticisms of government policy. The Indian Left and the Rashtriya Swayamsevak Sangh (RSS) attacked the 'soft' policy of announcing at the highest political level that India would be willing to sign the CTBT conditionally. Mr Brajesh Mishra, Principal Secretary to the Prime Minister, announced, on 11 May 1998, a willingness to consider acceptance of parts of the CTBT provided that there was reciprocity by the US and the other P-5 states.

Prime Minister Vajpayee gave a similar sign in his appearance before the UN in September 1998. The softness in India's policy is revealed in the list of US conditions in the Strobe Talbott–Jaswant Singh talks. These are: (1) sign and ratify the CTBT without conditions, and do so quickly. (2) Halt all production of fissile material. (3) Participate in the Committee on Disarmament on Fishban. (4) Exercise restraint in the development, flight testing, storage, basing, and deployment of missiles and aircraft, that is, in all delivery systems. (5) Define Indian security requirements at the lowest possible level and clarify the meaning or requirements of India's quest for a 'minimum, credible nuclear deterrent'. (6) Tighten export controls and bring them up to international standards. (7) Develop the Indo–Pakistani dialogue.[18]

The softness of Indian policy was also revealed by the lack of transparency about the Indian requirements of a viable nuclear infrastructure to support a posture of credible deterrence. Retired Indian Admiral Ramdas was critical of Indian claims, and he highlighted the requirements of a nuclear doctrine, command and control, early warning, intelligence, and other elements of a nuclear posture.[19] Indian economists questioned if the budgetary support existed for such a big undertaking.

The scope and depth of the Indian debate can be assessed further by examining the attitude of Indian scientists to the post-Pokhran II nuclear question. This section is based on confidential interviews with Indian scientists which were conducted between September 1998 and March 1999. They indicate a dysfunctionality in the Indian nuclear debate because of the following. According to insiders, a majority of Indian scientists were against the NPT regime. The reasoning was that it was discriminatory. It was necessary to maintain India's independence and sovereignty in terms of having the right to develop India's technological and scientific frontiers and technological choices. Also, the Indian scientists were sensitive about the problem of harassment in NPT/NPT-equivalent arrangements. Despite this pronounced attitude against the NPT, the scientists, by and large, did not anticipate the weaponization of India's nuclear programme (unlike their acceptance of the weaponization of India's missile programme); and they did not anticipate the impact of the China and Sino–Pakistan question on India's nuclear behaviour. So there was a dysfunctionality between recognizing the American factor in the context of NPT/NPT-equivalent arms control and a lack of recognition of the weaponization imperative in response to the weaponization factor, the China factor, and the Sino–Pakistan factor. A caveat to the above is that the Indian scientific community was divided. The physicists welcomed the weaponization as a consequence of their lobbying since the 1980s, while Indian biologists wanted to sign the CTBT. There were several reasons for the opposition to weaponization. It was deemed to escalate tensions in the subcontinent and to provoke an arms race. Secondly, the Indian governments' willingness to sign the CTBT was deemed to be similar to the cynical behaviour of the NWSs, that is, 'do the tests first, satisfy your security requirements, and then talk about restraint and disarmament'. Acceptance of this approach was seen as a way to lose the moral ground. Finally, the economic costs of weaponization had to be calculated against the pressing developmental needs of India. The position of Indian scientists revealed subtle but fundamental differences. One position sought to stop weaponization and to stop deployment in South Asia. Another held that India must not sign the CTBT because it was NPT-equivalent and a signature created a cynical cover to keep nuclear weapons; that is, the CTBT signature was a pro-nuclear weapon ploy. In this view, the correct position was not to sign the CTBT (for reasons cited earlier) and not to produce and to deploy nuclear weapons in India. This was seen as a good package that maintained the integrity of the traditional Indian policy of conditional self-restraint and principled opposition to NPT/NPT-equivalent arrangements (see Figure 8.1).

The opposition of some Indian scientists—no statistics are available about the number of vocal ones and the number who form the 'silent majority'—reveals several themes in their opposition. The first theme is that the Indian tests in May 1998 were more a political event than a scientific one because it is harder to build and maintain nuclear reactors than it is to build and explode nuclear bombs.

The second theme is that nuclear weapons do not guarantee Indian national security. This is a political judgement by some Indian scientists, and it raises a fundamental issue. Are they qualified to make such a judgement or should it be left to the elected Indian political leaders and to the military professionals? On the other hand, if scientists are to offer such judgements, they speak as citizens and as 'politicized scientists' rather than pure scientists. The argument here about the contribution of weaponization to Indian security centres on whether or not Pakistani nuclear testing negated the Indian achievement. The answer depends on whether the emphasis is on the Indian tests as a political event—in which India was unique as the sixth nuclear power—or whether the tests are emphasized as a scientific event—in which case the issue of the yields and nature of weaponization become important.

The third theme concerned the political role of the Department of Atomic Energy (DAE) and the Defence Research and Development Organization (DRDO). Both were proactive politically in two ways: first they urged the government to conduct nuclear tests and to weaponize India's nuclear programme. Secondly, they indicated that no further tests were required, and hence, there was no scientific reason not to sign the CTBT. Many in the scientific world considered these views as political and military judgements which even senior heads of the scientific community were not qualified to make. However, such proactivity was not new for Indian scientific leaders. H.J. Bhabha had argued that China had made a great impression on Afro–Asian and Western opinion by its nuclear tests and India too needed nuclear weapons for its security and prestige. Before Pokhran I, Homi Sethna (then head of the DAE) was talking to Americans about the nature of the minimum deterrent. Dr Raja Ramanna's autobiographical account, *The Years of Pilgrimage*,[20] also made the case for testing.

Figure 8.3 is a critical subset of the CTBT debate. It involves scientific judgements about India's ability to sustain its technological independence in the nuclear sphere even if it adopted the CTBT. This figure goes to the heart of the question: does India have the means now to maintain a credible, minimum nuclear deterrent? The term 'minimum' is not in official statements. Given the context of Chinese, Pakistani, and US nuclear activity (in Diego Garcia and elsewhere), 'minimum' has an elastic, evolutionary meaning that depends entirely on the distribution of military power and the pattern of strategic relationships in India's strategic neighbourhood. 'Credible' nuclear deterrence is also context-specific. 'Credibility' depends on who is supposed to be credible (say India) in relation to a threatening power (say, China,

Pakistan, and the US—alone or in combination). Credibility relies on independent technical parameters, that is, on the reliability of the design of a nuclear weapon that being thermonuclear, tactical atomic weapons, booster fission, sub-critical capacity, and computer simulation capacity. The latter two refer to stockpile maintenance capacity, and the ability to develop new weaponry and technology. Apart from Admiral Ramdas's criticisms (discussed earlier), there are other points of view. Dr P.K. Iyenger, former head of the DAE, holds a pro-weaponization view and believes that India needs more testing to develop a full range of weapons including Tactical Atomic Weapons (TAWs). In this case, the CTBT is a problem as it forbids testing. On the other hand, Dr Gopalakrishnan, former head of Indian Atomic Energy Regulatory Board, takes an anti-weaponization view. He believes that India lacks a credible nuclear deterrent capability. Dr Chidambaran, the present head of the DAE, however, believes that India possesses a credible deterrent capability including TAWs, and on this basis, it can sign the CTBT. Given that the US has a full-blown stewardship programme to test the reliability and safety of its nuclear weapons in the foreseeable future, and given that the Indian debate among scientists and others raise doubts about India's nuclear infrastructure and the need for more testing if the requirements of a credible deterrent are to be validated, it appears that the Indian official position follows China's initial position about minimal, credible deterrence when it joined the nuclear club. This makes political sense but its technical validity is arguable. The implication is that more testing may be required even if technical work is being done in secret to develop a credible deterrent.

Figures 8.1, 8.2, and 8.3 reveal a volatility and a lack of equilibrium in the Indian nuclear debate. One suggestion for equilibrium lies in the Chinese and the Canadian demand which requires a unilateral roll-back of India's nuclear and missile programme. We argue that having crossed the line in May 1998, the Chinese–Canadian demand is untenable. So, the next possible point of equilibrium is for India to unilaterally adopt a policy of non-weaponization and non-deployment. This would keep the nuclear weapons option open and it would necessarily combine with a policy not to formally accept the CTBT. This approach to equilibrium, however, is problematic for two weighty reasons. This first is that non-weaponization would increase the technological gap between India and the nuclear powers in the absence of a programme for weaponization that relates to concrete threats and contingencies rather than abstract research or scientific problems. It is one thing to name China and Pakis-

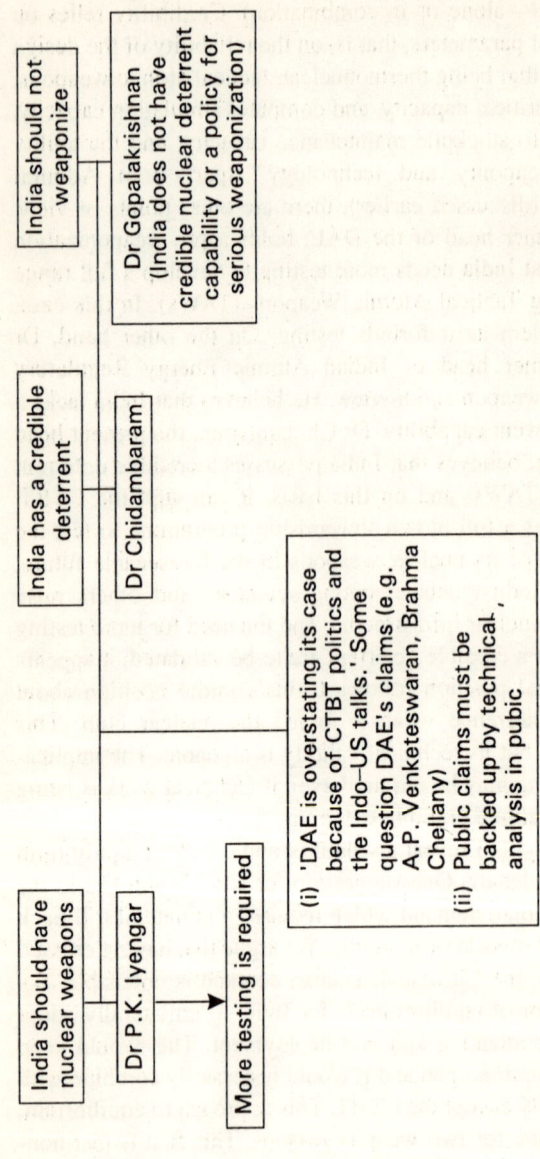

India should not weaponize

Dr Gopalakrishnan
(India does not have credible nuclear deterrent capability or a policy for serious weaponization)

India has a credible deterrent

Dr Chidambaram

India should have nuclear weapons

Dr P.K. Iyengar

→ More testing is required

(i) 'DAE is overstating its case because of CTBT politics and the Indo–US talks.' Some question DAE's claims (e.g. A.P. Venketeswaran, Brahma Chellany)
(ii) Public claims must be backed up by technical, analysis in pubic

FIG. 8.3: The Indian Scientists (and Intelligentsia), the CTBT, and Weaponization

tan as the public enemies and to require the scientists to deal with scientific issues in a specified and time-bound policy context, and quite another to retain the nuclear option in an academic mode. A weaponization stance provides a concrete policy context or framework so that scientific activity is coordinated with military planning. Here, the weaponization mode requires continuous coordination between the scientific, military, and political establishments in war and in peace to ensure that the distribution of military and technological power is favourable and manageable in the context of the pattern of India's relationships—hostile or friendly—with the powers. Weaponization also requires continuous attention to technological innovation and scientific discovery in the international sphere. Furthermore, a declared policy of non-weaponization or an undeclared one inhibits the development of a national nuclear doctrine and the physical nuclear infrastructure with command, control, communications, early warning, and intelligence components. Lastly, non-weaponization signals a lack of political resolve to the international community (and especially to enemy powers), and such a stance also demoralizes the scientific and the military constituencies who will be the actual users of weaponized technology when the need arises.

Non-deployment also conveys a lack of seriousness about the enemy. Deployment indicates that the enemy's nuclear capabilities and intentions are taken seriously. Deployment also helps the enemy concentrate the mind on the deployment, to factor it into the costs and requirements of its own defence, and to seek negotiated reductions if these are deemed necessary. Deployment must be, as far as it is practical, non-provocative but it must also be militarily effective.

Towards a New Debate and Equilibrium

An equilibrium must be found beyond the parameters of the debate outlined in Figures 8.1, 8.2, and 8.3; this search for new parameters and an equilibrium must take into account the organizational framework and political culture of the Indian strategic and scientific 'debates'. In its real sense, a 'debate' implies a process of engagement that requires professional and open confrontation and creative tension on a matter of public importance; a debate has a social purpose. A debate on a complex issue like the role of nuclear weapons in India must inevitably be multidimensional that takes an integrated view of the relationships between different factions and forces. Indian strategic 'debates' are usually fragmented and unintegrated for three reasons. First, the Indian political establishment does not know how to lead a debate, and how to participate in one except in an *ad hoc*, reactive, and fragmented manner. Secondly, the bulk of Indian scientific activity is conducted by national laboratories and institutes. A 'mind your own business' attitude prevails in these establishments. Hence, the system of the government establishments is compartmentalized and secretive. H.J. Bhabha and V. Sarabhai had robust internal, high-quality systems for decision-making. Figure 8.4 shows the general pattern and context of Indian science 'debates'.

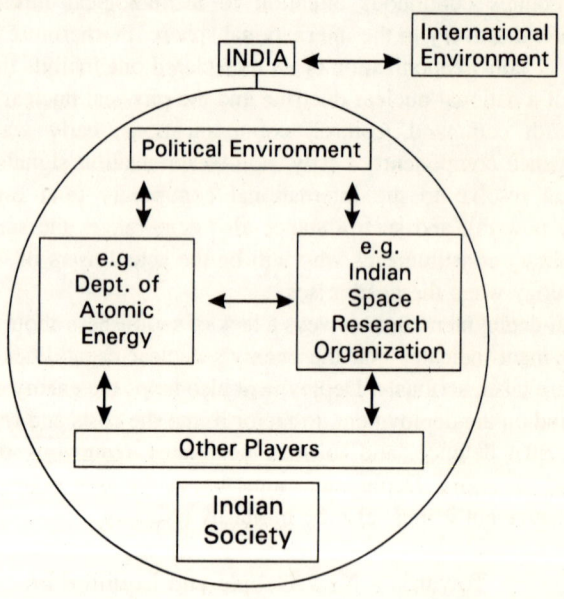

FIG. 8.4: Context of Indian Science Debates

Under Bhabha and Sarabhai, the Department of Atomic Energy (DAE) and the Indian Space Research Organization (ISRO) respectively worked well, but the environment was weak—as a consequence of difficult or unstable internal political and economic conditions, as well as weak political leadership styles and direction (or lack of it). The mini-state represented by DAE and ISRO in Figure 8.4 worked and continues to do so but its functioning depends on the integrity of that state. The timeliness of decision-making by DAE and ISRO can be enhanced if the political 'environment' in Figure 8.4 supported the development of Indian atomic and space science and if international pressures were managed. The Vajpayee government did so in authorizing Pokhran II and the Agni-II tests. But this kind of strength in the 'environment' is rare.

The third reason for the fragmented, unintegrated nature of Indian scientific debates is that Indian scientists play three different roles: they act as politicians—then their advice has political content and is weak in its scientific rationale; they act as social advocates—then they offer judgements to the press which are outside their professional competence; finally, they act as scientists who are solving scientific problems. Indian scientists' debates are often contaminated by political activity and social advocacy.

To move towards an integrated strategic debate within India, and to be taken seriously as an outward-looking international force by the world community, the participants in the debate should take into account the following:

(i) Before Pokhran II, there was a national consensus against accepting the CTBT on the grounds that it was an NPT-equivalent arrangement, but at the time, there was no publicized consensus about Indian nuclear weaponization. After Pokhran II, the majority Indian political opinion (the attentive public) is mostly pro-Indian bomb. (The P. Bidwais and K. Bajpais are a small vocal minority.) But there is now a debate about signing or not signing the CTBT, when, and under what conditions.

(ii) Keeping the nuclear option has had a general all-parties consensus about it, but now the debate has to shift to a different plan: should India produce and deploy nuclear weapons, and against whom; and what should be the size of the arsenal?

(iii) To be taken seriously as an outward-looking international force in Asia and in world affairs, the Indian political class has to revise the language and the parameters of the debate within India and it requires a strategy to manage its fallout at the international level. To do so, the underbrush of faulty premises should be cleared. Several Indian premises of the Nehru–Gandhi dynastic era will have to be discarded. Table 8.1 lists the Nehruvian premise, and then recommends the change.

TABLE 8.1.
Faulty Premises in India's Strategic Discourse

Nehruvian	*Recommended*
That global peace could be achieved through global nuclear disarmament; that peace could be achieved by goodwill rather than by armed struggle and coercive diplomacy.	Be prepared to fight if you want no war, an extended and a stable cease-fire with an enemy, and eventually a political settlement.
That unilateral Indian self-restraint in the nuclear and missile sphere gave India moral authority.	Unilateral *self-restraint* is often seen as weakness in the realpolitik-driven world. Seek *negotiated restraint* instead. That reflects the interests of negotiating partners.
That a discriminatory non-proliferation regime could be challenged and contained by diplomatic rhetoric; that powerful opposition to the regime was necessary on the moral plane, and it could be effective politically.	A majority of the states including the NAM countries are comfortable with a discriminatory international politics as long as their economic and strategic interests are protected; here opportunism is the driving element, not principle.
Great Powers would help India in time of a military crisis because of common interests; India was protected by the international balance of power or the pattern of alignments. Hence, India could spend less on military security and more on developmental security.	There is no guarantee that outside help would be forthcoming in a crisis. It is risky to depend on fortunate external circumstances. Self-help, deterrence, and ability to fight at a time and place of one's choosing is essential.
That India is big and no one dared to attack it.	Even if the major powers dared not invade India, the problem of encircling India militarily, challenging Indian interests by mounting external diplomatic, economic, and military pressures was the real challenge to India's diplomatic prestige, military and economic security, and the psychological well-being of the population.

(Contd.)

Table 8.1 Contd.

Nehruvian	*Recommended*
That the Third World and NAM was important as an international political and moral force, and that the 'South' could function as a line of pressure against the 'North' and that the 'South' could shape global power relations; that narrow partisan interests could and should be subordinated to world community norms and interests.	Globalism is dangerous because it creates false expectations; and it is unnatural because the nation-state is still the primary international institution in world politics. Hence, it is necessary to engage in the international dialogue by articulating Indian strategic priorities rather than global norms. Furthermore, the emphasis should be on building relationships with the Great Powers rather than NAM/Third World countries who had nothing to offer to India.
That India could be independent in its thinking and have an independent policy without paying the price of maintaining conventional and nuclear armament; that power struggles were avoidable and could be settled without armed forces or coercive diplomacy.	Real independence requires conventional and nuclear explosives capability; power struggles are inevitable and can be settled only by coercive means.

In other words, by completely denouncing the Nehru–Gandhi dynastic foreign policy line, and by shifting to a consideration of our recommended list, Indian strategic planners would find it easy to place the nuclear question in the context of the evolving balance of power situation in Asia. The durability of nuclear weapons as the ultimate source of deterrence in the world today can be established in this way. Unless the issue is located in the context of statist Asian strategic politics and modern military technology, the dysfunctionality and the fragmentation of the Indian strategic debate will continue to produce navel gazing rather than an integrated strategic analysis.

ENDNOTES

1. Owen Lattimore, *The Situation in Asia* (Boston: Little Brown, 1949), pp. 3, 4, 21, and 52.
2. Thérèse Delpech, 'Nuclear Weapons and the "New World Order": Early

Warning from Asia?', *Survival*, London: IISS, Winter 1998–9, p. 57. See also pp. 61–3 for the nature of the Sino–Indian strategic rivalry and China's attempts to contain and encircle India—diplomatically and militarily.

3. Paul Dibb, *Towards a New Balance of Power in Asia*, Adelphi Paper 295, IISS (Oxford: Oxford University Press, 1995), p. 10.

4. Lattimore, *The Situation in Asia*, p. 13.

5. Delpech, 'Nuclear Weapons and the "New World Order" ', pp. 59–60.

6. Ibid., p. 67.

7. For Axworthy's far-reaching statement, see 'India's Nuclear Testing: Implications for Nuclear Disarmament and Nuclear Non-Proliferation Regime', extract in *CANCAPS Bulletin*, no. 18, August 1998, pp. 10–11. For China's views, see interview by the PRC ambassador to India, Zhou Gang, 21 April 1999. Here the ambassador demanded that India should abandon its nuclear programme and accept the NPT and CTBT immediately and unconditionally. For a detailed appraisal of China's stance and its implications, see the insightful analysis by Thérèse Delpech, 'Nuclear Weapons and the "New World Order" ', pp. 57–74. For a detailed assessment of international reactions, also see A. Kapur, 'India after Pokhran II', in A.J. Wilson and Amita Shastri, eds, *Post-Colonial States of South Asia* (London: Curzon Press, forthcoming).

8. Harald Müller, 'The Death of Arms Control?', *Disarmament Diplomacy*, no. 29, London, August/September 1998, p. 2.

9. Ibid.

10. Ibid., p. 4.

11. Swapan Dasgupta, 'Line to Washington', *India Today*, 1 March 1999.

12. 'Can the Chinese Army Win the Next War', summary, 1993 meeting of the Chinese Central Military Commission, Beijing, unpublished, p. 6.

13. Ambassador Zhou Gang, 'China's Policy of Reforms and Opening up', *Key Issues*, vol. 1, no. 2, November 1998, p. 56.

14. Reproduced in full in Rediff Interview, 3 May 1999, p. 2, my emphasis.

15. J.F. Burns, 'India's New Defence Chief Sees Military Threat', *New York Times*, 5 May 1998.

16. Ashok Kapur, 'Indian Strategy: The Dilemmas about Enmities, the Nature of Power and the Pattern of Relations', in Y.K. Malik and A. Kapur, eds, *India: Fifty Years of Democracy and Development* (New Delhi: APH Publishing, 1998), pp. 341–72.

17. Official statement. Also see, 'India must say "NO" to CTBT and FMCT' (interview with Arundhati Ghose), *Frontline*, 3 July 1998, pp. 31–2.

18. 'US looks to India's Emergence as a Global Power', *The Times of India*, 13 November 1998, p. 13.

19. L. Ramdas, 'Pokhran II and its Fallout', *Frontline*, 17 July1998, pp. 86–8.

20. K. Subrahmanyam, 'Indian Nuclear Policy—1964–98', in Jasjit Singh, ed., *Nuclear India* (New Delhi: Knowledge World, 1998), pp. 26–53, is a good account of the Indian policy. Raja Ramanna, *Years of Pilgrimage, Autobiography* (Delhi: Viking Penguin, 1991).

Appendix A

History of Scientific Activity in India before 1947[1]

1876	The Indian Association for the Cultivation of Science (Calcutta)
1890	Botanical Survey of India
1899	Haffkine Institute
1905	Agriculture Research Institute (Pusa, Bihar; transferred to Delhi, 1936)
1906	Forest Research Institute (Dehra Dun)
	Central Research Institute for Medicine
	Medical Research (Kasauli)
1911	Tea Research Institute
	Indian Institute of Science (Bangalore, supported by J.N. Tata)
1913	Indian Science Congress Association
1916	Zoological Survey of India
1917	Bose Institute (Calcutta)
1921	School of Tropical Medicine (Calcutta)
1923	Dairy Research Institute (Bangalore)
1924	Cotton Technology Lab (Bombay)
1927	Malaria Institute (Delhi)
1928	Nutrition Research Institute (Conoor)
1930	Academy of Sciences (Allahabad)
1931	Indian Statistical Institute
1934	Institute of Public Health and Hygiene (Calcutta)
	Indian Academy of Sciences (Bangalore)
1935	National Institute of Sciences

[1] A. Parathasarthi and Baldev Singh, 'Science in India', conference paper, *India, The First Ten Years*, University of Texas, Austin, 6–9 December, 1990.

1936	Institute of Sugar Technology (Kanpur)
1938	National Planning Committee (India Congress Party)
1939	Jute Research Institute (Calcutta)
1942	Council of Industrial and Scientific Research (Government of India)
1943	Professor A.V. Hill, Review of post-war Indian scientific and industrial research
1945	The Tata Institute of Fundamental Research (Bombay, supported by D. Tata Trust)
	Education Department review to consider establishment of Institute of Technology on the lines of Massachusetts Institute of Technology (vs)
1946	Research Committee on Atomic Energy (Government of India)
	Institute of Palaeobotany (Lucknow)
1947	Shri Ram Institute for General Industrial Research (Delhi)

Appendix B

Prime Ministers of India and Their Tenure in Office

	Prime Minister	*From*	*To*
1.	J.L. Nehru	August 15, 1947	May 27, 1964
2.	G.L. Nanda	May 27, 1964	June 9, 1964
3.	L.B. Shastri	June 9, 1964	January 11, 1966
4.	G.L. Nanda	January 11, 1966	January 24, 1966
5.	Indira Gandhi	January 24, 1966	March 24, 1977
6.	Morarji Desai	March 24, 1977	July 28, 1979
7.	Charan Singh	July 28, 1979	January 14, 1980
8.	Indira Gandhi	January 14, 1980	October 31, 1984
9.	Rajiv Gandhi	October 31, 1984	December 1, 1989
10.	V.P Singh	December 2, 1989	November 10, 1990
11.	Chandrasekhar	November 10, 1990	June 21, 1991
12.	P.V. Narasimha Rao	June 21, 1991	May 16, 1996
13.	A.B. Vajpayee	May 16, 1996	June 1, 1996
14.	H.D. Deve Gowda	June 1, 1996	April 21, 1997
15.	I.K. Gujral	April 21, 1997	March 18, 1998
16.	A.B. Vajpayee	March 19, 1998	17th April 1999
17.	A.B. Vajpayee	October 13, 1999	Present

Index